# The Psychology of the Social

D0732556

The differences between individual and collective representations have occupied social scientists since Durkheim, whose classic article 'Individual and Collective Representations' was published a century ago. In the twentieth century, the social psychological theory of social representations has been one of the most important theories of the social, with the influence of social representations scholars such as Serge Moscovici (who contributes to this book) attested to by the work of social scientists worldwide. *The Psychology of the Social* brings together leading scholars from social representations and related approaches, including discourse analysis, to provide an integrated overview of contemporary psychology's understanding of the social. Each chapter comprises a study of a topical issue, such as social memory, social discourses about racism, intelligence, and education, or representations of the self in different cultures. These studies exemplify the theory of social representations and make connections between social representations and the central concerns of psychological research, including attribution, everyday knowledge, memory, the self, culture and ideology. They also emphasize the links to be made between social psychology and educational and developmental psychology. Taken together, the chapters offer an alternative programme for social psychology as the psychology of the social.

UWE FLICK is Professor of Empirical Nursing Research at the Alice Salomon Fachhochschule (Alice-Salomon-Polytechnic) in Berlin and also teaches at the Technical University of Berlin. Previously he taught at the Free University of Berlin and the Medical University of Hanover and has held visiting research positions in Paris and London. His recent publications include *An Introduction to Qualitative Research* (1998), and a number of books on social representations, which have appeared in German, English, French and Japanese.

# The Psychology of the Social

*Edited by*
Uwe Flick

**CAMBRIDGE**
UNIVERSITY PRESS

PUBLISHED BY THE PRESS SYNDICATE OF THE UNIVERSITY OF CAMBRIDGE
The Pitt Building, Trumpington Street, Cambridge CB2 1RP

CAMBRIDGE UNIVERSITY PRESS
The Edinburgh Building, Cambridge, CB2 2RU, United Kingdom
htt;://www.cup.cam.ac.uk
40 West 20th Street, New York, NY 10011–4211, USA    http://www.cup.org
10 Stamford Road, Oakleigh, Melbourne 3166, Australia

Originally published in German in the series 'Rowohlts Enzyklopädie' as
*Psychologie des Sozialen*
by Rowohlt Taschenbuch Verlag GmbH, Reinbek bei Hamburg
and © Rowohlt Taschenbuch Verlag GmbH
First published in English by Cambridge University Press 1998 as *The
Psychology of the Social*
English-language edition © Cambridge University Press 1998

Printed in the United Kingdom at the University Press, Cambridge

Typeset in Times 10/12pt [CE]

*A catalogue record for this book is available from the British Library*

ISBN 0 521 58159 1 hardback
ISBN 0 521 58851 0 paperback

# Contents

# Contributors

MARTHA AUGOUSTINOS
Dept of Psychology
University of Adelaide
GPO Box 498
5001 Adelaide
South Australia
Australia

FELICE CARUGATI
Università di Bologna
Dipartimento di Scienze
  dell'Educazione
Via Zamboni 34
40126 Bologna
Italy

JOSE LUIS GONZALEZ CASTRO
Facultad FICE
Alto de Zorroaga, s/n, 2011
San Sebastian
Spain

MARIO VON CRANACH
Psychologisches Institut der
  Universität Bern
Muesmattstr. 45
CH-3000 Bern 9
Switzerland

WILLEM DOISE
Faculté de Psychologie
24, Avenue du Général Dufour

CH – 1204 Genève
Switzerland

AUGUSTÍN ECHEBARRÍA ECHABE
Facultad FICE
Alto de Zorroaga, s/n, 2011
San Sebastian
Spain

ROB FARR
Dept of Social Psychology
London School of Economics
Houghton Street
London WC2A 2AE
United Kingdom

UWE FLICK
Alice Salomon Fachhochschule
Alice-Salomon-Platz 5,
D-12627 Berlin
Germany

ROM HARRÉ
Subfaculty of Philosophy
10 Merton Street
Oxford, OX1 4JJ
United Kingdom

MILES HEWSTONE
University of Wales College
  of Cardiff
PO Box 901

Cardiff CF1 3YG
United Kingdom

LENELIS KRUSE
Psychologisches Institut der
 Universität Heidelberg
Hauptstr. 49–54
D-69117 Heidelberg
Germany

HAZEL ROSE MARKUS
Dept of Psychology
Stanford University
Stanford
CA 94305
USA

SERGE MOSCOVICI
Ecole des Hautes Etudes en
 Sciences Sociales
105, Boulevard Raspail
F-75006 Paris
France

GABRIEL MUGNY
Faculté de Psychologie
24, Avenue du Général Dufour
CH – 1204 Genève
Switzerland

DAPHNA OYSERMAN
Wayne State University,
Detroit
USA

JUAN ANTONIO PÉREZ
University of Valencia
Psicología Social
Facultad de Psicología
Av. Blasco Ibañez 21
46010 Valencia
Spain

JONATHAN POTTER
Dept of Social Sciences
Loughborough University
Loughborough
Leicestershire LE11 3TU
United Kingdom

PATRIZIA SELLERI
Università di Bologna
Dipartimento di Scienze
 dell'Educazione
Via Zamboni 34,
40126 Bologna
Italy

CARLO MICHAEL SOMMER
Psychologisches Institut der
 Universität Heidelberg
Hauptstr. 49–54
D-69117 Heidelberg
Germany

MARGARET WETHERELL
The Open University
Walton Hall
Milton Keynes
United Kingdom

# Figures and tables

**Figures**

**Tables**

# Acknowledgements

The idea for this book was developed while the editor benefited from a grant of the Deutscher Akademischer Austausch Dienst (DAAD) and the Maison des Sciences de l'Homme (Paris) in 1991, which allowed him to work as a research fellow at the Maison and the Ecole des Hautes Etudes en Sciences Sociales in Paris.

The editor wants to thank Serge Moscovici for his consultations, which have helped to make this book a reality, and Gerard Duveen for his assistance in preparing an English version of this book and especially for the editor's introduction and chapter.

Chapters 5 and 14 were translated from French with the assistance of a grant from the Maison des Sciences de l'Homme (Paris) and the French government.

# Foreword

*Rob Farr*

This year marks the centenary of Durkheim's classic article on the difference between individual and collective representations (Durkheim, [1898] 1974). His primary objective in writing the article was to differentiate sociology (the study of collective representations) from psychology (the study of individual representations). His sharp distinction between the two disciplines created an opportunity for social psychology to develop within the context of either discipline. This generated an identity crisis for social psychologists which they have been unable to resolve in the course of the present century. At the close of the century there are sociological as well as psychological forms of social psychology with few points of contact between the two.

One solution to the problem posed by Durkheim is to declare that social psychology is the study of social representations. This was the strategy adopted by Moscovici ([1961] 1976) at the start of the modern era in social psychology when he published his pioneering study *La Psychanalyse: son image et son public*. This initial study was as much a contribution to the sociology of knowledge as it was an introduction to the concept of social representation. Moscovici's choice of Durkheim as an ancestor for this tradition of research indicates that Moscovici considers it a sociological rather than a psychological form of social psychology. Social representations are intermediate between collective and individual representations. While they may comprise a unique object of study for the social psychologist, their investigation inevitably involves one in being able to inter-relate sociology and psychology. If ancestors are able from beyond the grave to influence the affairs of their devotees then Durkheim will help ensure that social representations are not explained in terms of individual representations.

Although the term 'representation' does not appear in the title, the volume edited by Flick is germane to a consideration of Moscovici's response to the challenge posed by Durkheim. In his contribution Moscovici presents a very full account of the transition from collective to social representations. He describes in detail the influence of Lévy-Bruhl as well as of Durkheim on the developmental psychologies of Piaget and Vygotsky. The developmental perspective is important in accounting for the stability of cultures. It is also useful in identifying how collective representations are transmitted from one generation to the next. The contribution by Moscovici is conceptually challenging in regard to the relations between sociology and psychology and historically interesting in regard to the development of the theory of social representations. The developmental perspective is well represented elsewhere in the volume in the contributions of Doise, Mugny, and Pérez on the social construction of knowledge and of Carugati and Selleri on the differing discourses of parents and experts concerning intelligence and child development.

It is highly appropriate that the editor of the volume, Flick, is a social psychologist with a background training in sociology. The objects which are the focus of interest in the book which he has edited are explicitly social and cultural. This clearly differentiates it from a rival volume in social psychology covering many of the same topics (namely, Fraser and Gaskell, 1990). The appearance of the word 'belief' in the title of the rival volume privileges a psychological over a sociological form of social psychology. The appearance of the word 'knowledge' in the title of the present volume has the reverse effect, i.e. it privileges a sociological over a psychological form of social psychology. The theory of social representations, for example, is more central to the present volume than it was to its rival. The sociology of knowledge is a distinct field of study in its own right. As noted above, *La Psychanalyse* was a contribution to that particular field of study.

Belief has to be the belief of an individual, i.e. it is a psychological term. Knowledge can exist in a purely physical form, e.g. the volumes of an encyclopedia. Knowledge in this form is a cultural artifact rather than a social phenomenon in the strict sense. A representation is social, I would say, if it is, or has been, in two or more minds. The key question is: How does it get out of one mind in a form that can be picked up and interpreted by another? Centuries may elapse between these two events, e.g. the Renaissance corresponds to a rediscovery of the texts of the Ancient World, which had been preserved in the libraries of monasteries, mostly unread for centuries. The Renaissance, in its turn, led to the period between the Modern and the Ancient Worlds being re-presented, retrospectively, as The Middle Ages. I have chosen print as a medium for the expression of representations. Sommer, in his contribution to the volume, argues that television is a powerful new medium for the generation of social representations and he illustrates his argument by references to punk and to chaos theory. Text, inevitably, is language based. Television permits the transmission of images as well as text.

This is the first volume available in English which approaches the study of social representations through the medium of knowledge and language. There are six chapters devoted to the study of knowledge in its various forms and six to the study of language, with the former being more coherent, overall, than the latter. The forms of knowledge covered comprise von Cranach on social systems; Flick on everyday knowledge in social psychology; Hewstone and Augoustinos on social attributions; Doise, Mugny, and Pérez on social construction; Echebarría and Castro on social memory, and Oyserman and Markus on the self. The section on language and discourse is more heterogenous in its composition. Harré raises various epistemological questions concerning the nature of social representations while Potter and Wetherell, in their contribution, distinguish between discourse analysis and social representations. The topics covered in the two chapters on discourse analysis include media coverage of the Gulf War, racism (Potter and Wetherell); changing scientific conceptions of intelligence and cultural models about development (Carugati and Selleri). Augoustinos deals with ideology; Sommer (see above) with the mass media and Kruse with social representations of man in everyday language.

In origin, social representations was a French tradition of research (Farr, 1987a). It is, today, a multi-lingual enterprise with a substantial body of literature now available in Italian, English, Spanish, and Portuguese. The contributions in the last two languages come from South America as well as from Europe. There is now a growing literature in German on the topic. The present volume first appeared in German, and I believe I am correct in saying that it was the first text in that language to introduce the theory of social representations. There are links of a theoretical and historical nature between the collective representations of Durkheim and the objects of study in the ten volumes of Wundt's *Völkerpsychologie* (1900–20), i.e. language, religion, customs, myth, magic and cognate phenomena. Whilst Moscovici, in his theory of social representations, modernized Durkheim's conception of collective representations there was no comparable move, in Germany, to modernize Wundt's *Völkerpsychologie*.

The present volume is a welcome addition to the literature available in English on the theory of social representations. There are novel contributions in the present work from German academics such as Flick himself, von Cranach, Sommer, and Kruse. The salience of the sociological dimension is also, I believe, important. It is also good to see the prominence which Flick gives, in his substantive contribution (as distinct from his editorial introduction), to the sociology of Schütz.

# 1    Introduction: social representations in knowledge and language as approaches to a psychology of the social

*Uwe Flick*

## Introduction

If we start from the notion that the psychology of the social is, or should be, the issue for social psychology, then it seems trivial to entitle a book on social psychology *Psychology of the Social*. Yet, a review of the recent history and present state of social psychology gives the impression that the social does not have the status in social psychology that might be expected. Anyone concerned with understanding social problems and ways to tackle them rarely thinks of looking to social psychology for the concepts they need, and social psychological research has found little resonance for its results in public discussions (as in the scientific pages of newspapers). Although social psychology has always dealt with the relations between the individual and society or (in other words) with the subject in its social environment, neither current textbooks nor the discussions in most social psychological journals offer answers to questions such as: What part do social and collective attributions play in everyday life, and how can they be studied psychologically? What social discourses of racism circulate in everyday life? How does social development or the social construction of knowledge proceed? What do we know about everyday knowledge of social systems? Which psychological concepts can explain how ideologies function? Which forms of social memory can be studied in a culture? How do representations of selfhood vary in different cultures? What role does the image of the 'new man' play in everyday life, in the media, and in ordinary language? How do new media influence our representations, our image of reality? What is the relevance of everyday knowledge for research in social psychology, and what is the relevance of social psychology for everyday knowledge?

On the one hand, disillusion about social psychology's contribution to answering these questions may be a consequence of its choice of a more or less closed paradigm to guide and structure its current research, a paradigm which (according to its critics) obscures rather than explains the social. The study of social cognition – the central approach in recent

1

social psychology – is more or less exclusively concerned with information processing within the individual and with the ways in which social influences disturb these processes[1]. On the other hand, social psychology has attracted greater attention for its regular crises than for any results and answers it has produced.

### Crises and turns in social psychology

The recent history of social psychology has been marked by various turns or even crises, which, rather than progressing in a linear sequence, have occurred more or less in parallel over the same period of time. These turns will be briefly sketched here before outlining approaches which illustrate alternatives for a psychology of the social capable of responding to the kinds of questions listed above.

#### *The historical turn in social psychology*

The beginning of this turn is primarily linked to an article in which Gergen (1973) described social psychology as history rather than as natural science. He argued that the objects of research in social psychology have constantly and decisively changed to a considerable degree. It seems impossible therefore for social psychology to formulate in a positive way any a-historic regularities, that is any psychological laws whose validity could be independent of historical situations. Gergen suggested that to a large extent these changes are determined by the way in which psychological knowledge has itself entered everyday knowledge, so that social actions have already been influenced by psychological theories before they become the objects of study for social psychologists. Following Gergen it is not only the historical relativity of social psychological objects and results which have been discussed, but also their cultural relativity, the sense that both objects and results are shaped by, or depend on, the culture in which they occur (see Oyserman and Markus, chapter 7 this volume).

At the same time as Gergen's article other critical stock-takings of social psychological research mourned its lack of sensitivity for the contexts of research (Israel and Tajfel, 1972), or the loss of society in its perspectives and the theoretical deficits of its research (Moscovici, 1972). There were also demands that social psychology should connect with relevant theoretical developments outside psychology, such as symbolic interactionism (Harré and Secord, 1973). Together with Gergen's critique these arguments initiated a crisis in social psychology which lasted throughout the 1970s and 80s (see Rijsman and Stroebe, 1989). In the long run this crisis – or at least the discussion about it – led to three consequences:

- A mainstream emerged in social psychology which – while engaged in the other turns described below – is trying to continue the empirical programme of social psychology without being too impressed by the discussion of crisis and relativity. Zajonc (1989) has complained strongly that the discussion inaugurated by Gergen has failed to produce any heuristic consequences for research, but has prevented promising students from entering social psychology and funding agencies from increasing social psychological research budgets.
- Outside the mainstream, however, movements such as Gergen's (1985) social constructionism or the discursive psychology of Harré (see chapter 8 this volume) or Potter and Wetherell (this volume) have emerged from these discussions.
- Lastly, the existence of two social psychologies has sometimes been considered a consequence of this turn. Distinctions have been drawn according to contents (e.g. between mainstream and social constructionism – see Rijsman and Stroebe, 1989), or locality (between American and European social psychology, in particular in the work of Tajfel, Harré and Moscovici – see the 'European' introduction to social psychology by Hewstone *et al.*, 1995, or the *European Journal of Social Psychology*) or by assigning social psychology as a discipline to psychology or to sociology (see Stephan *et al.*, 1991).

*The cognitive turn in social psychology*

Following the cognitive turn in general psychology, the 1970s and 1980s saw a similar turn in social psychology when the focus of research shifted from the observation of behaviours to the investigation of cognitive processes. As one of the initiators of this turn has recently emphasized, it was an attempt to establish 'meaning' as the central concept in psychology (Bruner, 1990, p. 2), even though he (like Graumann, 1988) has now reached the critical evaluation that it is information processing which is being studied, not meanings. In social psychology the dominant product of the cognitive turn has been social cognition, and in research domains such as the self-concept, attitude, stereotypes or attribution, social cognition has demonstrated the relevance of certain mental schemata for the processing of social information. For its protagonists, indeed, the cognitive turn has led to an 'integration of social psychology in psychology' and one of the leading protagonists of this view has celebrated social

cognition as indicating the 'end of crisis' (Strack, 1988, p.74). Nevertheless, for its critics, the cognitive turn has led to decisive losses for *social*
psychology:

- On the one hand, the cognitive turn has produced a cognitivism in social psychology (Graumann, 1988) in which the
  concept of cognition has been reduced from thinking to
  information processing, and where the study of the contents
  of cognition (what people think about or know of social
  contexts) has been replaced by the study of how information
  processing functions without social contents.
- On the other hand, the cognitive turn has led to a new
  individualism in social psychology (Graumann, 1988), in
  which the focus on the mental processing of information has
  created an even greater distance from social reality.[2] Questions
  of the 'sociality of human existence' have been ignored in
  psychology or 'passed to the social sciences' (Graumann,
  1988, p. 87). The relevance of communication and interaction
  for social action, and the relevance of social action for
  knowledge and thinking have been neglected. Finally, information processing models have rarely considered the evaluative aspects of information (Taylor, 1991, p.98).

Through its concentration on information processing, social psychology under the label of social cognition has lost any connection to the big
– social – questions, not least because of its own lack of interest.

### The linguistic turn in social psychology

A third turn in social psychology, linked to the linguistic turn in the
social sciences, has seen a dissociation from cognitivism. Here – mainly
in Britain – it is the communicative embedding of cognitive processes in
social psychological contexts which has been emphasised. Psychological
research has shifted from the experiment to the analysis of discourse and
conversation (Harré, see chapter 8 this volume; Potter and Wetherell, see
chapter 9 this volume). A parallel development – mainly in the United
States – is Gergen's 'social constructionism' which also has recourse to
linguistic principles and to Wittgenstein (1953), and is engaged in the
study of the social construction of reality from a (social) psychological
perspective. Here knowledge is no longer considered as something inside
people's heads but as something to be observed in their common
practices (Gergen, 1985). Memory is no longer understood and analyzed
as an individual cognitive process of retrieving information in the brain,
but, rather, as a social or collective process (Middleton and Edwards,

1990b; Echebarría and Castro, see chapter 6 this volume). Researchers from this perspective have been interested in social questions such as racism (Potter and Wetherell, see chapter 9 this volume) or ideology (Billig et al., 1988).

So far, some central developments of social psychology have been outlined which can be summarized as follows: following the cognitive turn, recent years have seen the emergence of social cognition research as the mainstream of social psychology (in both America and Europe); this paradigm has become increasingly restricted to the study of the individual and the ways in which they process information, and has thereby lost touch with the social of psychology. There are parallel approaches trying to reorient social psychology once more to social questions, and to re-establish links to contemporary social issues, which have been missing from the discipline of social psychology for some time. As a nucleus for such a *psychology of the social* there is now a prospect of an integrative basic theory in work on social representations, a theory which has anticipated the turns and developments outlined above and has developed its own research programme.

### Social representations theory as a basic theory for the psychology of the social

The theory of social representations, which is central to this volume, has integrated the three turns of social psychology to a programme of theory and research in a specific way: In dealing with knowledge this theory takes the (original) starting point of social psychology after the cognitive turn, returning again to the study of the meanings of objects and processes for subjects and groups, and to the social construction of meanings. In contrast to social cognition research, knowledge is studied as social knowledge. The formal functioning of information processing becomes less interesting than the contents of knowledge and their meaning for the individuals and groups being studied. The theory considers knowledge (both theoretically and empirically) in relation to the local, social, cultural, and historical contexts in which it is generated and used. Thus it is assumed that social representations as a type of knowledge are specific to modern societies, and are influenced by science as a main source for everyday knowledge (Moscovici, chapter 14 this volume; Flick, chapter 3 this volume). By taking account of the influence of scientific knowledge on everyday perception and thinking, social representations returns to the central theme of the discussions of the historical character of social psychology. Lastly, knowledge is not reduced to a purely cognitive phenomenon, as in information-processing models of the mind. Rather, knowledge is understood and studied both as the result and the object of interactive processes, and as a cognitive stock. Here we find a combination of the psychologies of knowledge and of language. As the chapters by Harré and Potter and Wetherell in this volume show, rather than presenting a clearly distinct alternative model to social cognition research, discursive psychology should be seen as enlarging and detailing a central aspect of the theory of social representations.

For the three lines of discussion outlined above – social psychology as historical, cognitive, and discursive science – social representations theory offers a model that takes into account the social and communicative character of social psychology as a psychology of the social.

### Social representations as a research programme

Moscovici ([1961] 1976) introduced the theory of social representations into social psychology with his study of the appearance and diffusion of psychoanalysis in French public life in the 1950s. The ancestors acknowledged in the formulation of the theory included Durkheim's ([1898]/1974) differentiation between individual and collective representations, Freud's psychoanalysis and Piaget's developmental psychology. Social representations are concerned with knowledge, understood as *social knowledge* which arises from people's membership in social groups. As well as this principle of knowledge being socially embedded, there is also the assumption of a social distribution of knowledge – *what* people know and *how* they know it depends on the social groups to which they belong. Originally, this question was investigated through the example of the emergence of scientific theories into everyday life, whereas later studies have been concerned with the social construction and representation of particular objects (e.g. health, illness, madness).

### *Definition and function of social representations*

A social representation traditionally is understood (see also Moscovici this volume) as

a system of values, ideas and practices with a twofold function; first to establish an order which will enable individuals to orient themselves in their material and social world and to master it; and secondly to enable communication to take place among the members of a community by providing them with a code for social exchange and a code for naming and classifying unambiguously the various aspects of their world and their individual and group history (Moscovici, 1973, p. xiii).

According to Moscovici (1984a, p. 24), the aim of every (social) representation is 'to make something unfamiliar, or unfamiliarity itself, familiar'. Social representations provide an instrument to cope with and classify new phenomena and changes in phenomena that are already known. In the process of social representation, two concepts, *anchoring and objectification*, are seen as central.

The first process means 'to anchor strange ideas, to reduce them to ordinary categories and images, to set them in a familiar context' (Moscovici, 1984a, p. 29). A concrete illustration of this process can be outlined with the example of technological change in everyday life (see Flick, 1996). Up to a certain point, the strangeness of new devices and the arrival of new technologies is dealt with by integrating them into the categories and representations already held by the individual – and even more importantly – by his or her social context. By anchoring new objects in existing categories, these categories are modified step-by-step – they are enlarged, differentiated, united, or put in different relations to each other. This process of construction and classification is not limited to and does not take place merely inside the individual, but is embedded in social classifications and constructions. It is a process in which categories and classes available in everyday communications, accepted and conventionalized in the social or cultural context, are used or modified. Anchoring is understood as a social process drawing the individual into his or her social context and into the cultural traditions of his or her group (Billig, 1988, p. 6).

*Objectification* translates abstract ideas and concepts into a concrete image or links them to concrete objects (Moscovici, 1984a, p. 29). In this translation process a theory is reorganized so that some parts of it are omitted, while others are brought more sharply into focus. Thus, the opposition of the conscious and the unconscious and the process of suppression passed from psychoanalysis as a theory into everyday knowledge, while sexuality and libido, which are central concepts in Freud's theory as well, remained more or less omitted. In everyday expressions active roles are ascribed to the elements of this figurative nucleus – such as the unconscious or suppression – so that, for example, it becomes possible to speak of the unconscious and the conscious as being in conflict with each other.

### Main investigations

The social embedding and distribution of knowledge were themes in three paradigmatic investigations in which the theory of social representations was not only empirically applied and grounded, but also demonstrated through different methodologies.

Moscovici's ([1961] 1976) investigation pursued an analysis of the representation of psychoanalysis through a study of the mass media in France in the 1950s, and a questionnaire survey of over 2,000 respondents from different social classes. Although it was evident that psychoanalytic concepts and ways of thinking had broadly entered everyday life, it was also clear that only some aspects of the theory were retained in these representations, and that the perception of the theory differed from group to group. Finally, the study showed the specific resonance this theory found in the Catholic and Marxist press, i.e. in contexts based on different '*Weltanschauungen*'.

Herzlich (1973) interviewed eighty people from social groups differing in education and profession about their ideas of health and illness. Any claim about the representativeness of this sample was given up in favour of more flexibility and depth in collecting the data through open-ended interviews. Further, the aim of following the passage of one specific theory through society was abandoned. In fact, no *one* theory is used as a starting point, nor is the passage of parts of the theory reconstructed through media analyses. Instead, the study is focused on the subjective aspects of the genesis and meaning of social representations.

Jodelet's ([1989a]1991) study of the social representations of madness has often been discussed as the third paradigmatic example of research in this tradition (for example, chapter 8 by Harré in this volume). It was undertaken in a village in France, where for several generations a large proportion of the population has lodged mentally ill people from a nearby asylum in their own families. The income the villagers receive for taking in these 'lodgers' has become an important element in their domestic economies. Jodelet used participant observations, complementary interviews, and analyses of documents to explore these villagers' concepts of mental illness, madness and the mentally ill, as well as the way these concepts shaped everyday life in the village. She found that the central nucleus of the social representation of mental illness consists of a naive theory of madness, which is dominated by the fear of contagion and the loss of distance from the mentally ill. This structure at the centre of the villagers' representation of madness explained many of social practices she had observed in the village, practices which seemed contradictory in content and effect to the 'official' aim of housing these people. Once again, as with Herzlich, this study is neither focused on a specific theory nor is there a content analysis of the mass media. Jodelet's concern is with the changing discourses of madness and mental illness, which she examines in relation to the changing ways of dealing with the mentally ill in everyday village life.

### The psychology of the social as a framework for other disciplines in psychology

The psychology of the social outlined in this book is not a particular discipline of psychology aiming to promote specific empirical strategies for other psychological disciplines. That seems to be the strategy of social cognition research, which, with its methods and procedures, is striving to approach the methodological and theoretical standards of general psychology, endeavouring thereby to become linked to the cognitive sciences. To make this link it has also had to neglect the typical characteristics which identify a *social* psychology. In this book, social psychology is understood rather as a framework for some other disciplines in psychology, illustrating the social character of their objects. In the psychology of knowledge, for example, social psychology contributes a perspective based on the social distribution and construction of knowledge (see chapters 2 and 3 by von Cranach and Flick respectively) as well as the social construction of memory and remembering (see chapter 6 by Echebarría and Castro) or of everyday patterns of attribution (see chapter 4 by Hewstone and Augoustinos). In developmental psychology, it contributes insights about social influences in the development of children's knowledge and intelligence (see chapter 5 by Doise, Mugny and Pérez) and about the influence of changing scientific ideas of intelligence and children's development on parents' practices (see chapter 11 by Carugati and Selleri). By drawing attention to social and cultural differences in personhood, identity and selfhood (see chapter 7 by Oyserman and Markus), it also contributes to personality psychology. Finally, it offers materials and insights to establish a relationship between the psychology of language and the psychology of knowledge, enabling these disciplines to connect with discussions in the social sciences about the role of language in everyday life and as a medium for the scientific study of everyday lives (see chapter 8 by Harré and chapter 9 by Potter and Wetherell).

### The contributions to this volume

This outline of a *psychology of the social*, which begins with the theory of social representations and relates this to social knowledge on the one hand and to language and discourse on the other, provides a framework for organizing the contributions to this volume. The first part deals with social knowledge in its various forms. *Mario von Cranach* outlines the specific qualities of knowledge of social systems. He uses various examples to explain the functions of such knowledge and of the social processes of remembering for action in different institutions. Social representations as a particular form of knowledge in social systems are juxtaposed to other concepts of knowledge in social psychology in a discussion of their function for individual and social knowledge. Following from this discussion, *Uwe Flick* examines the area of everyday knowledge. He looks first at its role in the research process in social psychology, and then compares different models of everyday knowledge (subjective and naive theories, personal constructs and cultural models) with the ways of understanding everyday knowledge in the theory of social representations. The emphasis is on the general theory of knowledge and the relations among different forms of knowledge as outlined in the theory of social representations. *Miles Hewstone* and *Martha Augoustinos* link attribution theory with the theory of social representations in order to develop an approach to both social knowledge and social attribution. They demonstrate the fruitfulness of their approach with concrete examples of everyday patterns of explanation ranging from health and illness to riots, poverty and unemployment. Social influences on the development of cognitive abilities and of intelligence in children are analysed by *Willem Doise, Gabriel Mugny*, and *Juan Pérez*. They show how the social construction of knowledge proceeds through processes of social marking and socio-cognitive conflicts. *Augustin Echebarría* and *José Luis Castro* examine different approaches to the study of social memory (Halbwachs, Durkheim, Vygotsky) to show, how processes of memorizing are influenced by membership in particular social groups, using the (differing) memories of historical and political events in different groups as examples. Finally, *Daphna Oyserman* and *Hazel Markus* pursue the question of how individual selfhood is determined by membership in a specific culture. They use differences between a western and a non-western culture (using the United States and Japan as examples) to show how a culture's dominant social representation of the self develops and differs and how people deal with contradictory representations of the self.

The second part of the book deals with *language and discourses as media of social psychology*. In his theoretical reflections, *Rom Harré* asks about the nature of the social in social representations. Starting from the discursive turn in psychology, he discusses different types and dimensions of social representations and analyses their functions in communicative processes. *Jonathan Potter* and *Margaret Wetherell* continue by comparing their approach of discourse analysis with that of social representations, outlining both common essentials in the basic principles and differences in concretely formulating and answering research questions in these approaches. To illustrate their approach, they employ various examples ranging from the way the Gulf War was represented in the media to studies of racism and the social construction of groups through linguistic practices. *Felice Carugati* and *Patrizia Selleri* return to questions of intelligence and development and sketch the differing discourses of experts and parents. They show how the changing scientific concepts of intelligence influence and also question parents' educational practices, and how everyday ideas and discourses about development evolve and change in different social contexts. The concepts of ideology and social representations are linked by *Martha Augoustinos* to arrive at an analysis of ideological representations. Her analysis starts from the social differentiation in ideologies and from their location in consciousness, language, and everyday practices. *Carlo Michael Sommer* considers an issue which is implicit in several other chapters – how social representations are both mediated and changed by the media. Using the examples of punk and chaos theory, he shows the influence of new media on social representations and how their production as social phenomena is determined by their presentations in the media. This is continued with reflections on television makers' representations of their audiences. The image of man in the media and in everyday language is studied by *Lenelis Kruse* to demonstrate the role of a social representation in everyday language and the way it changes.

In the third part, *Serge Moscovici* outlines the historical background of social representations research and links it with the anthropology of Lévy-Bruhl, the developmental psychology of Piaget, and the cultural-historic school of Vygotsky and Luria.

The chapters of this volume start from the theory of social representations, but this is not conceived of as some kind of a closed paradigm. Rather, it is linked with other theoretical approaches (attribution theory, discursive psychology, cultural models, cultural-historic school) to let both sides profit from these liaisons. The theory itself is enlarged or modified in some way in most of the chapters, which may demonstrate that the theory has not yet lost its dynamic, raising hopes that it will continue as a fruitful nucleus of a *psychology of the social*.

### Notes

[1] Social cognition may thus become an example of Thomas Kuhn's reflections on the genesis and limitations of scientific paradigms: 'A paradigm may even isolate the community from these socially important problems . . . because they

can not be expressed in the framework of the conceptual and instrumental tools furnished by the paradigm' (Kuhn, 1962, p. 51). Although the concept of paradigm seems problematic for approaches in psychology, it is explicitly employed by authors like Strack (1988) for this form of social psychology.

[2]  'Whether a hypothetical cognition is a 'representation' of social reality may not be decided from inside the model' (Graumann, 1988, p. 87).

*Part 1*

Social knowledge as an issue
in social psychology

# 2 The knowledge of social systems

*Mario von Cranach*

## Introduction

Every understanding of the world and of humankind, every meaningful thought or action, depends on knowledge. Hence not only individuals, but also human social systems which process meanings and act, possess knowledge. Where there is knowledge there must also be memory; and at any time, the given functions of memory in a social system determine what knowledge that system owns and can process – which also involves changing the knowledge itself. But there are many kinds of social systems – arrangements which are located between the twin poles of individual and society; they vary from culture to culture and are marked by varying structures and processes. Each uses and processes its knowledge in a different way and to a different end. And there are several different kinds of knowledge, which differ in content and in other ways: most particularly, in their functions. We need to know about ourselves and the world, but knowledge must, first and foremost, serve the needs of action; and there are different kinds of action. My purpose here is to analyse the differing functions of different kinds of knowledge in different kinds of social systems. This is a tall order: the subject is so complex that we are only now gradually beginning to understand the questions, and as yet we know few of the answers. In any case, I shall be asking my readers to grapple with a number of conceptual systems and classifications.

All the individual problems which emerge from this debate are interconnected; no matter where we enter into the debate we are forced to make certain assumptions. I shall begin by discussing some fundamental concepts which we shall be using repeatedly, and which give some indication of the paths we shall be following. Then, helped by some examples, I shall have more to say about social systems, their knowledge, and the function of that knowledge. Finally, I shall suggest some directions for future research.

## Some conceptual foundations for a theory

In order to proceed with our analysis we need to define the following concepts: *social system, society,* and *culture, multi-level structures and processes, knowledge, memory, action,* and *social development.* Most of them are also used in sociology; some are basic sociological categories, but I am approaching them from a psychologist's viewpoint, which turns them into something rather different.

### Social system

There are some excellent introductions to modern systems theory (e.g. Jantsch, 1980; Willke, 1991). Systems can be classified: the more developed, on the whole, the more complex. Higher systems may retain characteristics of the lower systems from which they have evolved, but by incorporating those characteristics they may also alter or overwhelm them (see von Cranach, 1990). In this chapter I shall be dealing with open and living (Miller, 1978), self-activating (see von Cranach, Ochsenbein and Valach, 1986), and human social systems. Each analysis will be based on certain key concepts. For systems in general, these key concepts will be structure, process, and function; for open systems, the degree of isolation or interconnection; for living systems, the fundamental categories of matter, energy, and information alongside the individual qualities of instability, self-activity, self-referentiality, and development; for human systems, sense and meaning; for social systems, interaction and synergy. 'Social system' is often taken to be a sociological concept and is linked with well-known names such as Robert Merton, Talcott Parsons, and Niklas Luhmann (cf. Gukenbiehl, in Schäfers, 1986, pp. 298–305 and 337–9). I shall be using it as a concept of social psychology, as a blanket term for different types of system such as dyads, groups, organizations, etc. Subsequently, these systems can be distinguished according to their individual characteristics and analysed more differentially.

### Society

This is also a primary sociological category. I take it to mean the most comprehensive of social systems. The term is largely irrelevant to psychological theory, because individuals in modern, 'pluralistic' societies are linked not to society as a whole, but only to their own subsystem. But as a social representation, 'society' can be very influential. Society is important as a super-system and, in particular, as a carrier for 'culture'.

## Culture

I take this to mean the human life world which is generated by society and its social subsystems. Its most important elements are knowledge systems (including values and norms) and material artefacts, which (like natural objects and phenomena) can carry varying degrees of 'significance'. (By *significance* I mean a reference to structures – including knowledge structures – functions and processes which are essential to the existence of the people concerned). For psychologists, the concept of culture is of little importance – except to cultural psychologists, who hitherto have always been on the margin.[1] We shall see whether we really do need this term.

## Multi-level

This concept refers to the fact that important processes like the processing of (always meaningful) information, interaction and development occur simultaneously on several different levels: the individual level and various social levels (cf., e.g., von Cranach and Tschan 1990).

## Knowledge

The modern psychology of knowledge is strongly influenced by artificial intelligence and computer technology (Mandl and Spada, 1988): it equates knowledge with information that has been stored. Underlying this is the 'information-processing' paradigm (Atkinson and Shiffrin, 1968), which describes the flow of information through a system of recall and processing points. The paradigm is based on a more or less technical idea of 'information', for example, an assumption that information has no 'meaning' for its carrier system – no more than a computer attaches meaning to the data it processes. The theory distinguishes between different types of knowledge on the basis of content, for example, 'declarative' (knowledge of content), 'procedural' (knowledge of actions and procedures), 'episodic' knowledge (memory of events), etc. Thanks to this concept of 'information', meaning is seldom considered to be important to the psychology of knowledge. Although in psychology there has been some critique of this argument (see, e.g., Bruner, 1990), in sociology 'meaning' is an absolutely fundamental category: Luhmann ([1984] 1995), for example, considers it as constitutive of the social system. For the purposes of my own research I assume that meaning is integral to human information processing. I define 'knowledge' as stored information which relates to important structures, processes, and functions in its 'carrier system' (the person in whose memory it is stored) and therefore triggers evaluative processes (knowledge always requires a carrier system, and is anchored in the structures of that system). Thus, if we want to discover the meaning of the knowledge, we must identify its carrier system. This involves not only individuals, but also all kinds of social systems. For the sake of clarity, my multi-level model distinguishes between 'sense' on the individual level and 'meaning' on the social levels: individual *sense* and social *meaning* (cf. also Rubinstein, 1977). Within the broad category of 'knowledge' it is possible to distinguish different types, classified according to their content and function; and we can also distinguish different carrier systems. Multi-level knowledge can have different meanings on different levels.

The information-processing model of cognitive psychology has yielded much that is of use to the present study; but I think it necessary to vary its terminology because of the complications introduced by the question of 'meaning'. Hereafter – until a better solution offers – I shall use the term *knowledge processing*, meaning the processing of meaningful knowledge.

### Memory

This concept is central to modern cognitive psychology, which often uses it in the sense of 'storage system', but also attributes processing powers to memory itself. Most psychologists distinguish between long-term and short-term memory, and also see the latter as the locus of processing and conscious representation. Only a small proportion of available knowledge is being consciously represented at any one time. Some theories postulate special 'sensory registers' which store the information temporarily while it is being perceived. There is a general tendency to postulate a particular kind of memory for each different recall function. In this essay, which focuses on the (meaningful) knowledge of social systems, I shall consider all individual memory functions under a single umbrella, so I cannot here go into the details of recall theory (for an overview see, e.g., Kluwe, 1990). It is important to realize that the memory processes can be analysed into three stages: the reception (encoding), storage (retention), and retrieval (decoding) of knowledge. These all involve processing, and therefore also *altering*, knowledge. Moreover, it must be clearly understood that (in our culture at least) only part of the available knowledge is retained as internal, mental 'memory': we make much more use of *external storage systems* – inscriptions, books, signs, documents, maps, electronic databases, etc. – which multiply the capacity of our mental recall many times over. To use them we need special encoding, storage, and retrieval processes, for example, reading and writing; however, as far as I know, these have never been studied as memory processes. Finally, it is also important to realize that mental memory processes are accessible only to the individual subject: they are *private*, and become *public* property through communication or transfer to an external storage system (cf. Echebarría and Castro, chapter 6 this volume).

### Action

The broadest possible definition of action might be 'the human form of behaviour'. It is possible to distinguish between various types of action, of which 'goal-directed action' has received the most scholarly attention. We defined it previously as 'consciously goal-directed, planned and intentional behaviour on the part of an actor, emotionally coloured, socially directed and controlled' (see von Cranach and Kalbermatten, 1987). In this sense, 'action' presumes knowledge. An 'action' is 'a unit of action which takes place in a socially defined situation and is directed at a goal'.

This definition reflects the current state of research: action has been conceived of and studied almost exclusively on the individual level, as goal-directed action by an individual human being. However, it seems increasingly likely that this concept is too narrow: there are in fact many types of action, and social systems can also be considered as acting entities (socio-psychological studies over the last few years include, e.g., Cranach *et al.*, 1986; McGrath, 1984, 1990; the concept has of course a long tradition in sociology.)

To begin with, we can distinguish long-term projects from actual, short-term actions (see von Cranach, 1993). *Long-term projects* occupy the interaction system for a fairly long time, usually with some interruptions. They have one consistent theme, but include a number (which may be considerable) of individual action types. *Themes* (cf. Pulver, 1991) are long-term projects with a recurrent thematics; they govern the cyclic structure of everyday life (e.g. cooking, eating, and sleeping on the individual level; regular meetings and team conferences on the social level). *Projects* (Little, 1983) are to a certain extent consistent over a long term: they focus on a specific event or process (e.g. 'building a house', 'completing a study', on the individual level; 'conquering the international market' on the level of a business undertaking). When dealing with long-term projects it should be borne in mind that the time horizon may alter according to the system level. For example, actions by social systems may include individual projects.

Many single actions are part of a long-term project. When classifying them we can ask (for example) what is their object, product, or goal, how they are energized or directed, whether or not the knowledge processing is public and how they relate to their environment. I distinguish six classes of individual action: *goal-directed action* (e.g. many actions at work), with various subclasses; *meaning-oriented action* (e.g. rituals); *process-oriented* action (such as dancing); *emotionally intuitive action* (like many everyday actions); *affective action* (e.g. a fit of anger); and *mental action* (which also includes deliberate refusal to act). Analogies to some of these classes can be found in social systems, but I shall not go further into that aspect here.

We shall now turn to the 'action of social systems'. Experience has shown that this concept presents certain difficulties. A cultural tradition going well back in western European history urges us to reduce social processes to individual ones. In my own discipline of social psychology, an authoritative study (Allport, 1924) elevated the individual standpoint almost to the status of a norm; the author's later qualifications (Allport, 1961, 1962) passed virtually unnoticed. This barred the way to a theoretical, system-based analysis of social data, and to the many answers which such analysis might have elicited. We have explained elsewhere how and why social systems can be treated as acting systems (see, e.g., von Cranach, Ochsenbein and Valach, 1986; von Cranach and Tschan, 1990). The action-related processes of social systems are to an extent analogous to the individual processes. Thus, action-related communication within groups is in many ways similar to action-related cognition in individuals. However, the organization of action in social systems is *quintessentially multi-level*, and on the lowest level we always find *individual processes*.

Social systems exist as units through their action, and it also essentially defines their structures. For example, a university exists to foster teaching and research, and will not endure for long if it loses these functions and obtains no others. Families provide mutual help and emotional support to their members and provide for the upbringing of children, and become purposeless if these functions are not performed. These are really functions on the social-system level; other functions may be on the lower-system level, for example, an employee of the university may view it as a kind of life insurance. The multi-level principle is again relevant here, and I would emphasize that individuals are always involved. Of course, social-system action also presumes knowledge. This brings us back to our multi-level concept of knowledge, as explained above.

## Social development

In systems theory, 'development' is seen as a continuous process in living systems, a necessary consequence of their existence in a state of imbalance. It is understood as progressive differentiation and integration. It is often intermittent, with alternating changes and plateaux, and may even occur in qualitative leaps. A crisis may provoke a reaction involving an un-differentiation, regression, or simplification of structures (for more on systems development see von Cranach, 1990). I shall refer to 'social' development because for my present purpose the connection between the development of individuals and social systems, i.e. multi-level development, is of the first importance. This does not mean that I shall ignore individual physiological development: this always has an influence on social systems (e.g. the development of a family as its children grow up, or the superannuation of the higher echelons of whole societies). Stages in development always involve both individuals and their social systems, and the developments in different levels are mutually determinant. They can be understood as circular processes in which knowledge and action change, each influencing the other (see Figure 2.1; and cf. Thommen, Ammann and von Cranach, 1988). I would suggest we use the term *multi-level co-evolution.* I shall return to this theme when discussing the function of knowledge (see below).

These definitions may serve as a framework for what follows. I have distinguished between different types of social systems, and between knowledge and action. We shall now proceed to examine the connection between them. My considerations may be summarized as follows:
1 Social systems store and process knowledge and perform actions. This involves multi-level processing. Knowledge and action are interconnected and jointly determine development.
2 Different types of social systems organize these processes in different ways. The systems also differ in what knowledge they store, how they store it (memory function), and how they use it.
3 The memory function depends on the characteristics of the knowledge-processing system; the type of knowledge stored depends on all the circumstances in which the system exists.

## A classification of social systems

To work successfully, real sciences (those concerning themselves with real situations, to which they refer continually and on which their methodology is based) must describe the objects of their concern; this assumes a need to distinguish among those objects and impose order upon them. (A

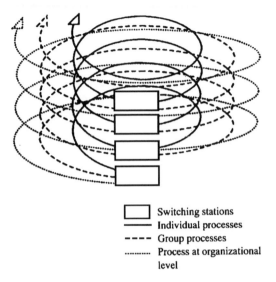

⬜ Switching stations
—— Individual processes
- - - Group processes
.......... Process at organizational
level

Figures 2.1a and (opposite) b.   We have schematized the multi-level developmental processes of individuals, groups, and organizations as a system of nested spirals, which are connected by switching stations (Figure 2.1a). The spirals emerge from circular processes. These run from knowledge via the multifold processes of action-preparing information processes (here called 'planning') to action. Actions and their results lead to learning from which the elaboration of the knowledge basis results (Figure 2.1b). The switching stations described here are: the multi-level organized knowledge system (see Thommen, Amman, and von Cranach, 1988), the communication during planning processes, the multi-level 'action' (with the included communication), and finally development related communication (taken from von Cranach and Tschan, 1991).

zoology that tried to do without the concept of 'animal' would find its scope severely limited.) My aim in this section is to distinguish among various types of social systems, but also to look for similarities: in a word, to classify them. Naturally, such distinctions are often made, but with no attempt to relate the concepts to one another, or to use them consistently. For example, 'group' in the literature can mean almost anything, from a three-man research group to a nation, or even a statistical aggregate.

In what follows I shall use two examples, to which I shall be returning at frequent intervals.

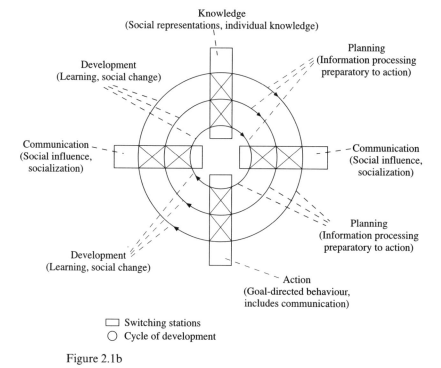

Figure 2.1b

*Notice of dismissal*

The protagonists are P, a professor at a Swiss university, his secretary Miss SE, his assistant A, and other employees, E1, E2, and E3. P holds a weekly conference with them to discuss problems and, if possible, find acceptable solutions. Others involved are the head of the university administration (HA) and a professional administrator, PA.

A took his first degree under P, and after that worked for him as a trainee. A few months ago, P was obliged to dismiss him on financial grounds (funds were very short, owing to government cutbacks), but, in view of A's family circumstances and their long association, he was reluctant to do so before A had finished his doctoral dissertation. A intends to finish in November, and he also hopes to continue working on a part-time basis. They agree that he should leave at the end of the year. A asks for a formal notice of dismissal so that he can apply for unemployment benefit if necessary (if he left by mutual agreement he might not be entitled to benefit.) Not until the last possible moment, at the beginning of December, does P ask his secretary to inform the university administration that A is leaving – only to learn that this is not legally possible. Apparently, A's employment contract is *permanent*, and can be terminated only after two months' notice. After some reflection and discussion with the other employees in the department, P decides to ask the administration to give A notice to leave at the end of February.

This little story contains the most important elements in the theoretical discussion which will follow: a number of individuals, interacting in dyads (P and S), groups (the department) and organizations (the university) and relating personally to one another (P and A). They base this interaction on previous knowledge of legal relationships and actual events, but they do not all have the same knowledge. The social configurations figure as negotiating units (the university as party to A's contract), and individuals sometimes negotiate on behalf of the social configurations (HA on behalf of the university). This negotiation depends on present knowledge (HA knows the conditions attached to A's post). Certain culture-specific assumptions are made throughout (e.g. the formal regulations which make a legal contract valid) – assumptions which would be unthinkable in a stone-age culture, for example.

### 'Christmas'

The Smiths (father John, 34; mother Catherine, 31; daughters Elizabeth and Sandra, 8 and 6; son Mark, $1\frac{1}{2}$) are celebrating Christmas. After some long and multifarious preparations, with all due respect to national customs and their own habits, the festivities have begun, and every member of the family takes part. A family is more independent than a university department: it is not so closely bound up with the social super system; it has other functions; personal relationships are much more important; and so on. But we can also discern some parallels: a social organization as an acting unit; individuals acting and interacting on behalf of this organization; a group within which we can distinguish dyads (mother and child, husband and wife), etc. In this example, too, the role of knowledge is transparently clear. Without 'cultural representations' (what does Christmas mean? what is a Christmas tree for?), 'values' (how far are we going to take part in the conspicuous consumption, the consumer orgy?), 'practical knowledge' (how do you make a Christmas cake?) and 'personal knowledge' (if Elizabeth is given a doll, must Sandra be given one too?), the festivity will not be a success. That is all that need be said for the moment.

I now propose a rudimentary classification for social systems (see Figure 2.2). It concentrates on distinguishing among the different levels within the system. Within this distinction there are various subclasses,

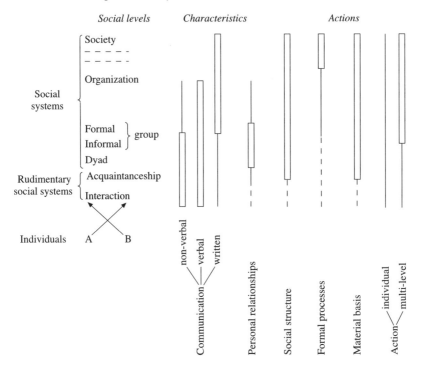

Note: Vertical lines show distribution of characteristics:

| ¦ Existing | | Important | ☐ Central point of the characteristic |

Figure 2.2   A classification of social systems

which I shall consider briefly later. My distinguishing criteria are printed as column heads. Their individual significances will become clear from the subsequent discussion. Here I am distinguishing between more permanent 'structures' and temporary 'processes'. The 'social levels' (first column) are based on individuals, single people. 'Rudimentary' systems are structurally less developed than 'full' social systems.

Now let us consider the social levels one by one. All social systems consist of individuals, and all their processes are also individual processes (like the actions of P, A, and HA, or father, mother, and children in our examples). But they are not just individual processes (the university ends the employment relationship; the family celebrates Christmas). To put it another way, they can no more be reduced to individuals than a wood can be reduced to its individual trees. Most people would readily accept the latter idea; but when it comes to sociology, this intrinsic truth is opposed to individualistic tendencies, which are deeply rooted in our culture (cf. Oyserman and Markus, chapter 7 this volume.)

Individuals interact, and so the social begins. (John and Catherine got to know each other in a bank, when she was behind the counter and John was a customer.) Here we are not so interested in the systemic character of the *interaction*, which has been examined in many studies of verbal and non-verbal communication (see, e.g., Watzlawick, Beavin, and Jackson, 1967); but we must insist that interaction can both be a (rudimentary) social system in itself and also take place within higher social systems. Repeated or intensive interactions lead to *acquaintance-ship*, which is already much more structured. (John began to go more and more frequently to the same window in the bank.) As our examples show, acquaintanceship includes interaction and contains a measure of personal relationship; and it already has a 'material basis' (the bank counter). This material basis brings in the 'environment'.

A *dyad* is an established one-to-one relationship with a fully developed personal relationship (one partner is important to the other as an individual, and this includes the relevant emotional processes), a social structure (e.g. roles, a hierarchy), a well-developed material basis and multi-level interaction – the dyad begins to act as a unit (it is easy to imagine how John and Catherine's relationship developed).

*Groups* are small social systems containing several persons: this makes their structure more complex than the dyad's, because they allow (for example) coalitions, three-cornered relationships etc. They are *acting* social systems and, as in a dyad, personal relationships are very important. Furthermore, we distinguish between informal and formal groups. In informal groups, formal processes are less important, and their structures and actions are less formalized. Formal groups are formal mainly because they are embedded in a higher, and therefore more strongly formalized, social system. Our examples illustrate this rather well. The Smith family is an informal group. Their rule system (who does what) is nowhere written down, and (with some exceptions) their interactions do not need any particular form in order to be effective. The university department is another matter: hierarchy and distribution of roles are determined by rules, ordinances, work contracts, and so on, and so the potential actions of group members, and the group as a whole, are prescribed and circumscribed. Finally, all groups (like social systems in general) require a material basis: what would happen to the Smiths without their nice house, or to the department without its well-equipped faculty building?

Lastly, *organizations* can subsume dyads and groups; hence they are usually rather larger. Thus our department is part of a faculty, which is part of a university. Families in our society are a noticeable exception: they all have the same structure in law, but apart from that they are only in principle subordinated to 'public institutions', the community or the state, and then only in certain precisely defined relations. They are protected by a certain autonomy which makes them difficult to interfere with even if they infringe social values or laws (child abuse, marital rape, etc.). The most important characteristic of organizations is that personal relationships within them are subject to *formalisation*. This may to some extent be caused by their size, but it is also quite clearly one of the purposes of the organizational form to introduce a certain objectivity into the shifting and unpredictable texture of personal relationships, and make structures and processes independent of individuals. This means that individual group members can, to an extent, be interchanged or substituted for one another. Thanks to formalization, structures and processes are, at least in part, governed by formal, fixed rules, and the outcome of processes like interaction and transaction is *invalid* unless it follows these formal rules. Thus John can ask Catherine for money informally if he has forgotten to withdraw any for the weekend; but if P asks HA for a couple of hundred dollars for a guest lecturer, he is unlikely to get them unless he follows the correct procedure: the request will have to have the prescribed form, the budget item must be correctly described, there must be a written receipt, etc. Of course, HA knows perfectly well what P wants – but unless there is a formal request, he will be unwilling or unable to grant it.

More and more attention is being drawn – rightly – to the importance of informal processes in organizational action: for example, any organization may be paralyzed by a 'work to rule'. But it seems to me that discussions of 'formal' and 'informal' organization are riddled with uncertainties: observers often fail to notice that informal processes take place on group or dyad level, and these are parts of the organization itself. My multi-level concept can clarify matters here. If communications within an organization are formalized, this will of course make formal writing more important. Recall processes – minutes, memoranda, filing, mainframe computer – will also be highly formalized. The material presentation of data takes precedence over knowledge processing. The organization is the most complex form of social system, below society itself, that will concern us in these pages.

It is possible to make further distinctions within this classification of social systems. Among groups we can distinguish working groups, families, leisure-time groups; among organizations, profit-oriented undertakings, public administrations, schools, voluntary associations, etc. Each has its own structure and function, which will affect their memory processes and knowledge.

We could summarize this part of the discussion as follows:

4 Social systems can be ordered into a hierarchical, multi-level system. On each level we will find particular patterns of structure and characteristic processes.
5 The higher levels subsume the lower levels and their characteristics, and add further characteristics of their own.
6 Further distinctions can be made on each separate level.

### Memory and knowledge in social systems

*Recall processes*

I have differentiated among social systems and claimed that they differ in their methods of knowledge processing. Their recall processes also differ. The multi-level principle applies again here: these processes always include individual processes on the individual level, but on the social levels, procedures are more numerous than, and sometimes different from, the sum of individual processes.

Wegner (1986) has shown, in his work on 'transactive memory', how this applies to dyads. Partners in a dyad remember different aspects of a given stock of knowledge according to their role in the dyad: they 'divide the labour' of knowledge processing. If necessary, they use each other as external knowledge-storage systems. In order to extract information from an external storage system one must know its label and location: thus partners must have some idea of who ought to know what. In a communicative exchange, they pool their respective funds of knowledge, a process which may alter the initial input. This is the essence of the theory of transactive memory (cf. Echebarria and Castro, chapter 6 this volume).

The dyad now possesses a stock of knowledge different from that of its individual members. It has *more* knowledge insofar as, following the familiar principle of *gestalt* psychology, 'the whole is more than the sum of its parts'; but it has *less* knowledge if its members withhold information or seldom discuss it, for example if a taboo is involved (Ochsenbein and Schärer, 1994), or if they misunderstand each other. Moreover, it is only to be expected that there will be 'process losses' during the communication process, as in any kind of common action. Finally, the dyad possesses another stock of knowledge, insofar as the content of the knowledge changes during communication. This knowledge of the dyad can (depending on the role structure) be used subsequently in actions, or in individual or dyadic knowledge processing.

We can use our existing examples to illustrate the procedure. In course

of the dismissal process, the administrator asks the professional administrator, PA, to show him A's personal file. She finds it using her own
memory plus external storage systems (a register or computer). When
they discuss the current decision process in the next meeting, HA and PA
call to mind some similar cases, and HA knows what legal precedent
applies. He comes to a decision, which PA conveys to the professor's
secretary: 'We can't repudiate the contractual relationship: P will have to
give the usual period of notice, which takes us to the end of February at
the earliest.' This takes place within a dyad, which is part of an
organization, and therefore formal. Intimately related dyads, like John
and Catherine, function in a similar way, but external storage systems
and formalised sequences will be far less prominent in their recall
processes.

The recall processes of groups follow the same basic pattern, but
groups have a far more complex structure, and their communications can
take place either collectively, or in subgroups or dyads. This leads to an
unequal distribution of knowledge, not only because different individuals
know different things and have different roles, but also because of the
location in time and space of current communication patterns. We must
therefore assume that the recall processes of groups are considerably
more complex (cf. Echebarría and Castro, chapter 6 this volume).
Unfortunately, there has been little empirical research on this as yet.

Organizations are larger, more complex, more materially based and
more formal than dyads and groups, and all these characteristics affect
their recall processing. Knowledge is more unevenly distributed in large
and complex structures: indeed, this inequality is often a part of the
legitimate order, more or less formalized by the formality of the
structure, whereas in groups it is a mere matter of fact. (Catherine and
John may have the same amount of knowledge about Christmas; at least,
there is no good reason why not. HA, as a member of the university
administration, knows more than PA about long-term university policy,
and this is quite legitimate and to be expected.) The complexity of
organizations produces another characteristic: they are subdivided not
only into individuals, but also into social subsystems (groups, depart-
ments, etc.), each of which has a role matching the division of labour
(Katz and Kahn, 1978) and possesses knowledge. (The university administration, on behalf of which HA acts, knows the 'procedure' for
dismissing A; and the administration acts on behalf of the university as a
whole.) Therefore our previous remarks must be extended to multi-level
recall processes: this involves many practical difficulties, but none of
principle. The importance of the material base is clear from the greater,
and formally necessary, use of material-storage systems. Moreover,

formalization also filters out a good deal of information and admits only certain approved content into store – usually anything which concerns the relational aspects of social processes. (John and Catherine will remember for years how the children reacted when they suggested cutting down on the Christmas celebrations and giving the money to charity. On the other hand, A's personal file gives no hint of how P reacted emotionally to H's decision; indeed, the whole procedure, which is quite informal, is not mentioned at all, and leaves no trace in the memory of the organization.)

This brings me to an important point. Recall processes are important for an understanding of the processes of social systems because they are represent part of its knowledge processing (as they do on the individual level), and they thereby alter the knowledge itself in a more or less systematic way. The effect is similar to that of the influences on individual perception processes in our initial example, and can be labelled 'selection', 'accentuation', 'completion', and 'organization'.[2] Certain items of knowledge are similarly selected in the course of encoding, storing, and decoding: some parts are emphasized, missing items are added, and the whole is organized in terms of content and function. We can assume – and this is very important – that these changes will depend on the characteristics, structures, and functions of the processing system; indeed, this is one reason why we embarked on a classification of social systems.

This argument could be extended. In some earlier studies, for example, I pointed out an analogy between *conscious individual knowledge processing* and *open group communication*. However, in research on recall processes, conscious processing is seen as a characteristic of short-term recall ('working storage system'). On these terms, transactive memory could be understood as *short-term group memory*. The only structures which could be considered as analogous to long-term memory would be the psychological memories of participants, or the social system's material storage.

So far, our analysis has been theoretical, with little empirical data to go on. We may summarize as follows:

7 The recall processes of social systems (encoding, storage, decoding) will alter the knowledge of those systems (selection, accentuation, completion, organization) in ways depending on their characteristic structures and processes, following general principles of knowledge processing. This will involve several system levels, mainly through communication or the use of material storage.

*Knowledge content and function*

What do social systems actually 'know'? What knowledge do they possess, and how do they use it? These are the questions we will deal with in the last part of this chapter.

*Forms of knowledge and their classification*

It is obvious from everyday experience that there are different kinds of knowledge. In the seminal works of knowledge psychology, which is currently a very active branch of psychology, different words are used for different types of knowledge, but there is no generally recognized classification. Most authors distinguish on the basis of differences in content or function, or both. The terminology is very general, however, because research psychologists are more interested in processes than in content (or even function). The fundamental distinction in current research is between *factual (declarative) knowledge* and *procedural knowledge*. There is also *meta-knowledge*, the general knowledge required to control and plan transactions. These knowledge types may be related to a common area of life, or a given problem, and are then described as *area-specific*. Alongside these we may rank *heuristic* knowledge, which 'shapes and directs sequences of processes' (Dörner 1988), and *episodic knowledge* of past events. Other classes of knowledge are the *conceptual*, *taxonomic*, and *ontological*.

Social psychology also uses several concepts implicitly or explicitly related to knowledge.[3] I have summarised their characteristics in Table 2.1. With two exceptions, I have used the definitions of two representative textbooks and a reference book. This simplified overview allows us to draw some conclusions about the current debate. However, we must not forget that the sources are of very different natures: the chapters in Hewstone, Stroebe and Stephenson (1995) and Frey and Greif (1987) were mostly written from the viewpoint of traditional, individual-oriented social psychology, whereas Witte's textbook (1989) was based on systems theory. Hence Witte's definitions assume a multi-level approach.

This is, of course, a greatly simplified description of what these terms are and how they are connected. They are used in very different ways, and this has given rise to much debate and discussion. I could find no available synopsis, and realized I would have to make my own. Even such a simplified overview may prove useful, however, when we are considering how far the various terms are capable of describing the knowledge of social systems.

First let us see whether we can use them to describe social events, and if any gaps remain. Since we have no empirical research to go on, we

Table 2.1. Socio-psychological constructs relating to knowledge

| Characteristic \ Construct | Script | Prototype | Value and value-orientation | Self-concept | Norms and rules |
|---|---|---|---|---|---|
| Object | actions | circumscribed objects and facts | broad classes of objects and facts | 'own person', 'self' | actions |
| Short definition | schematic knowledge as basis for routine action | category which best represents its object | basic representation of what is desirable or undesirable | terms, theoretical representations, viewpoints, self-esteem | rules for actions, partly sanctioned |
| Function | active function | simplified identification of objects | guidance of the affective subsystem; coherence of cognitive subsystem | core of personality; cognitive and active functions (coordination and interpretation) | conformity to society, action-related functions |
| Carrier system | individual | individual | V: society (culture); VO: individual | individual; group | individual |
| Source | Hewstone *et al.* (1995) | Hewstone *et al.* (1995) | Witte (1989) | Frey & Greif (1987) | Hewstone *et al.* (1995) |

must return to our previous examples. Let us look first at the knowledge terminology of general psychology.

We will begin with the 'notice of dismissal'. P and A agree that A's period of service will terminate at the end of the year. Both assume that they know each other – their personal qualities, lifestyles, etc.: they have *personal knowledge*. Both know – from a different viewpoint and imperfectly – the demands and possibilities of the current situation: they have *factual knowledge*, which includes knowledge of previous events (*historical knowledge*). These stocks of declarative knowledge stem from personal experience in the social context of their faculty. P and A each have their own ideas about the right way to proceed: they have procedural or *transactional knowledge*. This can also describe social knowledge on the individual level: P's desire to obtain a written notice of

| Social attitudes | Naive, subjective, everyday theories | Group beliefs | Ideology | Social represen-tations |
|---|---|---|---|---|
| social facts, prob-lems, groups | social and other facts, actions, psychic processes | the in-group, and facts impor-tant to it | social facts affecting the interests of the social system | (a) problematic social facts (b) actions |
| (a) cognitions, emotions and action-related dispositions (b) evaluation of facts | layperson's quasi-theoretical conceptual system | theories and concepts of 'groups' which relate to the groups them-selves and stablize them | systemically ordered know-ledge claiming to be true; prejudiced, not subject to analysis | social know-ledge relating to a problem area |
| knowledge func-tion (perception, evaluations); action-related function disputed | integration of knowledge, action-related function | individual con-forms to 'group'; stabili-zation of 'group' | knowledge func-tion, conforms to the group | stabilization of personality by construction of a central area; organization of knowledge and actions |
| individual | individual | individuals (group unclear) | social systems, individuals | unclear: indi-vidual or social system (rarely culture) |
| Hewstone et al. (1995) | Hewstone et al. (1995) | Bar-Tal (1990) | Witte (1989) | Frey & Greif (1987) |

dismissal is based on the widely known fact that in order to qualify for unemployment benefit in Switzerland, one must give proof that one's employment was not terminated due to misconduct.

Now let us turn to the socio-psychological terminology outlined in Table 2.1. The behaviour of both P and A depends on *social attitudes*. P's attitude, acquired over many years of service, is that budget resources must be used sparingly; A, as the father of a young family, knows he is responsible for their social welfare. Note that A is thinking and acting solely on his own behalf, whereas P also represents a social unit: in this context (and later, when he dictates the letter to HA) his knowledge appertains to his professorial chair.

The decisions taken by HA and his colleague, PA, show even more clearly how the social system is represented in this nexus. The administration, as a suborganization of the university, takes decisions on the latter's behalf. Their factual and action knowledge (A's appointment is for an unlimited period, so he must be given a period of notice) is that of the university as an organization, and is stored formally on the administrative level as *material knowledge* – personal file, regulations for the employment of assistants. The regulation is also an expression of society's *social representations* of the social rights of employees, which perhaps boils down to a social attitude held by HA and PA: 'Professors tend to be disorganized and capricious; it's up to us administrators to make sure that everything is done properly.' (This attitude probably includes some 'stereotypes' – categories which structure perceptions of certain groups of people.)

The regulation itself is, first and foremost, a *norm* or collection of norms. But it also represents a standardized set of instructions governing day-to-day transactions within the university: on the organizational level, a kind of *script*. However, it is very likely that HA and PA do not need actually to consult the regulations, because they have dealt with similar cases before. As individuals and as a dyad they possess (in connection with the prototypes and the scripts) *episodic knowledge*, i.e. they remember potential precedents for the current procedure. Maybe only one of them knows the precedent; maybe both remember bits of it and piece them together: this would be an example of *transactive memory* as defined above.

Now to the 'Christmas' example. There is no need for me to describe it in detail, as there can scarcely be a reader who cannot supply examples of the various classes of knowledge from their own experience of Christmas. Here again, we find all the classes of knowledge defined in the literature. There are differences, however: unlike the university (an organization), the family uses much less knowledge from material storage systems, excepting a few elements from known scripts, such as a cake recipe. The biggest difference, however, is that the family uses a kind of knowledge which we have scarcely mentioned up to now: *customs*. Customs constitute a kind of hierarchical system: within the overall system of Christmas customs common to our culture there are regional and subcultural customs, within which families usually develop their own habitual rites. Embedded in this context there are further classes of knowledge, for example, the prototypical Christmas tree and the script of the individual Christmas ritual. *Thus, knowledge systems include different types of knowledge.*

This short exercise seems to show that the terms developed by General Psychology are adequate to describe types of knowledge in everyday life. But what about the system behind them? To answer this question we will need to look somewhat more closely at the terms listed in Table 2.1. Our first impression gleaned from this table is probably accurate: basically, the knowledge-related terminology of social psychology can be applied to that the knowledge-psychology characteristics discussed above, but the terminology is far more specific. It relates to different contents and has a very different scope. The boundaries of these terms may be indistinct, or they may overlap; moreover, they do not cover the entire field, for they leave a number of gaps (for example, there are no terms for things like social or private customs which are handed down by tradition). The carriers of knowledge are almost always individuals; social systems are seldom mentioned, and when they are, there is no mention of memory functions. The functions examined mostly relate to individual cognition (perception, judgement, emotions, evaluations) and individual transactions; social systems include stabilization, integration, and demarcation. In fact, this overview shows the terminology to be unsystematic: the terms were developed and adopted in the service of definite, but limited, research aims.

From our point of view this is, of course, unsatisfactory. To research into the knowledge of social systems, its content and function, we need something which is at least minimally systematic. However tentative our remarks may be, we must always try to bring our terminology into better order. Otherwise we will never be able to reorganize the field as a whole, with its tens of thousands of studies, its hundreds of monographs and textbooks, representing the life's work of so many specialists. We cannot hope for a utopia, but we can try to find some overarching category which will include all the others. It must be wide-ranging and capable of sufficient expansion to encompass all the knowledge of social systems. It will have to take account of the dynamic role of knowledge in relation to action and development. It must be applicable to all classes of multi-level support systems. Finally, its relationship to other knowledge constructs must be clear.

The category best able to fulfil these criteria is that of social representations. Its content is the broadest (apart from that of 'subjective theories', which can be seen as single-level social representations); its content can include virtually everything of importance to its support systems (cf. the surveys in Wagner, 1994). It includes the important aspects of its objects and imposes internal order on them. The concept is dynamic, predicated on change and social transformation: social representations can be seen as a basis for transactive knowledge, and can be developed into a model for social development (cf. von Cranach, 1992). Moreover, its relationship to other knowledge constructs has already been extensively discussed. Jodelet (1984) and Semin (1989) have discussed it in relation to prototypes; Breakwell (1993) to the concept of self; Doise (1989) and Wagner (1994) to social attitudes; Flick (chapter 3 this volume) to subjective theories; and Aebischer, Deconchy and Lipanski (1991) and Augoustinos (chapter 10 this volume) to ideologies. Paez and Gonzales (1993) discuss its relationship to scripts, prototypes, social attitudes, and ideologies – and this is only a selection from the relevant material. Both individuals (as in most studies) and social systems (Thommen, Ammann and von Cranach, 1988; Thommen, von Cranach and Ammann, 1992; cf. von Cranach, 1992) have been considered as carrier systems for social representations. At this point, however, the concept requires further development.

### The functions of knowledge

Human knowledge serves two functions, action and cognition. To act is to influence both the world and oneself; to have cognition is to make an image (though not necessary an accurate one) of the world (world picture) and of oneself (self-portrait). The two are actually inseparable, bound together in a circular process whereby knowledge guides action, and action creates and alters knowledge, and therefore cognition (that is what we call 'learning'). Therefore these circular processes are essential for development. This principle was applied to the ontogenesis of thought by Piaget ([1936] 1953, [1937] 1954), and to its phylogenesis more recently by Klix (1992); both, of course, include an abundance of detail and discuss many other possible viewpoints. The same principle also applies to social systems, so long as we take a multi-level approach (see Figure 2.1, in which I attempt to represent this notion). The coupling of knowledge and action is vital, because human beings cannot survive unless they act. The same, as aforesaid, applies to their social systems.

Human cognition can, however, stand alone, and the impulse towards it can be disconnected from action and become an autonomous motive. Knowledge systems are created which build their own rules from their own structures and construct more or less abstract, very elaborate, world pictures, and self-portraits. That is also a kind of 'learning'. It happens overwhelmingly in the context of social systems, and its results are then labelled 'culture' (under which label we must remember to include material storage systems and other cultural artefacts). This sort of cognitive development is a universal characteristic of human life; its ultimate expression is the sciences, in which researchers work within their own disciplines to modify the world pictures and self-portraits within our culture. However, such cognitions also affect action in technological disciplines, economics, and in daily life. They also influence everyday knowledge – individual and social representations – and in an altered form they become common property and guide everyday actions. The transformation of science into universally shared social knowledge was the first topic of research into social representations (Moscovici, [1961] 1976).

The connections between knowledge and action are fundamental truths. Unfortunately, they are often neglected by psychologists and social scientists busy with their own research, perhaps because their own activity is so strongly focused on cognition. The cognitive function takes pride of place in the literature on social representations. I myself would give priority to the active function, for reasons I have explained above (and see also von Cranach, 1992). My examples make this very clear. However, little practical research has been done in this area as yet.

I shall now summarize the conclusions from this section as a series of propositions:

 8  The terminology used by psychologists and social psychologists to discuss knowledge do apply, in principle, to real, existing operations of knowledge processing. They cover a wide spectrum of facts, but give rise to serious problems of delimitation and leave some areas uncovered. We still lack a coherent, systematic and comprehensive classification.

 9  'Social representations' seems particularly well suited as a super-ordinate terminology for knowledge.

10  The chief function of knowledge is to foster action and cognition; each of the latter influences the other.

11  Any future classification of knowledge should take better account of the multi-level nature of knowledge processing.

### The theory of social representations: suggestions for further development

'Social representations' is one of the most innovative and influential concepts of modern social psychology, and is therefore worth developing further. My first suggestion aims at widening the scope of the theory. It was, of course, Moscovici ([1961] 1976, 1984a) who extended and modified Durkheim's theory of 'collective representations' ([1898] 1974, [1895] 1982). Durkheim saw social-knowledge, especially social knowledge systems, as free-standing, super-individual collective images which could not be reduced to individual facts. His 'collective representations' did not only include science, religion, and mythologies: indeed, they extended (as Moscovici complained) to all forms of human knowledge. Moreover, he saw them as stable and unalterable. Moscovici's social representations, on the other hand, were a more limited and dynamic concept, which is especially applicable where there is change (hence the change of name: cf. Moscovici, chapter 14 this volume) 'Social representations' means structured, connected knowledge on a social level, applied to a specific nexus of problems, developed and shared by individuals. Social representations help in the further processing of knowledge which is already available, but hard to understand and therefore threatening. 'The purpose of all representations is to make something unfamiliar, or unfamiliarity itself, familiar' (Moscovici, 1984a, p. 24). The most important of the consequent changes are the result of 'anchoring' (relating unfamiliar ideas to familiar ideas and images via individual classification and appellation), or of 'objectification' (turning abstract forms into concrete representations, e.g. by developing a 'figurative nucleus').

Making the concept more dynamic in this way seems attractive at first sight, but in fact it overshoots the mark. 'Familiar' and 'unfamiliar', 'threatening' and 'safe' are not polar opposites, but the end points of a series of fine gradations; real, existing knowledge consists of multi-dimensional portraits or complex structures, in which many different qualities are mingled and given many different expressions. The familiar goes hand in hand with the unfamiliar. Even processing does not move naturally from the unfamiliar to the familiar; and the familiar can become suddenly alien. Moreover, these representations are structurally similar: even the most solidly familiar representations have a figurative core, around which peripheral assumptions will cluster. So I can find no compelling reason for the important but misleading decision to exclude traditional and familiar knowledge (such as the Christmas customs in our example) from the theory. We need not worry about dynamics: they stem from the carrier system, which is a dynamic, pluralistic, multi-level society, and so cannot be suppressed.

My second suggestion aims to put the problems of multi-level knowledge processing into perspective. Hitherto, social representations have been defined as societal knowledge developed and modified by individuals through interaction. Unfortunately, however, the meaning of 'societal' and 'interaction' is quite unclear. We need to be much more specific about the relevant carrier system and the way it processes knowledge. These distinctions are very important. As we have seen, the structures and functions of the carrier system determine its knowledge-processing capabilities (e.g. the recall process), including their contents, functions and results. Catherine and John discussing whether to cut back on their Christmas celebrations are quite a different proposition from a government suppressing the festivities altogether, as has happened in more than one country. A few years ago we attempted to account for these differences by introducing the concept of 'Individual Social Representations', i.e. social representations on the individual level (Thommen, Ammann and von Cranach, 1988); but even this differentiation is far from comprehensive. At present, researchers are faced with at least two problems: more in general, we must study how different carrier systems process knowledge and how the processes inter-relate; more in particular, we must identify the support systems of particular social representations and analyse their functions and processes on more than one level.

My third proposal bears on the action-related function. Moscovici himself stressed the function of cognition: 'When we study social representations we study man, insofar as he asks questions and seeks answers or thinks, and not insofar as he processes information, or behaves. More precisely insofar as his aim is not to behave, but to understand' (Moscovici, 1984a, p. 15). Other studies do refer to action-related functions (e.g. Guimelli, 1993), but come to no significant conclusions. As I have tried to show, such studies betray a misunderstanding of the terms on which social systems exist. It seems to me that work on the active function in social representations is currently on two levels. First, there are *general action schemata*, which underlie the typologies described above: they are rooted in social representations, which are the common property of our culture (cf. von Cranach, 1993); this assumption is now for the first time being confirmed by concrete research. Alongside these there are *object-specific action schemata*, which underlie individual actions (cooking a dish, doing a particular piece of work, etc.) and are actualized in their 'operative image systems' (Oschanin, 1976, quoted after Hacker, 1986). These also rest on social representations (see, e.g., Thommen, Ammann and von Cranach, 1988). Both urgently require further research. Once again I will draw my own conclusions:

12 If 'social representations' is to become the core of a theory of social knowledge, the theory of social representations must be refined and extended. In particular, the habit of limiting it to dynamic forms of knowledge must be reconsidered; assumptions about knowledge processing by carrier systems on different levels must be further refined and more prominence must be given to the active function of knowledge.

Here I end my remarks. Knowledge is nourished by continual development. This applies in particular to the theory of social representations, which takes development as its own subject of study. I have set out my proposals at the end of each section of this essay. In conjunction, they constitute a plea for an ecology of human social systems, their knowledge and their actions.

## Notes

I am grateful to Peter Beck, Uwe Flick, and Guy Ochsenbein for their criticisms and suggested improvements. This chapter was translated from the German by Rosemary Morris.

1  Anglo-American cultural psychologists seem to be interested principally in the differing behaviour of individuals in different cultures (Shweder and Sullivan, 1993); their German-speaking colleagues seem more interested in integral explanations based on action psychology (Boesch 1991; Lang 1992). Both strains make some use of semiotic concepts and methods (cf. also Oyserman and Marcus, chapter 7 this volume).

2  I am assuming that these concepts describe general categories of changes which take place during recall processes.

3  I have not included terms used in ecological or cultural psychology which relate to knowledge stored in *material artefacts*. Lang (1992) discusses various individual and socio-cultural functions of such knowledge. In principle, this term could be used for knowledge on any social level.

# 3 Everyday knowledge in social psychology

*Uwe Flick*

### Starting points

This chapter explores the theme of everyday knowledge and its relevance for research in social psychology. There are two starting points one can take for such considerations – a historical and a recent one. First, the historical one: Bartlett (1932, p. 239) defined 'social psychology as the systematic study of the modifications of individual experiences and responses due directly to membership of a group'. In this way he already designated the study of the social transformation and, thinking further, the social construction of individual experience as a central topic for research in social psychology. What follows will clarify the ways in which analyzing everyday knowledge offers an approach to this issue.

The more recent starting point comes from the study of 'social cognition', which has been one of the main fields of research in social psychology for a long time. From a critical assessment of recent research on cognition and its main model, human thinking as information processing, neurobiologist Francisco Varela (1990, p. 97) draws the conclusion that 'we are forced to accept that cognition can not be understood appropriately without taking into account everyday knowledge and that this everyday knowledge consists of nothing else but our physical and social history'. It follows that a central need and precondition for research in human thinking is the study of everyday knowledge, its content and structure, its social constitution, and its function – regardless of whether this research takes a cognitive or a social psychological focus. Bruner (1990, p. 35) describes such a *folk psychology* 'as a system by which people organise their experience in, knowledge about, and transactions with the social world'.

While everyday knowledge may be localized on different levels, there may also be diverse ways of differentiating it. Both of these features are inter-related and both are taken into account by the approaches to everyday knowledge discussed in this chapter – through the ways in which it is conceptualized theoretically (in a model), through the forms of their methodological access to it (in empirical research) and in the way its mundane practical function is understood (as everyday phenomenon).

The following discussion of 'everyday knowledge' begins with some considerations of the function of everyday knowledge in the research process and of the social construction of everyday knowledge. Second, there is a discsussion of some elements of the history of research on everyday knowledge. Finally, the main streams of recent research on everyday knowledge are briefly outlined, and a first attempt made to offer a systematic comparison.

### Everyday knowledge in the research process

According to the epistemology of Ludwik Fleck ([1935]1979 – see also Moscovici, chapter 14 this volume), everyday knowledge plays a part in every research process at two main steps. Scientists formulate most of their questions and define most of their theoretical concepts on the basis of everyday knowledge, their own or that of their fellows, using what Fleck calls 'pre-ideas'. Fleck shows that scientific knowledge (not only in the social sciences) is determined by its historical and social contexts, which influence, *what* can be found and, above all, *when* this is possible. Knowledge from beyond the narrow specialist knowledge of the discipline leaves its marks on such pre-ideas as well, for example, certain moral values, mundane assumptions, and stereotypes. According to Fleck, the observations researchers make and the facts they find are formed by the 'thought style' prevalent in the 'thought collectives' in which they are participants. This style of thinking depends on and is influenced by social styles, such as national styles of research and thinking, as well as by the everyday knowledge existing in that historical period.[1] Fleck argues that the results of research become relevant only when they emerge into public opinion, and as they become part of current public or mundane stocks of knowledge they also become vulgarized (Roqueplo 1974). They also react upon subsequent research and its questions while they are diffused through society.

Everyday knowledge can also become relevant in another way for social psychological research, as an issue for research itself. Figure 3.1 illustrates these three functions of everyday knowledge in the research process.

### The social construction of everyday knowledge

General questions about whether and how knowledge is socially constructed are asked in various contexts (see Doise, Mugny and Pérez,

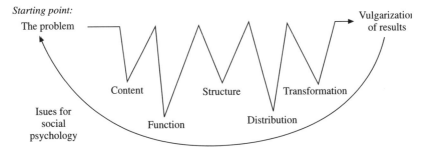

Figure 3.1   Everyday knowledge in the research process

chapter 5 this volume; Moscovici, chapter 14 this volume). One starting point for asking such questions about everyday knowledge is the work of the social philosopher Alfred Schütz (1966), whose theory takes as its premise that all our knowledge of the world, scientific or mundane, is a construction. Schütz (1966, pp. 62ff.) distinguishes first-degree constructions, which are made by actors in the social field, from second-degree constructions, which are those made by the scientist on the basis of such everyday constructions. For Schütz, everyday knowledge is organized and constructed through processes of selection and typification.[2] Why this should be seen as a *social* construction can be outlined in three ways.

First, there is social mediation in the acquisition of knowledge, where processes of social *conventionalization* of knowledge and thinking (see also Bartlett, 1932) play an influential role. As Schütz writes, 'I am taught . . . also how typical constructs have to be formed in accordance with the system of relevances accepted from the anonymous unified point of view of the in-group' (1962, pp. 13ff.). There is a parallel here to the epistemology of Ludwik Fleck ([1935]1979), who also holds that every kind of knowledge and understanding should be conceived of as a social rather than as an individual phenomenon. Central to his theory are his concepts of the 'thought collective' ('a community of persons mutually exchanging ideas or maintaining intellectual interaction', Fleck, [1935]1979, p. 39) and the style of thinking typical for it (which delimits what can be thought and what is accepted as knowledge at a certain time and in a certain social context), which influence not only scientific knowledge and perception, but also everyday knowledge.

Second, because it is socially mediated and conventionalized, everyday knowledge cannot be construed in terms of privacy or subjectivity. According to Schütz 'this world is not my private world but an intersubjective one and that, therefore, my knowledge of it is not my private affair but from the outset intersubjective or socialised' (1966, p. 7). The idea that social groups are constituted by the everyday knowledge or representations of a certain object shared by their members is central to research on social representations. Differences in professional everyday theories in the field of work demonstrate the influences of professions on their members' thinking (see Flick, 1989). Finally, 'cultural models', in the sense of D'Andrade (1987), are investigated to show how individual cognition and thinking are influenced by the culture and common models in it (several other chapters in this volume also develop this point, see chapter 7 by Oyserman and Markus; chapter 14 by Moscovici; chapter 11 by Carugati and Selleri; chapter 4 by Hewstone and Augoustinos).

The third essential aspect of the social construction of everyday knowledge is its *social distribution*. Schütz argues that there are differences between the worlds of different subjects, because, 'not only, *what* an individual knows differs from what his neighbour knows, but also *how* both know the 'same' facts' (1966, p. 14). A comparable idea is formulated in a different context by Putnam (1988, p. 24), who argues for a 'linguistic division of labour', according to which the same word (Putnam uses 'gold' as an example) is furnished with very different meanings depending on whether an expert or a layperson uses the word. Moscovici (1991) has taken up this idea and thought about a cognitive division of labour. With Goodman (1978), finally, such stocks of knowledge differing in their structures and points of reference may be understood as different 'versions of the world', produced by these stocks of knowledge.

With respect to the social distribution of knowledge Schütz (1966) distinguishes three ideal types of knowledge, that of the expert, the ordinary person and the well-informed citizen. But the social distribution of knowledge should not be understood as a clear hierarchy. Rather, the difference between experts and laypeople can vary according to particular issues or specific aspects of knowledge. As Schütz again puts it, 'I am an "expert" in a small field and "layman" in many others and so are you' (1966, p. 14). For example, the knowledge of a particular illness developed by chronically ill patients or their relatives often exceeds the knowledge of the doctors treating the patient. Compared with their physician, patients or relatives develop a sort of expert knowledge for this case, while leaving the layman–expert relation undisturbed for other diseases and cases (see the contributions in Flick, 1991a, 1993, for further details).

A social psychological analysis of the social construction of everyday knowledge needs to address questions such as: What do certain individuals or groups know about a specific domain or object and on which social factors does this knowledge depend? Across the versions of the world incorporated in it, everyday knowledge reveals the construction of subjectively and socially shared meanings. To fulfil this promise, empirical approaches to everyday knowledge need to be selected so that:

- room is left for the specificity of the cases under study, rather than assuming that there is a single principle of functioning which is generally valid (Flick, 1990); an assumption which is commonly made in much of the recent research in social psychology using the paradigm of information processing (and which Bruner, 1990, Graumann, 1988, Varela, 1990 Moscovici, 1991, have all recently criticized);
- the social context, in which this knowledge is acquired and used is taken into account and knowledge is not reduced to a private affair of an individual subject;
- evaluative and emotional aspects of knowledge are taken into account, so that, as Charles Taylor has put it in his discussion of recent research in cognition, 'the original informational input is deprived of its evaluational relevance and presented as a mere registration of 'facts' (1991, p. 98);
- and, finally, the internal structuring and complexity of knowledge is taken into account instead of attempting to analyse single cognitions or the information they contain.

Taken together, these points provide the basis for comparing and evaluating research programmes on everyday knowledge.

### Research on everyday knowledge: historical and recent approaches

The themes just outlined provide a starting point for a brief review of theoretical models of everyday knowledge in social psychology, and research approaches to this issue. In what follows this is done first more retrospectively, then more comparatively for recent approaches.

### *Kelly's psychology of personal constructs*

George A. Kelly (1955) coined the programmatic formulation 'Man the scientist'. His research on personal constructs starts from the notion that scientific and everyday knowledge are generally comparable. Everyday knowledge is seen as a system of (individual) constructs. Scientific reasoning and knowledge provide a model to explain everyday thinking and knowledge.

### Heider's psychology of interpersonal relations

Contrary to Kelly, Fritz Heider makes the point, that 'scientific psychology has a good deal to learn from common-sense psychology . . . fruitful concepts and hunches for hypotheses lie dormant and unformulated in what we know intuitively' (Heider, 1958, p. 6). Central to Heider's approach is his insistence on seeing 'language as a conceptual tool' (1958, p. 7) and the analysis of the concepts on which interpersonal behaviour is based. Increasingly, the research tradition which has grown up around Heider's work has become concerned with formal studies of processes in causal attribution (for more details see chapter 4 by Hewstone and Augoustinos, and chapter 14 by Moscovici).

Both these schools of research have contributed essential presumptions to recent studies of everyday knowledge, particularly ideas of hierarchical structures of knowledge and the notion that activities are structured by subjective constructs. These presumptions have been taken up in the concept of subjective theories (see below).

### Naive theories of behaviour

As well as research on implicit personality theories (Bruner and Tagiuri, 1954), Laucken (1974) has also used the model of scientific theories to conceptualize everyday knowledge. He describes naive individual theories as 'specific filling-outs' and individual concretions of a generic frame theory, i.e. the naive theory of behaviour. Laucken, too, uses analyses of linguistic material as an empirical approach.

More recent empirical approaches to everyday knowledge can be summarized under the headings of subjective theories, cultural models, and social representations.

### Subjective theories

Studying subjective theories emphasizes their implicit argumentational structure and comparability with scientific theories. The main interest in this research is everyday knowledge which is specific for certain topics, domains, or professions, for example, counsellors' subjective theories of trust. Subjective theories comprise not only causes and circumstances of events and situations, but also their consequences, and results and target ideas about how cope with them. They provide the basis both for defining situations and for positional coding (Dann, 1990).

In the case of counselling, for example, it could be demonstrated that counsellors' subjective theories provide stocks of knowledge for identi-

fying different types of initial situations in consultations, target representations for prototypical situations of counselling and their conditions
as well as representations of how to produce, at least approximately,
these conditions in the given situation. Analysing situations of counselling activities demonstrates how counsellors act according to these
stocks of knowledge, which are individual but also typical of their
profession, and how they use them for coping with actual and new
situations.

A problem in this approach is the one-sided orientation of scientific
theories as models for everyday knowledge and the clearly individual
focus on knowledge as a *subjective* theory. In addition, this approach
pays too little attention to the construction of reality through the
formation and use of such knowledge, so that the role played by socially
or culturally shared stocks of knowledge remains unclear in this research
(see Flick, 1987).

### Cultural models

At the borders of linguistic and cognitive anthropology knowledge is
seen as culturally mediated and shared, thus enlarging the perspective for
examining everyday knowledge. D'Andrade (1990, p. 65), for example
assumes, 'that culture consists of learned and shared systems of meaning
and understanding . . . Through these systems of meanings and understandings individuals adapt to their physical environment, structure
interpersonal relationships, and adjust psychologically to problems and
conflicts.'

Central features of such 'cultural models' are their hierarchical structure, the interlocking of different models with each other, and, finally,
their limitation in size and elements resulting from the processual
capacity of short-term memory. Additionally, there is the mundane
presupposition that everybody starts from the same model, so that
interpretations based on it are taken as facts (D'Andrade, 1987, p. 113).
The way to reconstruct these models is through the analysis of natural-
language expressions, as D'Andrade (1987) illustrates in his study of the
'folkmodel of the mind'. But in this study he assumes that the model is
valid for the USA and western Europe, an assumption which is grounded
in comparisons with representations from other cultures. The concepts of
schema and of cognition he uses follow too closely the way these terms
are used in research in the cognitive sciences and artificial intelligence.
The range of these models, for example, in the terminus *cultural model*, is
overestimated, as is their universality. Thus D'Andrade assumes a
*unitary* cultural model of the human mind within Western societies,

instead of exploring variations within these cultures through the differentiation of models in diverse social groups.

These two approaches furnish models for reconstructing and presenting idiosyncratic everyday knowledge (subjective theories) or culturally specific everyday knowledge (cultural models). Both approaches offer sufficiently structured complex models. Subjective theories, however, are so focused on the particularity of cases that they are unable to offer an adequate account of their social embeddedness. On the other hand, cultural models, precisely because they take culture as the reference point, fail to differentiate social embeddedness sufficiently to account for the different social embedding of individual knowledge which can be registered. Finally, because these models are more or less based on cognitive psychology, they do not take sufficient account of the social construction of (everyday) knowledge and the processes through which this is achieved. From the point of view of a psychology of the social, where the main interest is to focus on social knowledge, these perspectives have to be enlarged and more clearly differentiated. The approach of social representations may open a way to do just this, and in the following boxes the definitions used by these three approaches are compared:

### Subjective theories

Subjective theories are 'cognitions relating to the self and the world constituting a complex aggregate with an (at least) implicit argumentational structure; these cognitions fulfil functions parallel to those of objective "scientific" theories, namely those of explanation, prediction and technology'. (Groeben and Scheele, 1982, p. 16)

### Cultural models

'A cultural model is a cognitive schema that is intersubjectively shared by a social group. Such models typically consist of a small number of conceptual objects and their relations to each other.' (D'Andrade 1987, p. 112)

## Social representations

> '. . . a specific form of knowledge – common knowledge – whose contents show the operation of generative processes and socially marked functions. More broadly, it refers to a form of social thinking. The social marking of contents or processes of representations refers to conditions and contexts in which those representations reveal themselves in communication and through which they circulate and to the functions those representations serve in interactions with the world and with others.' (Jodelet 1984, pp. 361–2)

### Social representations as an approach to study everyday knowledge

The theory and studies of social representations originally dealt with the way scientific knowledge is popularized, the way in which it enters or replaces mundane, socially shared stocks of knowledge. Beyond that, a differentiated idea of everyday knowledge, its genesis and diffusion in society is outlined. Implicitly and explicitly, a theory of knowledge is developed, which deals especially with the relation of the various forms of knowledge.

### *Social and collective representations*

The starting point for the elaboration of the concept in Moscovici ([1961]1976) is Emile Durkheim's ([1898]1974) juxtaposition of individual representations as objects of psychology and collective representations as objects of sociology. For Durkheim, there are parallel juxtapositions of the individual vs. society and of instability vs. stability. This threefold polarity was made concrete in Durkheim's study of suicide ([1897]1952) in the thesis of anomie as the loss of the stability which a collective representation may give to the individual. Durkheim's ideal of a collective representation was the Catholic faith before the Reformation (Moscovici, 1984b, p. 950). The characteristics of such a collective representation are that, first, it is shared by all members of a society, second, there is a high degree of stability across several generations, and, lastly, that it is static (Moscovici, 1988a, p. 218).

Compared with this, social representations are more socially *differentiated*; there are several versions, forms, and types of social representations. To return to the same example, several religions now co-exist, with both cooperation and competition between them. Thus, the stabilizing influence a single religion had on society as a whole is lost. For the individual, this influence is at least reduced insofar as with the appearance of alternatives the question which now confronts them is whether to believe at all, and what to believe. Another major difference is the assumption of the dynamic of social representations. In contrast to classical religions, social representations are fed from various sources, mainly, but not only, the various sciences. On the other hand, a transformation of the knowledge received from such sources is typical of social representations. The kind of transformation of both the contents and the forms of knowledge varies in different social groups and contexts. This idea is taken up by Sperber (1985, p. 75) in his suggestion of an epidemiology of social representation, which should deal with how knowledge spreads and changes in the process of spreading.

Whereas collective representations are ascribed a *stabilizing* and *homogenizing* effect for both society and the individual, social representations have a differentiating effect and increased dynamics. Thus, Moscovici (1988a, p. 221) distinguishes *hegemonic, emancipated*, and *polemic* representations as subtypes of social representations. Hegemonic representations are shared by all members of a structured social group without being produced by them and are closest to Durkheim's model. Emancipated representations are generated through exchange and participation in certain ways of interpreting things, but have lost their close relation to a specific group (of experts for example) and turned into mundane knowledge. For example, everyday knowledge of mental illness is influenced by both special medical knowledge and laypeople's practical experience with the phenomenon as well as public opinion about it. Polemic representations become relevant for participants in social and political conflicts. Correspondingly, in comparison to collective representations, the function of social representations shifts from group coercion and group cohesion to communication and action and to the transportation of meaning and symbols (Moscovici, 1984b, p. 951).

From this brief description it should already be clear that, contrary to Durkheim's concept, social representations are not simply *given*, but are produced by individuals in social contexts or groups in a transformative process of interpretation and ascription of meaning.

### Social and individual representation

This relation can be addressed in two ways. Within the theory of social representations we can ask about the way in which the relation between individual and social knowledge is construed (see chapter 2 by von

Cranach in this volume). For this question, social representations define a framework for individual thinking and knowledge and for their social distribution. It is no longer, as with Durkheim, simply the conceptual juxtaposition of individual and social representation, because, 'what counts is not the separateness of individual representations but the transformation each individual imposes on group representation and the converse' (Moscovici, 1984b, p. 950). Individual and social representations are put in an interactive relation and individuals are seen as their 'producers and users . . . all in one' (Moscovici, 1988a, p. 233).

From a comparative perspective we can ask how the model of social representation is distinguished from other models of individual representation, such as individual and social cognition, mental models, subjective, naive, or implicit theories. What is it that makes social representations distinct, and therefore particularly instructive for a psychology of the social? An answer to this question can be drawn from examining the ways in which *social* representations differ fundamentally from models of individual representation:

First, social representations are social with respect to what is represented. This is also the case for social cognition research, but this approach is restricted to the study of general principles of human information processing applied to social relations. Social relations for this model usually means the interpersonal interaction, and the focus of attention is usually the biasing or impeding influences on the functioning of information processing resulting from social stereotypes or biases (see, for example, the discussion of the fundamental attribution error in chapter 4 by Hewstone and Augoustinos).

Second, social representations are social with regard to their genesis in everyday communication among individuals and among social groups:

The word 'social' was meant to indicate that representations are the outcome of an unceasing babble and a permanent dialogue between individuals, a dialogue that is both internal and external, during which individual representations are echoed or complemented. Representations adapt to the flow of interactions between social groups. (Moscovici, 1984b, p. 951)

This can be seen in studies of the genesis of social representations. Moscovici ([1961]1976), for example, in his analyses of French media was able to examine the way in which psychoanalytic terminologies have percolated into everyday knowledge. A second example is the study of social representations of nuclear power and its dangers by Galli and Nigro (1987). By interviewing children fourteen days after the reactor accident in Chernobyl and again after several months, they were able to show how these representations were generated and stabilized.

Third, social representations are social in their function and need to be studied with regard to this function. The task of social psychology is to demonstrate what happens when one form of knowledge is transformed into another – e.g. from science to everyday knowledge – and what effects these transformations have on communication and action (Moscovici, 1982, p. 139). Sustaining the mutual agreement inside social groups and their dissociation from outside is one of the most important functions of social representations. Jodelet ([1989a]1991, 1991) has studied the social representation of madness in a rural community which mainly survives by housing and caring for former patients of psychiatric hospitals. She demonstrates how rules for dealing with the mad, for excluding and integrating them, are derived from these representations in everyday life and are passed on to others – such as the children in the village. Reconstructing representations and particularly their change in the course of changes in mental illness, its phenomenology and treatment, illustrates both the content of these social rules and how they change. Revealing the unconscious and emotional aspects of the social representations renders comprehensible the implicit and explicit barriers errected around the mentally ill. The borders between social groups can be understood as the frontiers separating areas where social representations are shared from areas where they are no longer shared (see chapter 8 by Harré, this volume).

The concept of representation employed here is social first of all in the sense that social representations do not simply mirror an objectively given reality, rather, reality is socially constructed in the process of representation. Further, the concept of social representation does not assume a universal process of thinking and knowing, one which is optimally performed by scientists and only or less inaccurately present in everyday thinking. Such an assumption is made implicitly or explicitly by those models of everyday thinking and knowing which are based on scientific theories and modes of thinking, from attribution research to subjective theories. By contrast, Moscovici (1991) assumes a cognitive division of labour, in which the mode of thinking and knowing is determined not only by its content but also by the (social) function of the cognitive process.

### Social representations, science, common sense, and everyday knowledge

The origins of research on social representations were questions such as: 'What is the genesis of common-sense ideas about various scientific disciplines?' and 'What happens to a scientific discipline when it passes from specialists into society?' (Moscovici and Hewstone, 1983, p. 99).

Although this research was interested in everyday stocks of knowledge, the focus was different from that of Schütz (1966) or Heider (1958). Each of these authors assumed that scientific theories could develop from everyday knowledge. Social representations research has mainly been concerned with the reverse. Moscovici holds that archaic stocks of knowledge as common sense (as Schütz or Heider conceive of it) or myths in the classical sense have ceased to exist since the establishment of the sciences, and the popularization of their theories and results. Vulgarization (Roqueplo, 1974) of scientific ways of thinking (that is, the adoption of parts of scientific theories and results) led to a scientific rationalization of everyday thinking, knowledge, and life, which, in turn, led to the disappearance of certain forms of knowledge (Moscovici, 1984a, p. 29). Thus, the naïveté and the lay aspects of everyday thinking no longer hold, even though it is just these which are at least implicitly asumed in concepts of naive theories of behaviour (Laucken, 1974) or lay theories of health and illness (Raspe and Ritter, 1982). In this context, Moscovici (1982) maintains that we live in the 'era of social representations'. Where Heider (1958) or Kelly (1955) used the concept of a naïve scientist, Moscovici speaks of the 'amateur scientist' (Moscovici and Hewstone, 1983) to indicate the mass of people who obtain their knowledge of science from popularized adaptations in *Psychology Today*, *Scientific American*, or from the science pages of newspapers or from television programmes, or even from the representations of science in the cinema. People absorb their knowledge of science at first hand as readers or spectators engaged with these media, or at second hand through conversations with those who have already acquired such knowledge. This reception operates on the basis of the (parts of) scientific knowledge acquired in schools or through professional education, and on the transfer of ways of thinking and perceiving which such knowledge supports.

Figure 3.2 summarizes the relations among the different forms of knowledge implied in the theory of social representations. In this figure, Durkheim's collective representations are located next to myths and religions. The figure also separates the level of everyday life, where individuals and social groups produce reality, from the collective level, where knowledge is produced. Individuals and social groups do not have everyday access to this collective level, but a part of their knowledge is derived from it. Furthermore, pre-scientific areas of everyday life (that is areas which for reasons of time and locality remain outside the scope of scientific reason) are separated from areas where scientific reasoning has rationalized everyday life. As the figure indicates, scientific rationalization is always encroaching on common sense and religious forms of knowledge. Everyday knowledge emerges as the intersection of social

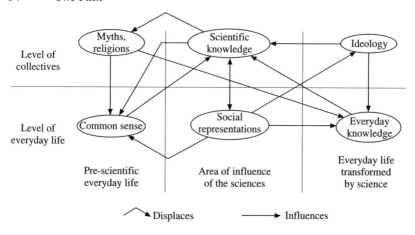

Figure 3.2    Forms of knowledge and their relations

and individual knowledge. The figure also shows the retreat of common sense and religious belief under the influence of science.

What does this perspective mean for strategies of research based on Schütz's and Heider's notion of scientific knowledge developing from common sense? Moscovici argues that common sense no longer exists as a clear-cut and separated counter-model to scientific knowledge, but that, perhaps to an extensive degree, it is derived from transformations of scientific knowledge. If this is the case, then the function of everyday stocks of knowledge as an epistemological source is not rendered obsolete, but the questions posed by Heider and Schütz need to be formulated in a different way.

First of all, the term 'everyday knowledge' is used here instead of common sense to take into account the influence of scientific rationaliza-tion. The heuristic potential of everyday knowledge for science can be seen in the fact that it is not exclusively based on vulgarized science but also draws on other sources such as traditional assumptions or beliefs. In her study of mental illness, Jodelet ([1989a]1991, 1991) has shown how myths and traditions or religious beliefs, and above all practical know-ledge influence everyday assumptions about health and illness. Similar processes can be seen in reactions to the appearance of Aids and the moral 'loading' of public and private discourses about it. Or again, the religious metaphors and archaic thinking used in dealing with cancer, such as the metaphor of 'God's scourge' (see Becker, 1986). As far as the transformation of scientific knowledge is concerned, the questions to be asked are what knowledge is transformed in which contexts into what everyday knowledge, how is it mixed with which other sources of knowledge, and how does it become relevant for human actions? Which problems are still solved in everyday life, although there are no scientific models and theories for analyzing and solving them?

Analyzing everyday knowledge provides information about its content and structure in relation to different social contexts, thus shedding some light on the social construction and distribution of mundane stocks of knowledge. Thus, analyzing everyday knowledge becomes a medium for studying social representations since this theory offers a theoretical and methodological perspective for this analysis.

### Definition of everyday knowledge

What should be understood here by everyday knowledge? It concerns stocks of knowledge that are less explicit and less defined than expert or scientific knowledge, but which are more complex and structured than isolated cognitions, even than so-called 'social cognitions'. Everyday knowledge is based on forms of archaic knowledge, which are replaced more and more, but by no means completely, by scientific knowledge. It is not merely lay knowledge, since scientists and experts also need it as an implicit basis and a supplement to their explicit knowledge. Finally, it is the medium for organizing the everyday experiences of individuals and social groups.

### Transformative circulation of forms and stocks of knowledge

The perspective of the transformation of scientific knowledge into everyday knowledge which is usually taken by studying social representations, needs to be completed by the Schützian and Heiderian perspective of studying the transformation and transformability of everyday knowledge into scientific knowledge, i.e. theories. In this way it is possible to formulate a comprehensive perspective of a transformative circulation of forms and stocks of knowledge. A central task of a social psychology of knowledge is to analyse this circulation and the conditions and processes of constructing reality that it engages. In relation to technological change (Flick, 1996), the main research questions are: Which stocks of knowledge are formed parallel to the entrance of technological developments and devices into everyday life? What role does (transformed) scientific knowledge play? In what ways can these stocks of knowledge, together with those which are formed independently of scientific knowledge, be used for formulating an everyday psychological theory of technological change? This process is indicated in Figure 3.3 in bold and enlarged type.

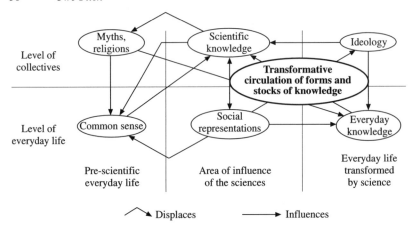

Figure 3.3    Transformative circulation of forms and stocks of knowledge

### Social representations, science and ideology

Finally, the question of the relations between social representations and ideologies arises repeatedly (see chapter 10 by Augoustinos). In a study of mass psychology, Moscovici (1985) demonstrated how certain scientific theories, such as Le Bon's theory of mass psychology ([1895]1947), were first vulgarized and then spread through social representations. Subsequently, they were taken up and functionalized by Mussolini and Hitler in the fascist ideologies in Italy and Germany. Similarly, Darwin's theories and the various evolutionary theories which followed became represented in the general population, and, insofar as the ideologies based on them fell on 'fruitful' ground, thus prepared the way for the unfolding of their terrific impact. For evolving modern ideologies, the vulgarization of certain scientific theories and the development of related social representations are a preliminary step. Using this knowledge as ideology is a way of functionalizing a social representation for political ends (Farr, 1987a). An ideology arises when a social representation is used for political and other purposes.

### Social construction and distribution of knowledge

Social representation, as opposed to the concept of representation in the cognitive sciences, is not restricted to the reproduction of a given reality but is constructivist in two ways. On the one hand, it makes no assumption about whether any reality 'as such' exists, but proposes that individuals and social groups produce this reality through interaction. On the other hand, the process of social representation is seen as a means of constructing reality (Moscovici, 1988a, p. 230). This close connection with communication and understanding means that representation is not construed as a purely cognitive process. The process of representation is transferred and extended beyond individual subjects into their social and interactive contexts. Social representation is enlarged from a subjective way of using individual-cognitive images to make sense of the world and find a secure place for oneself within it, to a social way of making sense of the world and finding a secure place in social groups and relations, employing the social reality which they produce and which they implicitly and explicitly confirm. This process of representation can also be found in certain objects and in the meanings they acquire, as Moscovici ([1988b]1993) demonstrates for the example of money. Another example of such a representation is the condom as a symbol (for the representation) of the (present) knowledge of Aids and its dissemination as well as its prevention. Social representations, as these examples indicate, always have a 'mental' and a 'material' side to them (Moscovici, 1987, p. 517).

Another aspect of the social construction of knowledge through the process of social representation is 'the fact that we mostly live in 'virtual' worlds . . . One might say that the transformation of these virtual worlds is another way of creating reality' (Moscovici, 1987, p. 517). These virtual worlds are, for example, represented in the discourse that is developed in certain professions or expert-cultures and which continues even without their members being in regular physical contact or encounters. As the example of medicine demonstrates, in such virtual worlds knowledge of various sciences (biology, psychology, physiology) is translated into the practical expert knowledge of a profession (medicine). This process of translation remains restricted to a profession, whose members do not necessarily have to be in direct contact with one another to ensure themselves of their professional knowledge or to exchange it. Through the application of these stocks of knowledge in medical practice, they enter everyday life and influence the existing (e.g. patients') everyday knowledge in relation to specific diseases, a process which should not question the monopoly for certain competencies of healing.

Studies of social representations trace the way in which such knowledge is transferred from the realm of science into the wider society, and how it becomes distributed across different social groups. The emphasis is on differences in the contents of the stocks of knowledge within different groups. In this way the theory of social representations rejects the concentration on formal aspects of thinking typical of contemporary psychology. Instead of attempting to examine formal aspects independently of meaningful contents, social representations theory and research address the question of how thinking produces meaningful contents and which means are used to do this. Knowledge is no longer localized in the individual but studied in its social use in processes of understanding and in its social contexts. Finally, a way to a *social* psychology of human thinking and knowing is opened, which stresses the distinctness of cognitive activities in different social contexts. The theory of social representations opens a psychological approach to the various versions of the world constructed in different social contexts. With this theory, we can proceed to develop a model of both the social distribution of knowledge and the construction of knowledge.

### Conclusions from comparing the models and research topics

The theory of social representations outlines a model of everyday knowledge which also encompasses a strategy for its examination. This model not only takes into account the social construction of reality through the ascription of meaning in everyday knowledge, but also takes into consideration the way that everyday knowledge is itself socially constructed through processes of transforming and conventionalizing knowledge (for example, in the passage from science into everyday life or certain domains of application in it). Finally, the model also takes into account the way in which everyday knowledge and its contents are socially distributed, assuming that there is a specific 'reception' of such knowledge by different social groups. Social groups diverge from other contemporary groups, or from social groups of other eras, through their everyday knowledge and its contents. The model offered by the theory is also sufficiently structured and complex to accomplish the analysis of such phenomena, as can be seen, for example, in the discussion of a figurative nucleus of the social representation of illness in Herzlich (1973) or Jodelet ([1989a] 1991).

Table 3.1 presents a comparison of social representations with the other models discussed earlier, in terms of the objects, points of reference, focus of research and the functions assumed by each model.

Finally, for a psychology of the social, we can sketch the following perspectives for research on everyday knowledge (which were presented initially in Figure 3.1):

- A first issue is the analysis of changes in the everyday knowledge of certain topics, i.e. developments of its contents, sources, and structure and the way it changes in confrontation with scientific or expert knowledge or religious belief systems.

Table 3.1. *Comparison of models of everyday knowledge*

| | Subjective theories | Cultural models | Social representations |
|---|---|---|---|
| **object of research** | a complex and structured model of everyday knowledge | a complex and structured model of everyday knowledge | a complex and structured model of everyday knowledge |
| **points of reference** | the individual and his or her knowledge | an entire culture | social groups |
| **focus of research** | internal structure of subjective knowledge | cultural influences on subjective knowledge | social distribution of knowledge |
| **mundane function of the model** | to allow the individual to act in the world | cultural anchoring of individuals' cognitive activities | to constitute and delimit social groups |
| **function of the model in research** | to understand the knowledge with which subjects act in the world | to prove cultural influence on individual cognition | to prove social anchoring and functions of knowledge |

- A second issue is its distribution in different social groups and cultures, and also the loss of importance it repeatedly suffers from the advance of scientific or professional knowledge, or its renaissance at times of crisis in medicine and science.
- A third question is the analysis of its function for everyday practices.
- Lastly, from a historical perspective, we could also study how the relevance of everyday knowledge changes for social psychology and its influence on the process of research, in order, finally, to arrive at a social psychology of knowledge in general.

### Notes

1 'So-called common sense, as the personification of the thought collective of everyday life, has become in this way a universal benefactor for many specific thought collectives' (Fleck, [1935] 1979, p. 109).
2 'The individual's common-sense knowledge of the world is a system of constructs of its typicality' (Schütz, 1966, p. 7).

# 4 Social attributions and social representations

*Miles Hewstone and Martha Augoustinos*

## Introduction

This chapter brings together two research traditions within social psychology which focus upon explanation in everyday life: attribution theory and social representations theory. Attribution theory is predominantly a North American theoretical perspective which seeks to understand the processes by which people attribute causes to their own behaviour and to the behaviour of others. Similarly, social representations theory, as founded and developed by Moscovici (1981, 1984a), emphasizes the explanatory function of the knowledge and meaning systems embodied by social representations. Both theories refer to a fundamental human need to understand and explain events, and in so doing offer a psychological perspective to the role of social explanation in everyday life. While both theories emphasize the importance of explanation in social life, the two theories are articulated at different levels of analysis (Doise, 1986). Attribution theory focuses primarily on the individual cognitive processes involved in making causal explanations, while social representations theory emphasizes the social and collective nature of explanations.

## Attribution theory

In his 1958 monograph *The psychology of interpersonal relations*, Fritz Heider argued that a fundamental feature of human thinking was the need to understand the causes of behaviour and everyday events. Understanding and making sense of behaviour and events allowed for some prediction and control over a complex social world. Heider construed ordinary people as 'naive' psychologists who developed a 'common-sense' psychology which they used to guide them through the vicissitudes of life.

A central premise of Heider's naive psychology was the distinction between two types of causal attributions: personal and situational. The

60

former refers to internal causal factors such as the disposition of a person, while the latter refers to factors external to a person such as situational forces. Heider commented on the tendency for people to overestimate the role of personal causal factors and to underestimate the significance of the situation or context. This has become known as the 'fundamental attribution error' (Ross, 1977), which we will consider in more detail later.

Since Heider's (1958) pioneering formulations about common-sense causal explanations attribution theory has undergone several extensions, the most notable being Jones and Davis's (1965) correspondent inference theory and Kelley's (1967) theory of covariation. Both these theories concern themselves with the processes by which people make causal attributions. Jones and Davis argued that the major goal in the attribution process is to make a correspondent inference; that is to infer that the behaviour of a person reflects an underlying stable trait of the person. Thus, an individual's angry outburst is attributed to an aggressive disposition or personality. This response is motivated, they argued, by a human need to view people's behaviour as intentional and predictable. The task is made difficult, however, in ambiguous situations where information is limited. In such instances, Jones and Davis argued that people look for cues to make causal attributions, such as the social desirability, role requirements, and choice of the behaviour. Similarly, Kelley (1967) emphasized that in many instances the making of causal attributions is a complex process requiring the perceiver to take many factors into account. He likened the ordinary perceiver to a naive scientist who uses complex statistical models like analysis of variance (ANOVA) to weigh up the relative influence of multiple factors when making causal explanations for behaviour and events.

What is most evident in this brief theoretical outline of attribution theory is that the attribution process has been conceptualized as an intra-individual phenomenon. Individuals are construed as information processors who attend to and select information from the environment, process the information cognitively, and then arrive at a causal analysis of the behaviour in question. There is little discussion in most attribution research of the social interactive and cultural context within which causal attributions are made. Attribution theory has therefore been criticized for being predominantly an individualistic theory requiring a greater social perspective (see Hewstone, 1983). As well as being very individualistic and cognitive in nature, critics have argued that attribution theory exaggerates the tendency for people to seek causal explanations for everyday occurrences and events. It has been suggested that people do not engage in such exhaustive cognitive activity as, for example, Kelley's ANOVA model would suggest, but rather that they use heuristics as short-cuts for making judgements and inferences generally and, more specifically, for attributing causality (Fiske and Taylor, 1991). Weiner (1985) has addressed this issue by examining whether people engage in spontaneous causal thinking or whether, in fact, the extent and nature of attributional activity that the research suggests is an artefact of the reactive methodologies used in attribution research. Most mainstream research in causal attributions requires respondents to indicate their agreement or disagreement with attributional statements specified by the researchers. There is a dearth of studies which investigate attributions and explanations in natural contexts such as in conversation, the print media, etc. In reviewing the small number of attributional studies which utilize non-reactive methodologies, Weiner (1985) concludes that people do indeed engage in 'spontaneous' causal thinking but mostly for unexpected events and non-attainment of goals (failure). This conclusion is consistent with that of others (e.g. Mackie, 1965, 1974; McIver, 1942) who have argued that people look actively for causal explanations for the unexpected or different.

### Social knowledge, representations and attributions

While there is agreement that expectations determine the extent to which people actively think about causes, there has been little research to date concerning where these expectations come from. It has been suggested that we must look to the contents of social knowledge itself in order to answer this question; an approach which is central to social representations theory. Moscovici and Hewstone have proposed that social representations should be viewed as the bases upon which attributions are made (Moscovici, 1981, 1984a; Moscovici and Hewstone, 1983). 'A theory of social causality is a theory of our imputations and attributions, associated with a representation . . . any causal explanation must be viewed within the context of social representations and is determined thereby' (Moscovici, 1981, p. 207).

Social representations form the foundations of people's expectations and normative prescriptions, and thus act as mediators in the attributional process (Hewstone, 1989a, 1989b). In a similar vein, Lalljee and Abelson (1983) advocate a 'knowledge structure' approach to attribution. Well-learned and consensual structures, such as highly organized event schemata or scripts (Schank and Abelson, 1977), do not usually evoke causal explanations because people come to expect the sequence of events that follow. People's prior expectations, beliefs, knowledge, or schemata will determine for what incoming social information they will need to engage in causal attributions. Information which is consistent with a person's schema or representation will not require an in-depth search for causality, given that the information is expected and therefore automatically processed. However, information which is inconsistent with expectations or existing knowledge will require a more detailed search for explanation (see Augoustinos and Innes, 1990). Thus social representations impose a kind of automatic explanation. Causes are singled out and proposed prior to a detailed search for and analysis of information. Without much active thinking, people's explanations are determined by their social representations (Hewstone, 1989b).

The social foundation of such automatic explanations is that they are learned and thus socially communicated through language. The use of cultural hypotheses to explain behaviour and events can be regarded as a kind of 'socialized processing' (Hewstone, 1983, 1989a, 1989b). Culturally agreed upon explanations eventually come to be regarded as common-sense explanations. Each society has its own culturally and socially sanctioned explanation or range of explanations for phenomena such as illness, poverty, failure, success, violence, crime, etc. People therefore do not always need to engage in an active cognitive search for explanations for all forms of behaviour and events. Instead, people evoke their socialized processing or social representations for expected and normative behaviour and events.

Such a knowledge or representation-based approach to attribution will necessitate the study of social knowledge itself. Research into the information base which people possess regarding particular social domains will reveal pre-existing knowledge structures and expectations which people use to filter and process incoming information. Instead of focusing exclusively on processes by which causal statements are generated, a knowledge-based approach to attribution would extend attribution research by studying the actual language people use when making attributional statements in naturalistic conversations and environments. Furthermore, such an approach may contribute to our understanding of the social origins of causal attributions and thus answer the often neglected question of where attributions come from (Pepitone, 1981).

## The social origins of the fundamental attribution error

A social representations perspective or knowledge-based approach to attribution can be applied to understand the social origins of the 'fundamental attribution error'. The tendency for individuals to over-attribute another person's behaviour to dispositional characteristics of the person, rather than to situational/contextual factors (Ross, 1977), is one of the most consistent findings in attribution research. Considerable debate and discussion has centred around the reason for this error or, perhaps more accurately, 'bias' (Harvey, Town and Yarkin, 1981; Kruglanski and Ajzen, 1983). Heider (1958) has argued that behaviour has such salient features that it tends to engulf the field, and Fiske and Taylor (1991, p. 67), in support of this cognitive explanation, describe how situational factors which give rise to behaviour, such as the social context, roles, or situational pressures, are 'relatively pallid and dull and unlikely to be noticed when compared with the dynamic behaviour of the actor'. The dominance of the actor in the perceptual field is, therefore, advanced as an explanation for this attributional bias.

More recently, it has been suggested that this dispositionalist bias is not a universal law of human cognitive functioning, but rather that it is deeply rooted in the dominant ideology of individualism within European and American culture (see Farr and Anderson, 1983; Moscovici and Hewstone, 1983; Bond, 1983; Augoustinos, chapter 10 this volume; Oyserman and Markus, chapter 7 this volume). The tendency to overestimate personal over situational causation was first noted by Ichheiser (1949) but, instead of viewing this phenomenon as an individual 'error' in cognitive judgement, Ichheiser viewed it as an explanation grounded in American society's collective and cultural consciousness (Farr and Anderson, 1983). The dominant representation of the person in Western liberal democracies is that of an important causative agent, over and above situational and contextual considerations. Political philosophers (e.g. Macpherson, 1962; Lukes, 1973) have posited the importance of individualism as an ideological doctrine specific to liberal-democratic societies and, most particularly, within American social, cultural, and political life. Lukes (1973) demonstrates how most areas of human activity in Western societies are imbued with these individualist tenets, including political, economic, religious, ethical, epistemological, and methodological concerns. The anthropologist Geertz (1975) has said the following about the individualistic representation of the person:

The western conceptions of the person as a bounded, unique, more or less integrated motivational and cognitive universe, a dynamic centre of awareness, emotion, judgement, and action organised into a distinctive whole and set contrastively both against a social and natural background is, however incorrigible it may seem to us, a rather peculiar idea within the context of the world's cultures. (p. 48)

### Culture and attributions

Indeed, research within the attribution tradition goes some way towards supporting this cultural view. Attribution research has found a significant tendency for dispositional attributions to increase with age in Western cultures. Whereas young Western children tend to make references to contextual factors to explain social behaviour, Western adults are more likely to stress dispositional characteristics of the agent (Peevers and Secord, 1973; Ruble *et al.*, 1979). Cross-cultural differences in attribution have been observed (Shweder and Bourne, 1982), with non-Western adults placing less emphasis on the dispositional characteristics of the agent and more emphasis on contextual/situational factors than Western adults. These developmental and cross-cultural differences have been explained within cognitive and experiential terms. For example, it has been argued that young children are limited in their cognitive capacity to make dispositional attributions because this requires the cognitive competence to generalize behavioural regularities over time. Similarly, it has been argued that non western adults are less likely to make dispositional categorizations because the cognitive capacity to do so is more likely to be associated with the experiential conditions of complex modernized societies (see Miller, 1984).

Miller (1984) points out that such explanations disregard the possibility that these developmental and cultural differences may 'result from divergent cultural conceptions of the person acquired over development in the two cultures rather than from cognitive or objective experiential differences between attributors' (p. 961). Western notions of the person are essentially individualistic – emphasizing the centrality and autonomy of the individual actor in all action, whereas non-western notions of the person tend to be holistic, stressing the interdependence between the individual and his/her surroundings. The developmental or age differences in attribution merely reflect the enculturation process – the gradual process by which children adopt the dominant conception of the person within their culture.

Indeed, Miller's (1984) research confirms this cultural hypothesis. A cross-cultural study was undertaken to compare the attributions made for pro-social and deviant behaviours by a sample of Americans and Indian Hindus of three different age groups (8, 11, and 15 years), together with an adult group (mean age = 40.5 years). Miller found that at older ages Americans made significantly more references to general dispositions ($M = 40\%$) than did Hindus ($M = <20\%$), most of these dispositions referring to personality characteristics of the agent. However, there were no significant differences which distinguished the responses of the 8- and 11-year-old American children from those of their Hindu counterparts (the difference was an average of 2 per cent). Within culture developmental trends indicated a significant, linear age increase in reference to general dispositions among Americans. By contrast, a significant linear age increase in references to the context was evident amongst the Hindus, who emphasized social roles and patterns of interpersonal relationships. As Miller points out, 'such modes of attribution may be seen to be reflective of Indian cultural conceptions in their emphasis in locating a person, object, or event in relation to someone or something else' (p. 968). Children displayed little cross-cultural differences in the number of contextual attributions they made. However, these were referred to frequently at younger ages in both Hindu and American children. Moreover, Miller found that these results could not be explained by the competing cognitive and experiential interpretations (see Miller, 1984, for details).

It appears, therefore, that the tendency to over-rate personal/dispositional factors of the agent in Western adults cannot be explained adequately by cognitive and experiential interpretations alone. The attribution 'bias' may not simply be a cognitive property or a universal law of psychological functioning – it may be culture specific. Though the agent of action tends to dominate the perceptual field for Anglo-Americans, the 'person' does not seem to enjoy the same degree of perceptual dominance amongst non-Western people.

The prevalence of personal explanations in Western societies has also been found in studies of causal explanations for success and failure: an area in which attribution research has been prolific. Most achievement attribution research uses Weiner et al.'s (1971) causal categories to study success and failure attributions, these being ability, effort, luck, and task difficulty. In a similar vein to Miller's cross-sectional research, but lacking a cross-cultural focus, is some Australian work which found an overwhelming preference among secondary-school students for personal over situational attributions when accounting for academic success and failure (Augoustinos, 1989, 1990; chapter 10 this volume). Students were more likely to endorse causal statements reflecting a candidate's intellectual abilities and effort in achievement attributions than causal references to external factors such as luck and task difficulty. Ability and hard work were regarded as necessary for academic success and their absence as instrumental in academic failure. This preference for personal attributions was evident for students from both ends of the socio-economic spectrum and was significantly more pronounced among the older students (13 to 14 year olds) compared with the younger students (16 to 17 year olds). This lends further support to Miller's developmental finding that internal personal attributions increase with age in Western cultures.

### Explanations for societal issues

It is clear that attributions or lay explanations for everyday behaviour, occurrences, and events are not only the outcome of internal, individual cognitive processes. Rather, some attributions can be seen to be truly social phenomena in that they are based on widely held and shared beliefs in the form of social and collective representations (Fraser and Gaskell, 1990). Just as Moscovici (1984a) has referred to a 'thinking society', Hewstone (1989a) refers to an 'attributing society' – the propensity of people to seek explanations within the predominant cultural framework, especially for societal problems and issues. Our explanations for social phenomena are not only shaped by culture but also by scientific and expert knowledge which proliferates everyday life. Increasingly, expert knowledge contributes to the stock of common-sense knowledge upon which people draw to understand social reality. The diffusion and popularization of scientific concepts throughout society is occurring at a rapid rate through the mass media. Thus, people can be regarded as 'amateur' scientists, 'amateur' economists, 'amateur' psychologists, etc., as they draw upon this information to explain a range of phenomena such as the greenhouse effect, a depressed economy, or problems in their interpersonal relationships. Some of this knowledge becomes an integral part of mass culture and, ultimately, what will come to be regarded as 'common sense' (Moscovici and Hewstone, 1983; Moscovici, chapter 14 this volume; Flick, chapter 3 this volume).

The attributions that people make for societal events and issues provide social psychologists with insight into a society's prevailing explanations or meaning systems. Research into lay explanations and attributions have focused on a number of social issues, some of which we discuss below. This review is not intended to be exhaustive but it does identify the social base from which explanations emerge and the manner in which explanations are linked to particular social and political identifications. Explanations are therefore not purely cognitive phenomena, but are social in origin, sometimes widely shared and shaped by socio-historical forces.

### Persecution and Conspiracy Theories

Throughout history the persecution of particular social groups has been a recurring phenomenon. Persecuted groups have included heretics, Jews, witches, lepers and communists, all of whom have been blamed and held responsible for a myriad of threatening events and social problems. Fauconnet (1928) argued that the main motivation for scapegoating is to punish those responsible for the event and thus prevent its reoccurrence. This points to the control function of societal attributions whereby negative events are attributed to identifiable and controllable causes. In medieval times witchcraft was popular as a theory of causality simply because witches could be identified and punished for their actions. Such a theory of causality was particularly satisfying, since it allowed for retribution and redress. As with the persecution of social groups, conspiracy theories provide a sense of control over events. Bains (1983) points out that if crises are attributed to identifiable groups and controllable causes, then simplistic remedies can be espoused. Poliakov (1980) refers to the inherent human appeal for an elementary and exhaustive causality as a 'causalité diabolique'.

Perhaps no other group throughout history has been victim to such elaborate conspiratorial theories as the Jews. The central theme of such theories is that all Jews everywhere 'form a conspiratorial body set on ruining and then dominating the rest of mankind' (Cohn, 1966). For example, the Jews were held responsible for the Black Plague which, between the years of 1348 and 1350, wiped out over one-third of Europe's population. The extent of the calamity was difficult for people to understand and, in an effort to come to terms with the destruction and to perceive the possibility of control over the situation, a Jewish conspiracy theory emerged. As Zukier (1987, p. 97) states, 'to many people, the Jews soon came to embody the explanation: the plague was but the monstrous unfolding of a Jewish plot to poison Christianity'.

Of course, beliefs in a Jewish world conspiracy were embodied in the anti-semitism of the Third Reich. Although the belief in a Jewish world conspiracy was far from hegemonic during Hitler's reign, it was shared by a significant number of Nazis (Merkl, 1975). Indeed, Hitler referred to Jews as 'bacilli' and viewed the systematic programme to exterminate the Jews as a battle waged against the elimination of an imaginary Jewish virus.

While the ideology and propoganda of the Third Reich is probably one of the most infamous and extreme examples of a conspiracy theory which was put in practice, such theories can be located throughout history. Indeed, many extreme contemporary organizations of the political right continue to espouse such explanatory accounts. Billig's (1978) research on members of the British National Front Party demonstrated the simplistic and all-embracing nature of conspiratorial accounts which were used to explain a plethora of social ills within British society. As

Wood (1982) warns, it is foolish to dismiss this pattern of thinking as irrational or pathological. Rather, it must be understood as a phenomenon grounded in the particular and specific socio-historical conditions of the time. What conpiracy theories point to is the essentially social and communicative nature of societal attibutions.

### Explanations for health and illness

Medical anthropology has traditionally concerned itself with how the experience of health and illness is understood and communicated within cultural collectivities. Each culture provides a specific set of meanings which people use to understand the experience of illness and its treatment. Kleinman (1980) refers to these meaning systems as explanatory models, in which identifying the aetiology or cause of an illness is a central component. For example, Evans Pritchard (1976) found that, among the Azande, all misfortune including illness and death was believed to be caused by witchcraft. While this may seem bizarre from a Western scientific perspective, Pritchard discovered that this particular explanatory model was able to answer a crucial question which Western scientific medicine cannot satisfactorily answer: the 'why me?' question. While Western medicine advances biological explanations for illness, it cannot explain why a particular person becomes ill at a particular point in time. While references to chance, luck, or the will of God are commonplace (Bulman and Wortman, 1977), the Azande have a ready-made explanation in that a witch targets a particular person at a specific time. In this way, illness explanations among the Azande also have a strong moral component.

With the increasing emphasis on preventive medicine, health and social psychologists have recently begun to explore the finer details of lay representations of physical illness in Western societies, the assumption being that such representations have important health implications, both attitudinally and behaviourally. Lau and his colleagues (Lau and Hartman, 1983; Lau, Bernard, and Hartman, 1989) have identified five themes or components of illness representations. These components are: identity – a label for the disease and its associated symptoms; time line – the course of the illness, whether it is acute or chronic; consequences – the short- and long-term effects of the disease; cause – factors which led to the onset of illness; and cure – prescriptions for recovery.

A predominant theme within this research has been the external/internal dichotomy in illness causation. For example, Herzlich's (1973) study on the representations of health and illness in France found that a prevalent view among her sample of eighty professional and middle class subjects was, that the urban way of life is a primary determinant in the genesis of illness. Many respondents felt that city life resulted in fatigue and nervous tension. This state, in turn, made the individual less resistant and more vulnerable to disease and illness. Mental disorders, heart disease, and cancer were illnesses most frequently referred to by respondents as being generated by the way of life. While illness was seen to be generated by the external environment, the individual was seen as representing the source of health. Illness was not viewed as an inherent part of the individual, but as something external to the individual. Thus health and illness were seen to be the outcome of struggle and opposition between the passive individual and an active factor: the way of life. Herzlich concluded that the representation of health and illness was structured around a number of opposing concepts: internal versus external, healthy versus unhealthy, natural versus unnatural, the individual versus society (see Herzlich, 1991).

An interesting extension of Herzlich's study is the work of Pill and Stott (1982, 1985) on concepts of illness causation and responsibility. Their primary motivation for exploring lay explanations of health and illness was the shift in public-health policy in Britain from curative to preventive medicine. Herzlich's research had already suggested that illness was not directly attributed to the behaviour of the individual, but was seen to be brought about through stress and the role obligations associated with everyday urban life. Pill and Stott explored whether people accepted the notion of individual responsibility in the maintenance of health, which is explicit in preventive health philosophy. Both studies concluded that, among working-class Welsh women, individual responsibility in the genesis of illness was given lower priority than external factors. The women were more likely to emphasize factors outside of the individual's control in the genesis of illness such as the environment, weather, pollution, heredity, germs, and infection. However, there were some women who mentioned lifestyle factors such as diet, hygiene, exercise, and rest as causative agents in illness. These women were also more likely to emphasize preventive health practices and were more willing to attribute moral blame to the individual for illness.

Pill and Stott's research suggests that people may be resistant to public-health experts' emphasis on individual responsibility for health care and the implementation of preventive health practices. It is unclear, however, to what extent such resistance is prevalent in groups other than working-class women in Britain. Furthermore, it is possible that with the increasing exposure of the public to preventive health issues, health-related attitudes and behaviour may change over time in accordance with this philosophy.

*Poverty*

Lay explanations for poverty have attracted considerable research, beginning with Feagin's (1972) American survey of around 1,000 randomly selected subjects. Feagin found that individualistic explanations for poverty (lack of thrift and proper money management, lack of effort and loose morals) were favoured over societal and fatalistic explanations (bad luck, lack of ability and talent). Feagin was struck by the extent to which his respondents primarily held the poor responsible for their situation and entitled his study 'Poverty: We still believe that God helps those who help themselves'.

Feather (1974), in an Australian study, found a similar preference for individualistic explanations, though the Australians were less likely to endorse individualistic explanations than Feagin's American sample. As well as an overall prevalence of individualistic explanations, both studies found demographic differences in preferences for explanations. Feagin found that respondents who were most likely to endorse individualistic explanations were white Protestants and Catholics, respondents over fifty years of age, those of middle socio-economic status, and respondents with middle levels of education. People most likely to endorse structural reasons for poverty were black Protestants and Jews, respondents under thirty years of age, and those of lower socio-economic status and education. The most striking group differences in Feather's study was that older respondents were more likely to support individualistic explanations than younger respondents. Other studies which found a predominance of individualistic explanations for poverty, and for these to be related to demographic characteristics include Caplan and Nelson (1973), Singh and Vasudeva (1977), and Townsend (1979).

In a British middle-class sample, Furnham (1982a) found that political voting patterns were related to explanations for poverty. Conservatives were more likely to rate individualistic explanations as important than Labour voters. In turn, the latter differed significantly from Conservatives in that they placed more importance on societal-structural reasons.

All the above studies have focused primarily on the views of adult respondents. The first study to investigate adolescent explanations for poverty was conducted by Furnham (1982b). He found that public (i.e. private) schoolboys were more likely to endorse individualistic explanations than comprehensive (i.e. state) schoolboys, while the latter were more likely to rate societal factors as more important. There were no school differences for fatalistic explanations. More recently, Stacey and his colleagues have investigated attributions for poverty in New Zealand adolescents. Stacey and Singer (1985) found that secondary-school students rated familial factors as most important in explaining poverty, followed by societal, individualistic, and luck attributions. This pattern of attributional preferences was also found in a sample of teenage university students (Stacey, Singer and Ritchie, 1989). Thus younger people are less likely to endorse individualistic explanations for poverty.

The relationship between age and explanations for poverty are consistent with the cross-sectional studies on causal attributions for positive and negative acts (Miller, 1984) and for success and failure (Augoustinos, 1989, 1990; chapter 10 this volume) which together, suggest that, with increased age, attributions within Western society become more internal and individualistic in nature. It is likely that with age, the dominant political, social, and economic values of individualism influence the nature of explanations people make for social issues such as poverty. Alternatively, it is also possible that people in general are placing less emphasis on individualistic causes for poverty. Feagin's (1972) study, for example, took place over twenty years ago. Even though he was dismayed by the prevalence of victim blaming in his sample, he concluded that his subjects in 1969 were more likely to support structural causes than the subjects in an earlier study in 1945. Thus beliefs and explanations for poverty may be changing over time. Of course, the only way to disentangle the developmental hypothesis from the historical one is to conduct longitudinal studies using different age cohorts, which has not been done in this area to date.

### Unemployment

Psychological studies on explanations for unemployment have not found such a pervasive influence of individualist explanations. Using Feagin's (1972) three categories of explanations (individualistic, societal, and fatalistic), which have characterized the work on explanations for poverty, Furnham (1982c) found that individualistic explanations for unemploment were least important, and societal explanations most important, in a sample of around 284 predominantly middle-class, well-educated Britons. His sample also included 100 unemployed subjects who had been unemployed for between 3 and 5 months. While significant differences were found between the employed and unemployed in their endorsement of various explanations, all subjects preferred societal over individualistic explanations. Both employed and unemployed subjects rated world-wide recession and inflation, together with the policies and strategies of British governments, as the most important causes for unemployment. Similarly, Gaskell and Smith (1985) asked a randomly selected sample of British male school leavers to respond to an open-ended question on the main causes of unemployment among young people, and their relative agreement to two fixed questions attributing responsibility for reducing unemployment to: (1) the unemployed themselves (internal) and (2) the government (external). External (societal) attributions of unemployment were considered more important than internal or individualistic attributions.

In an Australian study, Feather (1985) found a similar preference for external/societal explantions for unemployment among a sample of psychology students. Factors such as defective government, social change, and economic recession were rated as more important than lack of motivation or personal handicap on the part of those unemployed. However, it was also significant that one individualistic factor, which referred to the lack of skills and competence in the unemployed, was rated as the most important factor of all.

The above studies on unemployment also explored relationships between explanations and demographic variables, and political and value orientations. Needless to say, differences were found between employment status and political voting preferences in explanations by Furnham (1982c), a finding which received limited support in Gaskell and Smith's (1985) study. Feather (1985) found interesting relationships between explanations for unemployment and wider value orientations and attitudes. For example, conservative attitudes were related to the endorsement of individualistic explanations.

Overall, it seems that for unemployment, societal and structural factors are rated as most important suggesting the existence of a shared representation which attributes this problem primarily to social, political, and economic forces. It should be stressed, however, that, while external and structural factors dominate the explanations for unemployment in the studies reviewed, specific individual factors, such as skill and motivation deficiencies, have also been rated highly as reasons for unemployment. Kelvin (1984) argues that, as unemployment increases and becomes a major economic problem, individualist explanations for its occurrence are likely to become less important, as most people, particularly the media, focus on structural and socio-economic explanations. As with research on lay explanations for poverty, studies which examine historical trends in explanations for unemployment, with a specific emphasis on cohort effects, would be of considerable advantage (see Jennings and Markus, 1984).

### Riots

Few people will forget the television images of the chaos and mayhem in Los Angeles which followed the acquittal of the four police officers charged with assaulting black motorist Rodney King. As extreme and negative events, riots arouse interest and spontaneous efforts at explanation both by the media and by the general public. The May 1992 riots in Los Angeles were no exception, as social commentators and ordinary people around the world offered a variety of explanations for the intensity and extemity of the social unrest. Two psychological studies which have systematically investigated the causes attributed to riots will be examined in order to understand the underlying psychological nature of such explanations.

An early study of this kind was conducted by Schmidt, who investigated the nature of explanations advanced for the civil disturbances experienced all over the United States in the summer of 1967. Schmidt (1972) analysed the content of the print media's explanations for the riots and arrived at seventy-six different kinds of explanations. To determine the underlying structure of these explanations, Schmidt asked forty male judges to sort the explanations in terms of their similarity to each other. A multi-dimensional scaling analysis of the data found that the explanations could be differentiated along two major dimensions. The first dimension included explanations which referred to the criminal nature of the riots and the rioters. This included explanations which referred to the rioters as political extremists who were engaged in revolutionary behaviour. All these explanations emphasized the role of the rioters themselves. By contrast, the second dimension included explanations which referred to the social, physical, and economic conditions surrounding the rioting such as unemployment and poverty. Associated with these were explanations which stressed the Government's failure to improve the living conditions of the rioters which, in turn, led to the psychological characteristics of hopelessness, despair and frustration among the rioters.

Schmidt also asked independent judges to rate the seventy-six explanations in terms of the following properties: legitimate–illegitimate cause, internal–external cause, and social-institutional–physical-environmental cause. The two dimensions yielded by the multi-dimensional scaling analysis were significantly consistent with the way in which the judges rated the explanations as internal versus external. Explanations emphasizing the behaviour and role of the rioters themselves were more likely to be rated as internal causes, whereas explanations which emphasized the causal role of social and economic conditions were rated as external.

This dimension also correlated significantly with the legitimate–illegitimate ratings of the explanations. Internal causes were more likely to be rated as illegitimate, wheras external causes were more likely to be viewed as legitimate. Explanations regarded as social-institutional in nature included references to the failure of government policies and agencies, whereas physical-environmental causes made references to unemployment and slum living conditions.

Litton and Potter (1985) found a similar internal–external distinction in explanatory accounts of the St Paul's riots in Bristol, UK, 1980. Litton and Potter analyzed the numerous causal explanations which appeared in the print, radio, and television media and interviewed six people who were present at or involved in the riot. Again, explanations could be distinguished as internal, which located the cause of the riot in the people who took part in the dramatic event, or external, in that the social and economic circumstances of the rioters were emphasized. Litton and Potter (1985) argued that while at a general level there was considerable consensus about the available range of explanations to account for the riots, at more specific explanatory levels, there was considerable variation as to whether people fully or partially accepted or rejected these available accounts as having any legitimate explanatory power.

Litton and Potter (1985) demonstrate this with reference to two particular explanations for the riot: the role of race; and the effects of government spending cuts and amenities (see also Potter and Wetherell, chapter 9 in this volume). These authors demonstrated how these explanatory accounts were in some contexts actively 'used' to make sense of the riot, whereas in other contexts they were simply 'mentioned' as available explanations. Thus, despite the consensual range of available explanations for the riot, at more concrete levels there existed conflicting and contradictory accounts. This, however, is not surprising for a highly controversial and dramatic event such as a riot. A riot's very political nature and deviational salience ensures the generation of competing explanations, which are no doubt linked to particular social and political identifications. Indeed, Schmidt found in his study that the print media that identified with the political right and extreme left tended to advance internal explanations for the riots, whereas the centre-left media preferred external causal explanations. Furthermore, Schmidt found an interesting time difference in the nature of explanations for the riots. During and shortly after the riots, internal explanations emphasizing the nature of the rioters and their illegitimate actions were significantly more prevalent than external explanations. With time, the latter increased with frequency, as did references to the perceived legitimacy of the riots.

**Conclusion**

While the distinction between personal (internal) and situational (external) attributions is a central theme of both attribution research and of studies which have examined the content of lay knowledge and beliefs, there are conceptual and empirical problems associated with this dichotomy. The tendency is to conceptualize these attributions as being negatively related, whereas in reality people embrace and integrate both types of explanations. It is important to stress that, in most research, people make both kinds of attributions. Thus personal and situational attributions co-exist and should not necessarily be viewed as contradictory (Billig, 1982). Furthermore, in a qualitative analysis of the structure of explanations in political conversation, Antaki (1986) has found that single-cause explanations are rare, and that people make references to a number of attributions at different levels of explanation.

This chapter has tried to make clear that attributions or lay explanations are not only the outcome of individual cognitive processes but are also linked to social and cultural representations. Our belief systems, values, knowledge, and expectations form a background from which explanations are constructed and elaborated. In turn, social representations are shaped and influenced by socio-historical forces and by the ever-increasing contributions of scientific and expert knowledge to which we are exposed. By bringing together attribution theory, a theory which is predominantly concerned with the cognitive processes involved in making causal analyzes, and social representations theory, a theory which emphasizes the social and cultural context within which thinking is embedded, we have demonstrated the social-psychological nature of everyday explanations.

# 5    The social construction of knowledge: social marking and socio-cognitive conflict

*Willem Doise, Gabriel Mugny, and Juan A. Pérez*

## Introduction

It is commonly accepted that opinions are of a 'subjective' order, marked by the social attachments of individuals. It is, by contrast, common to consider cognitive, intellectual or perceptual tools as independent of such attachments. These are considered as being grounded in biology, as, for example, is assumed by the theory of intelligence as a 'gift' (Mugny and Carugati, [1985]1989), and stemming from a conception of knowledge as a 'simple' reflection of the objective world. The predominant conception in interactionist and developmental social psychology, on the other hand, is that all forms of knowledge are grounded in social interactions between individuals. In particular, it is marked by social representations of the tasks and of the social interactions actualised by an individual. Thus, knowledge of the 'physical' world is not independent of knowledge or representations of the social world. This chapter aims to demonstrate this in different ways, first through the social development of intelligence, and then through social influence on reasoning and perceptual judgements.

### Social interaction and cognitive development

*Elements of social developmental psychology*

A spiral causality accounts for the interdependence between social and individual regulations (Doise and Palmonari, 1984): at each moment in development specific competences allow an individual to participate in social interactions which can give rise to new competences which can then further enrich participation in other social interactions. The propositions which constitute the foundation for such a developmental social psychology (Mugny, 1982; Doise and Mugny, 1984; Perret-Clermont and Nicolet, 1988) are the following:

1 It is by coordinating their own actions and judgements with those of

others – that is through social interaction – that children are led to construct cognitive coordinations which they were unable to achieve individually. Thus, at a certain stage in their development, when they have the opportunity to accomplish tasks with peers or with adults, children succeed in accomplishing tasks at a stage of elaboration which they would be incapable of doing if they worked on them alone.

2 Once, having participated in social interactions, children then become capable of accomplishing these coordinations on their own. The resulting individual progress was observed after participation in both collective conservation tests (liquids, length, or number) and common spatial transformations or motor coordinations tasks (Perret-Clermont, 1980; Doise and Mugny, 1984).

3 Cognitive operations actualized on a given material or in a specific social situation take on more a character of stability and generality. In other words, they are transferable to other situations and other materials, providing evidence of children's authentic cognitive progress. This effect of the individual appropriation of cognitive operations has been confirmed, primarily through the use of different conservation tests (cf. Perret-Clermont, 1980; Doise and Mugny, 1984).

4 Social interaction is the source of cognitive progress because of the socio-cognitive conflicts which it generates. It is the simultaneous confrontation of different approaches or individual centrations during a social interaction which necessitates and engenders their integration in a new organization. To be a source for development, such a confrontation of responses does not imply that the opposing perspective should be cognitively more advanced than that of which a child is already capable; a child can benefit from responses of a similar level, even a lower level than their own, on condition that the centrations which flow from it are opposed to their own (Mugny, Lévy, and Doise, 1978). This social constructivism does not, therefore, assume any process of imitation or social learning from the responses of others.

5 For a powerful socio-cognitive conflict to take place, the participants in a social interaction must already dispose of certain cognitive instruments; in the same way a child will only profit from an interaction if they are already able to establish a difference between their approach and that of the other. This prerequisite competence means that some children benefit from some interactions, while those who have not yet attained this initial competence do not benefit from the same interaction. Experiments using motor-coordination tasks or the conservation of liquids have shown the role of this initial com-

petence and illustrated in a more general way that not every interaction is beneficial for every child. Social constructivism, then, operates on the basis of cognitive instruments and social competences
which the child possesses at a particular moment.

6 Regulations of a social nature which govern a given interaction can
constitute an important factor in the establishment of new cognitive
coordinations in this situation. It is precisely the intervention of such
regulations or social meanings during the cognitive coordinations
executed in the context of a particular task which is conceptualized by
the notion of social marking. This idea refers to the correspondences
which can be established between the social knowledge which char-
acterises the interaction between the protagonists actually or symboli-
cally present in a specific situation and the cognitive relations bearing
on certain properties of objects which mediate these social relations.

The research on social marking constitutes an extension of the earlier
research on the conflict resulting from different or opposed cognitive
approaches. A basic idea of this research is that an opposition can be
brought about within an individual between responses induced by social
knowledge and those induced by the principles organising their reasoning
about a given material.

A situation of reasoning will, then, be considered as socially marked
when an existing correspondence (or one which could exist) can be made
salient between the cognitive responses implied in the (correct) resolution
of a task (or in the way even an incorrect resolution is made by the child),
on the one hand, and the responses flowing from the social meanings
which are added to the properly cognitive aspects of the task, on the
other. The guiding hypothesis of the following set of research studies is
that certain social markings have constructivist effects on the mode of
resolution of a task and induce real progress in the reasoning of an
individual.

### Hierarchical differentiation and social marking

Piaget ([1965]1995) established a theoretical correspondence between
intellectual cooperation and relational autonomy (characteristic of relations among peers) on the one hand, and, on the other, between
intellectual constraint and heteronomy which characterizes relations
between the child and the adult. This conception allows the assumption
that egalitarian 'horizontal' relations would be more propitious to the
development of reasoning than the asymmetric relations in which
children are also engaged. A great many observations demonstrate
effectively that cognitive tasks involving children and adults risk being

resolved in purely relational terms, with the children, in particular, showing compliance in this respect, or simple imitation, at least when the adult lends themself to such dynamics (see, e.g., Mugny, De Paolis and Carugati, 1984). At the same time, it is also clear that the adult has the means which allow them to oppose such relational behaviours, and in particular can resort to questioning systematically children's responses, which comes back to the introduction of a socio-cognitive conflict (cf. Doise and Mugny, 1984, pp. 151–3). Furthermore, we should also note that if they take the form of reciprocal indifference, or introduce a constraining sociometric asymmetry (cf. Mugny, De Paolis and Carugati, 1984), relations among peers can also generate relational dynamics which block development. This is the reason why, for any developmental benefit, social interaction must at the same time secure a full unfolding of socio-cognitive conflict, and not merely introduce a purely relational solution in terms of agreement or disagreement.

A first study of social marking (Doise, Dionnet and Mugny, 1978) had shown how a hierarchical relation actually allows for the introduction of a constructivist social marking. In effect, since such a relationship assumes a differentiation between the child and the adult, implying a 'superiority' of the latter over the former, it is possible to establish a correspondence between this social differentiation and the responses to a cognitive task involving the conservation of an inequality. This experiment concerned the conservation of equal and unequal lengths. The subjects (aged about six years) were those who, in a pre-test, gave clearly non-conserving responses in a test of equal and unequal lengths. Thus, they did not recognize the equality (or the difference) of two objectively equal (or different) rods (or two bracelets) when the perceptual configurations were modified so as to be perceptually misleading. Only the conservation of the inequality of length task was included in the experimental session. For each configuration, the longer of the two bracelets was more or less deformed, leading the non-conservers to mistake the relative lengths of the bracelets: they judged them to be equal if their extremities coincided perceptually, and they judged the longer bracelet to be even shorter if its extremities were observed perceptually to be between those of the shorter bracelet. In the social-marking condition the child was told that they had to give one bracelet to the adult and one to themselves. They had first to give a judgement about the relative lengths of the bracelets (and justify this judgement), and then choose which bracelet was best for the experimenter and which was best for them. In the control condition without social-marking, the child had to choose which bracelet went best for each of two cylinders (whose dimensions were proportional to the wrists of a child and an adult). After each choice the bracelets were 'tested'. The experimental condition involved the child making an unequal choice in the context of a social relation where the adult could claim a bigger object than the child. A similar differentiation existed also in the control condition, but it was only functional and not directly social.

For each item two types of counter argument were introduced, since it was also a question of introducing a sociocognitive conflict. If the child made a mistake in their choice, they were asked why 'it didn't fit'. If the child, in spite of their erroneous judgement, nevertheless made the correct choice, the experimenter asked them to explain the discrepancy between their judgement and their choice. In other words the experimenter centered the child's cognitive activity on their own contradictions, without ever also suggesting a particular solution to them. Progress was assessed through two post-tests, the first immediately after the experimental phase and the second two weeks later, but always using a task without social marking.

The progress observed (subjects shifting from a non-conserving level to an intermediate or conserving level) was clearly distinct in the first of the post-tests. Although the material for the post-test was not socially marked, the subjects in the social-marking condition made progress (and, indeed, they also made progress on the conservation of the inequality of length), which then generalised to the conservation of equal lengths. Moreover, the same differences were also observed two weeks after the experimental phase. Thus, as this progress in reasoning illustrates, social marking has a strong share in generalized cognitive development.

### Cognitive effects structuring an egalitarian norm

Another set of research studies (cf. De Paolis, Doise and Mugny, 1987) suggests that the most coherent explanation for these constructivist effects is that of the socio-cognitive conflict introduced by the divergence – and hence establishing of a correspondence – between the solution suggested by social regulations or norms, on the one hand, and, on the other, the cognitive solution corresponding to the pre-operational cognitive strategies employed by the children participating in the experiments, or that suggested by the aid of the experimenter proposing an incorrect solution.

A conflict of the same type seems to be at work in experimental situations using tests of the conservation of liquids in a context of norms of equality (see, e.g., Doise and Mugny, 1984, pp. 69–72). For these tests the subjects were children who gave non-conserving responses to a test of equal amounts of liquids: if they accepted that two similar glasses contained the same quantity of liquid, when the contents of one glass were poured into another (narrower or wider) they considered that the amount of liquid was no longer the same, judging the quantity on the basis of the height of the liquid, without compensating for the width of the glass. These subjects then participated in the experimental session involving a task of distributing liquid (syrup or fruit juice). The aim of this task in socially marked situations was to reward two children who had worked equally hard and therefore merited the same amount of juice to drink. In the control situations, without marking, the aim was only to establish an equality between two quantities of liquid. Of course, in both types of conditions the two quantities underwent exactly the same perceptual transformations. Nevertheless, in the case of social marking, these transformations introduced a conflict with a social norm, since the perceptual appearances contradicted the equality of merits. In the other case, this social stake did not exist, and the conflict, if there was one, could only be the result of the eventual contradiction between the initial perceptual equality and the apparent inequality introduced by the pouring. The results showed that the first type of conflict is more effective for the enabling the child to understand that two quantities of liquid remain identical in spite of the perceptual transformations which they undergo during various transformations.

In his research Zhou (1987) used as an experimental task a variant on the test for conservation of discontinuous quantities described by Piaget and Szeminska (Piaget, [1941]1952). The experimenter asks non-conserving children to put the same quantity of sweets or beads in two equal or unequal glasses. He observed that the children were easily led to use a simple procedure to arrive at equality: they placed one element in turn in each glass. They often applied this strategy spontaneously when they had to distribute an equal quantity in two opaque glasses, into which they could not see, since the opening of the glasses was above their visual field. To do it, according to Zhou, the children applied a rule already well mastered: 'each one in turn'. In the post-test, the children who had used this rule did not generally make progress on a conservation of equal liquids task which did not involve social marking. They did not resist the perceptual transformations produced by pouring into unequal glasses. However, if the children had used the procedure 'each one in turn' during the experimental task with each deposit respecting a social agreement on equal sharing, then they made progress on the post-test. Must we, then, conclude that social marking has an effect in this way, without any intervention of socio-cognitive conflict being necessarily introduced? A type of sociocognitive conflict may, in reality, have played a role: the conflict generated by the experimenter through the use of counter-

Table 5.1 *Frequency of progress (+) and non-progress (0)*

| | With | | Without | |
| | | | Counter-argument | |
| | + | 0 | + | 0 |
|---|---|---|---|---|
| With social marking | 20 | 20 | 3 | 37 |
| Without social marking | 9 | 31 | 7 | 33 |

argument, or by producing a strong contrast between the expectations based on respect for the rule 'each one in turn' and the result obtained when the glasses are poured into two unequal glasses.

An experiment (Doise and Hanselmann, 1990) controlled the effects of these two types of conflict. Social marking was manipulated by asking subjects to distribute a quantity of marbles equally between two experimenters deserving exactly the same reward from an earlier task. In the conditions without marking, the distribution was made without any mention of equal rights. For the counter-argument, when the child replied correctly that there was the same quantity in two unequal glasses, the experimenter drew their attention to the difference in height between the two glasses, or when the child centred on only one dimension, the experimenter invoked the difference in the other dimension of height or width. In the absence of counter-argument the experimenter accepted what the child said without question. The 160 subjects were all non-conservers on a conservation of equal quantities of liquids task, but intermediary on a conservation of number task where they had mastered one-to-one correspondence. During the experimental task the children were all led to use the procedure one by one in order to assure the equality of distribution. Table 5.1 shows the frequencies of subjects who did or did not make progress on the first post-test (after Doise and Hanselmann, 1990).

The results show that social marking has a significant effect when it is accompanied by counter-argument. Social regulations therefore contribute to cognitive progress on the condition that they are used to orient a socio-cognitive conflict. We insist on the point that social regulation does not necessarily produce any cognitive change. When the regulation does not enter into any conflict with an individual centration, the child's habitual cognitive functioning is not put into question, and there is no reason to develop. On the other hand, socio-cognitive conflict produced by the divergence between responses induced by a social regulation and those derived from a cognitive approach can become a source of cognitive changes. We shall now see how in situations of social influence a cognitive change is equally produced in analogous situations.

### Social meaning of tasks and social influence

In these studies of social marking in cognitive development we have seen how certain types of social relations, even simply symbolized in the task, make possible the resolution of cognitive problems and logical tasks. A problematic of the same order has been approached in recent studies of social influence. These studies are close to those on the structuring effects of socio-cognitive conflict, notably because situations of social influence generally involve the existence of a divergence of judgements between two or more individuals. The conception we propose for the mechanisms of change which flow form these situations assume two basic hypotheses. First, that the contribution of information given by the other plays less of a role than the relation which predominates with them, and the mode of sociocognitive functioning which flows from this relation. Second, that the divergence has a different meaning according to the nature of the other, and the way in which they represent the task. This is exactly where the hypothesis of social marking in cognitive development rests. We shall begin the illustrations, however, with a paradigm which constitutes an extension of it.

### Social influence and reasoning

In a series of studies, Butera has asked whether social dynamics can be an explanatory factor for higher thought processes, such as, for example, inductive reasoning. He begins from the fact of the difference between majority and minority influence is a difference of kind (cf. Moscovici and Mugny, 1985): the majority most often secures a manifest, that is to say, immediate, public or direct, influence while the minority obtains a more latent, that is to say, deferred, private or indirect influence (Mugny and Pérez, 1991). From a similar point of view, Nemeth (1986) speaks of the activation of different modes of thought as a function of the status of the source. Faced with an interlocutor from the majority, individuals will function with a convergent thought, articulated around the position of the interlocutor. Faced with a minority interlocutor, divergent thought would be activated, based on parameters not necessarily present in the situation of confrontation.

One explanation is that these influences may proceed by activating different representations of knowledge: the majority would have its effects in a social field which it makes unidimensional through social regulations habitually associated with it, and which are governed by the necessity of consensus (one would speak of a representation of uniqueness; cf. Brandstätter et al., 1991). The minority, on the other hand, would have its impact through the plurality of the field which corresponds to it (representation of plurality). The hypothesis is, therefore, that individuals will tend to use forms of reasoning which correspond to the social structure in which they are inserted. Reasoning strategies aiming at the elaboration of ideas already presented and at the verification of predominant hypotheses would correspond to a social consensus made salient by a majority. On the other hand, a social structure in which an alternative is introduced (which occurs through a dissident minority) must induce reasoning strategies which take into account alternative hypotheses, and which envisage falsification.

The paradigm to test these ideas (cf. Butera et al., 1991–2) uses one of the tasks most classically employed to study processes of individual reasoning and scientific reasoning (Wason, 1960). Subjects have to discover the 'correct' rule (decided by the experimenter, for example, any two-figure number) with which a triplet of numbers (for example, 2–4–6) is compatible. A bias appears systematically when subjects have to propose a triplet to control the validity of their hypothesis: in spite of the diagnostic value of disconfirming strategies in this task, it is confirmation which is predominantly used in this type of task, as it is elsewhere in scientific practice (cf. Tukey, 1986; McDonald, 1990). For example, subjects who think that the rule is 'even numbers increasing by 2' propose 6–8–10, which is compatible with the experimenter's rule, but does not allow the subject to discover that their own rule is too specific and hence incorrect. Can majorities and minorities remedy this state of affairs?

In a first experiment (cf. Legrenzi et al., 1991; Butera et al., 1991–2) subjects were informed of the hypothesis ('each new number is larger than the preceding one') of people supposedly already asked, either the great majority of those already asked (specifically 88 per cent), or a small minority (12 per cent). In each trial a second series of three numbers was advanced, and presented as the triplet given by these people with the aim of verifying if their rule was well founded. This triplet was confirmatory for half the subjects (3–5–7) and disconfirmatory for the other half (7–5–3). In each trial subjects had then to give the rule which they thought underlay the initial series which had been proposed to them and a new triplet of numbers, and they wished to know whether or not it corresponded to this rule. After these problems subjects responded to some questions about their representation of the task. Finally, a post-test presented similar trials to the earlier ones. This time no information was given about the responses of the source.

The performances were evaluated from two points of view: that of the hypothetical rule and that of the strategy to test it. For the rule, it was either the same as that of the source (conformity), or the same rule but with some clearer specification (convergent cognitive work), or it was a new rule and evidence of divergent thinking. For the strategy to test the hypothesis, the triplet given by the subject either confirmed or disconfirmed the rule they themselves had proposed. There was confirmation when the triplet given by the subject could be described by the subject's hypothetical rule. Disconfirmation meant that the triplet did not correspond to the proposed rule.

Two effects were observed in relation to the rules. The same proportion of majority and minority subjects adopted the rule proposed by the source. On the other hand, differences appeared for the reshaping of the rule, which was more frequently the case during the experimental phase for subjects faced with the majority, and during the post-test for those faced with the minority.

In relation to the strategy for controlling the hypothesis, subjects benefited from 'useful' information given by the source using the strategy of disconfirmation, irrespective of its status. Subjects equally recognized the value of this strategy, even if its use remained infrequent. A difference appeared for the confirmatory sources: faced with the majority, subjects mainly used confirmation, while there was greater use of disconfirmation by those faced with a minority, a difference which persisted in the post-test.

From the point of view of the rules as much as the control strategies, the majority induced a mode of convergent cognitive functioning, taking inspiration from information coming from the source. Faced with a minority, subjects engaged more in a more divergent mode of socio-cognitive functioning, more open to new hypotheses, and also more frequently constructing an adequate (because it was more informative) strategy of disconfirmation. The complementary questions indicated that the minority had indeed induced a representation of the solution of the task as particularly tied to a consideration of different alternatives.

The representation of the source and of the task even appeared to constitute more important factors than the fact of knowing whether the source was correct or not. In another study (Butera and Mugny, 1992), subjects were told whether the rule of the majority or the minority was right or wrong. The results showed than even if subjects did then adopt the rule of the source more frequently, only the minority induced a control strategy based on falsification. In other respects, the analysis of the representation of the task again suggested that the minority generated a representation in multi-dimensional terms. This hypothesis was directly tested in a full factorial design (Butera et al., 1996). Subjects confronted with a majority or a minority were also told that the problems allowed either one single correct answer, or several possible answers. Results showed that it is when the source is a majority and the problem allows a single answer that most subjects adopted the majority's hypothesis and use confirmatory testing. On the other hand, it was when the source was a minority and the problem allowed several possible answers that most subjects gave alternative hypotheses and used disconfirmation.

The experimental results presented in relation to this new axis of research have enabled progress to be made in the definition of the relations between social regulations and cognitive functioning. The higher processes of thinking, such as the confirmation or disconfirmation of hypotheses, arise in different ways, according to the social interlocutors who have the role of providing either an example or a counter-argument. As with cognitive development, the other intervenes in an active way even in the construction of reasoning. These constructivist effects depend, however, on the correspondences established between the status of the interlocutor and the representation of the task. We shall give a last example.

### Anticipating consensus and the dynamics of influence

For this research we returned to situations of social influence similar to those used in the study of conformity (Asch, 1956; cf. Allen, 1965). The paradigm will be presented to test the merits of the hypothesis of uniqueness and plurality as preconstructs presiding over the social marking of situations of social influence. The specific hypothesis returns to the assumption that the dynamics of social influence resulting from a higher-status source, specifically the majority, flow from its correspondence with a social representation of the task as requiring unanimity. Three predictions were tested. First, that the dynamics of majority influence would only appear if individuals considered that the knowledge in question required unanimity. The other two predictions concerned the level of the regulation of the conflict which appeared in the case of divergence, when the expected unanimity was broken. The second prediction suggests that when there is a particular attraction between source and target, the search for unanimity will be more relational, and expressed at the level of socially manifest responses. The third suggests that when this is not the case the break in homology between source and knowledge will give rise to a constructivist effect: individuals will construct a new understanding to re-establish consensus.

The paradigm designed to test these correspondences was the following (cf. Brandstätter et al., 1991): during the experimental phase of influence subjects are confronted with a source (majority or minority, from the in-group or the out-group) who judges that an angle of 90° or 85° measures 50°. As with Asch (1956), this response is manifestly wrong. In a pre-test and post-test subjects also estimated the weight of an imaginary cheese represented by various angles. The manifest influence is measured by the reduction in the angles during the experimental phase, and the indirect influence by the reduction in weight of the figures in the post-test.

In the first study based on this model, either a majority (88 per cent) or minority (12 per cent) of people (who were shown to have made a mistake on a similar task) estimated as 50° angles which were either 90° or 85°. The idea was that angles of 90° would refer to an absolute demand for unanimity because of the *gestalt* represented by a right angle, while angles of 85° would leave room for some uncertainty. The former should favour majority influence and the latter minority influence. In fact, even when the source is explicitly presented as wrong, three significant effects were observed. First, the majority has a direct effect with angles of 85°: uncertainty is regulated by complaisance, since no indirect effect was observed. Faced with angles of 90° the majority has an effect, but uniquely indirect: manifest conformity is impossible, since the right angle is too pregnant, but the break in unanimity preoccupies the subjects to the point that they construct an object with a new property, in this case weight, which is compatible with the demand for unanimity. In the first case one can say that the regulation of the conflict is purely relational, while in the second it is properly sociocognitive. But in both cases it is the product of a contradiction between the anticipation of consensus and the majority status of the source. As for the minority, it obtains, as predicted, a latent influence in the face of angles of 85° (the weight of the figure then decreases), whose more open representation is more compatible with the minority status of the source.

A second experiment (Pérez et al., 1991) used only 90° angles, so as to ensure that any effects could not be explained simply by the degree of certainty associated with angles which were more (85°) or less (90°) difficult to evaluate. Two variables were manipulated. The first concerned the source, always a majority (88 per cent), and was defined as either in-group or out-group: an in-group source should induce a more relational regulation of the conflict, while an out-group source should induce a more sociocognitive regulation. Categorization was established on the basis of 'race'. In a supposed study of the similarities and differences

Table 5.2 *Evaluations of experimental angles (in degrees) and change in the weight of the cheese (in grams; − or + : direction of influence) (taken from Pérez et al., 1991).*

| | Majority | | | |
|---|---|---|---|---|
| | In-group | | Out-group | |
| Anticipation: | Similar | Different | Similar | Different |
| Angles | 80.9 | 88.7 | 88.9 | 87.3 |
| Weight | +33.5 | −27.8 | −187.3 | +296.1 |

between races, the majority was either white, like the subjects, or black. The anticipation of unanimity was introduced by instilling in the subjects the belief that scientific studies had demonstrated either a similarity or a difference in the perception of the races.

The results, shown in Table 5.2, show that the dynamics of positive influence only appear when subjects believed in the similarity of judgements described as the equality of perception between the races. When the source comes from the in-group, and in spite of its explicitly erroneous character, the residue of normative pressure (Deutsch and Gerard, 1955) tied to the categorisation was sufficient to induce the relational regulation which was expected: subjects re-established consensus by diminishing the angle, notwithstanding the perceptual evidence. This is not the case for an out-group source, which induces a constructivism about the object, hence the change in weight. Inhibiting the relational regulation only deepened the re-establishment of consensus made necessary by the representation of knowledge (Butera *et al.*, 1994).

### Conclusions

The studies reported in this chapter refer to two distinct domains of research: the social development of cognitive tools in the child, and social influence, traditionally studied among adults. In reality, they converge on many theoretical ideas which sustain them (Doise and Mugny, 1997):

1 At the origin of cognitive development, as with influence, is the working in one form or another of socio-cognitive conflict, which implies a *divergence* between an individual and one or more other individuals; disagreement about the same problem or the same object is thus at the root of individual changes.

2 In both domains, it is in effect the change which is the principal measure, and which theories aim to explain. This implies that the

individual is led to form judgements which they would not have done if they had not been confronted by a disagreement with others. A characteristic of these changes is that to a great extent they do not highlight a process of imitation, but a *constructivist elaboration* of new judgements and new forms of reasoning. Nevertheless, the resolution of conflict depends largely on the nature of the sources. Those of higher status, adults (in developmental studies), majority, or in-group (in studies of social influence), tend to induce a more relational regulation of the conflict, that is to say, a socially explicit re-establishment of consensus (imitation in developmental studies, compliance in social influence). Sources of an equal status (developmental studies) or inferior status, minority, or out-group (studies of influence) induce a more constructivist process.

3  In effect what predominates is the question of understanding if the knowledge on which individuals should converge is defined by its uniqueness or its plurality. The former attempts to induce a more convergent mode of thought (Nemeth, 1986), taking its inspiration directly from the response of the source, and the latter a more divergent mode of thought, which constructs on the basis of the knowledge of both parties. The relational regulation corresponds to a concordance between the higher status of the source and the anticipation of unanimity; constructivism to the concordance between a source of equal or inferior status and the anticipation of a plurality of knowledge (Butera *et al.*, 1996).

### Note

Translated from the French by Gerard Duveen.

# 6 Social memory: macropsychological aspects

*Augustín Echebarría Echabe and*
*José Luis Gonzalez Castro*

### Introduction

For centuries scholars in the Western world have been interested in the study of memory. Herrman and Chaffin (1988) reviewed different works on this topic written before Ebbinghaus, and located the first study on how to improve one's memory in the fifth century BC, which was entitled 'Dialexis'. From then onwards, those studies conducted on the subject of memory were fundamentally interested in the practical aspects of memory. It was only during the seventeenth century that there was a shift in interest from the practical to the theoretical aspects of memory. Although, as we see, there is a long history of interest in this topic, a more general interest on the impact of macrosocial factors (i.e. culture) on cognitive processes in general and memory in particular is quite recent (Jahoda, 1992). Nevertheless, as Jodelet (1992) states, social psychology's interest in this subject is but a decade old. To be more precise, we could say that the emergence of this interest is parallel to the emergence during the 1970s of social cognition as the dominant paradigm. (Markus and Zajonc, 1985; Fiske and Taylor, 1991).

Social cognition explains memory by using the concept of 'schemata', developed by Bartlett (1932) in his classical studies on memory. The epistemological bases underlying this approach to the study of memory are basically those which characterize 'cognitive science' as a whole (Gardner, 1985). We should not forget that cognitivism's gradual importance in social psychology is just another example of a more global 'cognitive revolution' which affects different areas. Cognitive science is a multidisciplinary approach which integrates philosophy, linguistics, psychology, anthropology, neuroscience, and artificial intelligence. Of all the characteristics which define this approach to cognitive phenomena, a certain number of them are also going to define the way that social psychology approaches cognition:

1 the acceptance that historical and cultural factors (in a word, social factors) are not necessary to explain human thought; and

2  the use of the computer as a metaphor for the human brain (Gardner, 1985). These same principles are those which orient the study of memory from the perspective of social cognition.

The purpose of this chapter is not to provide an analysis of this form of understanding and studying memory. For those interested in a detailed analysis of this position we recommend Fiske and Taylor's volume on social cognition (1991).

Nevertheless, many authors have felt somewhat disappointed with what social cognition has had to offer in the study of human knowledge. First of all, the idea that human beings are calculating processors in which emotional elements disappear was heavily criticized. This criticism has, of late, led to an increase in those studys concerning the mutual influences of moods and cognitive processes. However, the most important criticism which social cognition has faced, and the one which we find most important and pertinent for the aims of this chapter, is of its 'intrapsychic' nature, relegating memory's social aspects.

A characteristic phenomenon of 'social' cognition is its reduction of the social to a mere source of stimulation processed by the individual (Lave, 1991). Morgan and Schwalbe (1990) state this criticism in the following way: 'social cognition has not fulfilled its promise to show what is truly social about cognition . . . psychologists too often pursue individuals' cognitive activities within a structural vacuum, ignoring the influence of social environment . . . by limiting itself to issues of the mind as it functions within the individuals, social cognition has become strikingly asocial' (pp. 148–9). As Bakhurst noted (1990, p. 221), 'any statement proposing that memory is essentially a social phenomenon clashes with the individualistic conception of the mind which has dominated Western philosophy and psychology'.

In what is left of the chapter we will try to state 'another form of studying memory'. This approach, as with 'cognitive science', is multidisciplinary, being open to sociologists, psychologists, anthropologists, linguistics, etc. But, as opposed to the cognitive perspective, it will accept that the social (culture, history, groups, etc.) is the basis of all human knowledge. It is not possible to understand human thought by isolating the human being from his/her social and historical context.

### Memory as a social phenomenon

Halbwachs ([1950]1980) stated that individual memory was social because: (1) 'A man must often appeal to other's remembrances to evoke his own past' (p. 51); (2) 'He goes back to reference points determined by society, hence outside himself' (p. 51); (3) 'Moreover, the individual memory could not function without words and ideas, instruments the individual has not himself invented but appropriated from his milieu' (p. 51); (4) further, 'each memory is a viewpoint on the collective memory' (p. 48); (5) finally, social memory is always the memory of a group.

These quotations from Halbwachs will enable us to structure the rest of the chapter. We propose to study three areas related to social memory:

- social memory and society: in this section we shall review those authors who have studied the influence of macrosocial factors such as collective consciousness on individual memory;
- social memory and language: here we will study those authors who have stated that language is a central element in order to understand memory;
- social memory and the group: finally, we shall look into the subject of memory in view of the functions which it fulfils in a group.

### Social memory and society

Different authors have stated the existence of a directionality in the determination of memory, which would lead us from macro to psychological levels. We will now look into some of these authors, although space does not allow us to be too exhaustive on this subject.

#### Durkheim

Durkheim is one of the main exponents of this orientation. In his works ([1893]1984; [1912]1995), Durkheim studied concepts such as conscience, collective representations, and individual representations. He thought that individual representations were a result of individual consciousness (individual minds), while collective representations were a result of a *collective consciousness* (or social mind). This collective consciousness was defined as 'the totality of beliefs and sentiments common to the average members of a society forms a determinate system with a life of its own . . . [which] is independent of the particular conditions in which the individuals find themselves. Individuals pass on, but it abides' (Durkheim, [1893]1984, pp. 38–9). Each and every subject has two consciousnesses: a 'personal' one which defines his/her personality, and another one which is common to all society. Social cohesion is based upon the conformity of the personal consciousness to the collective consciousness.

For Durkheim, language occupies a very important place in the collective consciousness (Durkheim, [1912]1995). There is a concept in every word. Concepts condense all the knowledge and science accumulated by society over the centuries. *Concepts are collective representations.* Language and those concepts connected to it allow us to abandon the *simple representations* (feelings, perceptions, and images) which are ephemeral and alterable, and which are linked with those impressions which the external stimule produce to our senses. Concepts allow abstract representations, universal and non-alterable. Language, being as it is a system of concepts, is a result of a collective elaboration. It expresses the way in which a society as a whole understands the objects of experience. This system of concepts finds its way of expression in the vocabulary of our mother tongue.

As for social remembrance, in his analysis of totemic religions, Durkheim ([1912]1995) states that traditionally we have incorrectly thought that the most important aspect of religion (indeed of any kind of social-belief system) was its cosmology, the representations and beliefs which define it, and that the rituals and commemorations were merely the exteriorization, the external and material aspects of these beliefs. As opposed to this, Durkheim believes that the 'cult is not merely a system of signs by which the faith is outwardly expressed; it is the sum total of means by which that faith is created and recreated periodically' (p. 420). In other words, a commemoration is not just a reminder of the past, it is what creates and recreates the memory of the past. The role of a commemoration is very important because it gives a community unity and personality, by means of it a community is aware of its existence; it is the way by which we can reaffirm, on a regular basis, those feelings and collective ideas which define a society. The emotional component of a commemoration is of utmost importance. In this way, in these meetings and gatherings, the individuals reaffirm collectively their common *feelings.*

### Halbwachs

Halbwachs's work ([1950]1980) is possibly the most important example of applying Durkheim's ideas to the study of memory (Duvignud, 1968; Lieury, 1978). In order to present Halbwachs's ideas we will take into consideration his book *The collective memory* ([1950]1980). For this author memory is social because other people (a) help us increase our confidence in the exactness of our memories, and (b) take us into a reality in which we are never alone.

Nevertheless, even though remembrance is collective, not everybody remembers the same things. Each person's remembrance represents a different point of view of the situation. In the same fashion, the different groups which compose society share different memories of the same events inasmuch as their perspectives and views differ.

Halbwachs ([1950]1980) rejects the existence of a totally individual memory. The difference between *collective memory* and *individual memory* is a matter of degree; 'each memory is a viewpoint on the collective memory . . . The succession of our remembrances, even our most personal ones, is always explained by changes occurring in our relationships to various collective milieus – in short, by the transformations these milieus undergo separately and as a whole' (pp. 48–9). During a person's life span he or she becomes part of different social groups; some are stable (i.e. family), others are constantly changing and have a short life span. Each group may give the subject a different view of the things which have happened in the past. The individual memory will in the end be the result of the multiple crossed social influences which affect a person as a member of different social groups. This influence may give memory an idiosyncratic aspect. As we get involved with different social groups memory is transformed.

Halbwachs differentiates among at least three types of memory: (1) internal, personal or autobiographical; (2) social or collective; and (3) historical memory. The biographical memory would represent one's past in a more dense, continuous, and complete way, while the historical memory (defined as a series of events which have happened to a large number of individuals) would represent the past in a more schematic and reduced fashion. Nevertheless, biographical memory does have recourse to historical memory. Halbwachs contrasts historical memory to social or collective memory. 'Generally history only starts when tradition ends and the social memory is fading or breaking up . . . The memory of a sequence of events may no longer have the support of a group . . . may become scattered among various individuals lost amid new groups for whom these facts no longer have interest because the events are definitely external to them' ([1950]1980, pp. 78–9); social memory disappears and the only way to keep those memories is through history. History and collective memory are different in at least two aspects: (1) collective memory is anchored in a group's consciousness, never exceeding the group's limits, and (2) while there is only one history, there is a co-existence of various collective memories.

As Moreau de Bellaing states (1985), for a long period of time, any interest in Halbwachs's work in particular or collective memory in general, was relegated owing to the existence of a dominant empiricist conception which silenced this type of analysis.

One of the most important authors who have followed Halbwachs's ideas has been Gerard Namer. In his book *Batailles pour la mémoire* (1983), he exemplifies Halbwachs's ideas in the study of commemorations in France from 1945 onwards. He states that a commemoration represents an election, a preference for some events, and a rejection and forgetfulness of other events. In the study of social memory the analysis of *what is forgotten* is very important. Namer analyses two forms of memory: the Gaulliste memory and the communist memory. Both these memories adopt different starting points, they resort to different omissions, and they stress the importance of different events and people. De Gaulle is shown as someone who continues a French historical tradition which has its origins in Joan of Arc, Louis XIV, Napoleon and the Empire, the 1914 war, the 11 November armistice, the Second World War and the Resistance, and finally ends in his own figure. On the other hand, the communist memory starts off with the French Revolution, is followed by the nineteenth-century revolutions, specially the Commune, and reaches up to the Second World War Resistance. In both these cases of memory reconstruction there is a sense of continuity with periods which are condensed and periods which are forgotten.

Namer (1983) states two important aspects of social memory: (1) first of all, it is based on forgetfulness; (2) second, memory is above all *emotion, affect*. The most important aspect in a commemoration is not that the event is remembered as it was, but the emotional significance attached to this memory.

As we can see, Durkheim, Halbwachs, and Namer all agree that commemoration is a central element in the social reconstruction of memory. To commemorate some event also implies, on one hand, to rewrite history, and, on the other, to relive common feelings. In the words of Morin (Atlan and Morin, 1988, p. 126), 'a commemoration is not only a rememoration; it is even more than a revitalization, it is a regeneration. The events which are commemorated . . . arise in the present the impact which it had (the event) in the past when it was present.'

Atlan (Atlan and Morin, 1988, p. 127) also states that the re-elaboration of the past through a commemoration is easier when the personage or event to be remembered has been transformed into a *myth* instead of just being an object of scientific science. 'The mythical transfomation adds a number of potentialities which did not exist but which, as potentials, leave the door open to any re-creation during the commemorations which may take place during the following centuries or millenniums.'

Nevertheless, the social evocation of the past does not always have to adopt the form of a more or less official commemoration. There are sometimes ordinary routines which are forms of social memory. For example, De Madariaga (1988) exemplifies this point by showing how a child's game is the vehicle by which the image of the 'Moor', associated with a knife and death, which has lingered for centuries, is perpetuated.

A contemporary example of this orientation in social psychology would be Pennebaker's study (1993) of collective memory. Without actually citing Durkheim, this study is an example of both Halbwachs's and Durkheim's theoretical and methodological influence. Methodologically (and bearing in mind Durkheim's study on suicide), Pennebaker compares macro data (statistics on crimes committed in different cities; time which has elapsed between the occurrence of certain historical events and the building of commemorative monuments, etc.). The communicative interaction is an important element in the organization and assimilation of an event in the collective memory. Moreover, a shared discussion is a common fact in any large-scale event which affects an important segment of a given society.

The author also establishes a parallelism between individual memory and collective memory when stating that, by definition, those events which are important for individual memories should also be necessary for collective memories. Historical events may not affect an entire society's collective memory in the same way. He thinks that there is a critical period in the construction of one's identity, which is the period which lies between twelve and twenty-five years of age, in which national events have a stronger impact on memory. So, this age group would be those who would record, in a stronger way, certain historical events in their collective memory. This idea of the higher impact of national events during adolescence and up to around the age of twenty-five years, is supported by the studies of Schuman and Scott (1989), who state that those events experienced during this age period are in a position of primacy in memory because this is a period in which a person breaks free from the 'natural world' of infancy and is introduced into a more extensive 'political and social world'.

By linking collective memory to an age group, Pennebaker is able to explain those regularities in the sociological data with which he works. On the one hand, he finds that the period of time which normally elapses between a national dramatic event and the building of some kind of monument to remember it is around twenty to thirty years. If we think that those who are remembering the event now are those who were adolescents, young men, and women then, and that it is now when they have the necessary financial possibilities to build any monument, we will be able to understand this regularity.

In spite of the strong criticism which they have had to suffer, both these concepts of consciousness and collective memory have reached the present day. Quoting Jahoda (1992, p. 192–3), 'while this term [group mind] as such has ceased to be respectable, the notion persists under other labels, and the kind of problem it was intended to solve remains'. For example, Rubinstein (1982) favours the notion of 'group mind' as 'an antidote' to the individualising tendencies present nowadays in subjective sociology.

Rebaudiries (1987) stresses the role of collective memory as a tool with which to confront situations of acculturization and assimilation. Jeudy (1986) emphasizes the constant struggle which societies undergo (defending their national heritage) with the aim of keeping their identities and collective memories.

*Vygotsky*

From a totally different perspective we have the Marxist tradition, which stresses the importance of the forms of production in the determination of the psychological processes. An example of this idea could be Engels ([1876]1968, p. 358), who states that 'labour created man'. First of all, work and later words were fundamental in the development of the brain and in evolving from an ape to a human being. The progressive development of the superior cognitive processes as a result of the mutual relationship between work–language–cranial evolution bring about more complex social organization systems. This importance given by Engels to the tool, inasmuch as it implies a mediated and not direct relationship with the world, is again firmly stated by Soviet psychology, especially the socio-historical school, of which Vygotsky is the main exponent (see also Moscovici, chapter 14 this volume; Harré, chapter 8 this volume). Nevertheless, Vygotsky did include in his analysis an element which clearly distinguishes him from the rest of the authors encompassed in this school: *the central role given to language in cognitive development* (Vygotsky, 1978, [1934]1986; Riviere, 1985). Vygotsky thinks that a primitive intelligence is already present in the anthropoids. This intelligence is seen as the capacity to use rudimentary tools (sticks, etc.). He also believes in the existence of some type of language with a particular morphology, and which fulfils basic social-regulation functions in certain animals. Phylogenetically, this intelligence and this language have a different development. But, 'although children's use of tools during their preverbal period is comparable to that of apes, as soon as speech and the use of signs are incorporated into any action, the action becomes transformed and organized along entirely new lines' (Vygotsky, 1978, p. 24). In other words, the higher cognitive functions will emerge as a result of the external activity mediated by the tool (here we can see

Engels's influence), and language. The tool implies a mediated relationship with the environment or context. For Vygotsky, a sign is another
type of tool with which to relate and transform the environment. The
sign and the tool have in common their mediating function. What
differentiates them are the ways in which they orient human activity: the
tool is externally oriented and must produce changes in an external
object, while the sign has an internal orientation (Vygotsky, 1978).
Meaning is arbitrary and conventional. A child will acquire the capacity
to handle this tool (language) by implication in the linguistic practices of
their environment. Language, which initially, the same as a gesture, is
external, will progressively interiorize itself. Internalization for Vygotsky
is 'the internal reconstruction of an external operation' (p. 56). It is in
this way that language will become an instrument for contact and
control, not only with others and the external world but also with oneself
(consciousness emerges – see Harré, chapter 8 this volume).

With regard to his conception of *memory*, Vygotsky (1978) differentiates between two types: (1) natural memory, whose characteristic is that
it forms an immediate impression of things, owing to a retention of
experiences on the basis of mnemic traces; and (2) a social memory, in
which the storing of experiences is not determined by external stimulation
but by signs. This memory is so 'logical' that to remember is to think.
For Vygotsky, language allows us to synthesize present and past; to unite
elements of past experiences with the present.

Owing to the importance which Vygotsky gives to language, some
authors (Riviere, 1985; Bakhurst, 1990) have stated that his orientation
was clearly cultural-semiotic. Even though Vygotsky does give language
a great importance, he constantly states the importance of social activity.
He affirms that the internalization of socially rooted and historically
developed activities is precisely the point or fact which gives human
psychology its apecific character.

### Social memory and language

It is probably the social constructionist approach which has studied the
subject of language and social knowledge most extensively. These
authors criticize the cartesian paradigm which dominates social cognition
(Markova, 1982). As Harré has pointed out, in the cartesian paradigm,
to remember is considered a mental process, and memories, being mental
phenomena, are considered to be internal (see Harré, chapter 8 this
volume).

Social constructionism has sought to emerge as an alternative to the
dominant empiricism of social cognition. Instead of paying attention to

the intention, implicit rules (schemata) which find their adequate form of expression in language, they intend to study language in itself, perceiving language not as a capacity which one may have, but as a shared activity which is performed (Gergen, 1985).

On the basis of this conversational perspective, 'psychological realities' such as thought and memory will be understood as *language games*, defined as complex interpersonal processes which include conversational practices (Harré, 1989b, and chapter 8 in this volume). The psychological constructs will be extracted from the human brain and included in a communicative interaction. Following Harré (1989b), a person is a localized point; he or she is a point in space in which a speech act may occur. These speech acts are not in the individual but in the dyad, triad, etc., 'conversation is the primal human reality, and in the individual "minds" are not substances but privatized conversations' (Harré, 1989b, p. 449). Those concepts used to refer to ' "the contents of the psyche," those powers, motives, intentions, needs, wants, urges, tendencies, and so on, that are endowed with the capacity to direct human behaviour have no ontological status, but appear to do so because they are objectified through linguistic practices. They are essentially reified by-product of human communication practices' (Gergen, 1994, p. 85).

Coulter (1985) also criticizes the social cognition paradigm for forgetting that memory and forgetfulness, like other mental predicates, are *praxological* (based on practical actions), intersubjective, belong to the area of public language and have communicative functions. For example, forgetfulness fulfils social functions, it is an evasive technique, avoiding responsibilities in normal life. In other words, 'it is an organized moral phenomena' (socially), and there are rules with regard to what may and what may not be forgotten (Coulter, 1985).

Gergen (1987; Gergen and Gergen, 1983, 1988; Marlowe and Gergen, 1968) has studied the narrative linguistic practices displayed in the construction of a particular type of memory: autobiographical memory. This author states (Gergen and Gergen, 1983, p. 255) that when a subject asks him/herself about his/her past, he/she imposes order and stability on this same past through 'narrative forms'. Each culture sets a series of rules with regard to the ways of reconstructing our autobiographical memory. Moreover, this biography must be *socially negotiated* (Gergen and Gergen, 1983, 1988). This auto-narrative construction of the past may only subsist if the other social interlocutors adopt a specific and adequate support role.

Ross and McFarland (1988) state the existence of implicit theories of stability and change, which are specific to different cultures and which guide these auto-reconstructions.

Close to this orientation we find the *rhetorical* perspective which has been developed by Billig (1987, 1989, 1990). This author states that 'there is nothing specifically different in thought that may be opposed to argumentation' (Billig, 1987, p. 110). Private thought is modelled by public argumentation, and as a consequence possesses a dialogical character. With regard to memory, he thinks that the concept of collective memory is important in the study of ideology. 'Ideology would be a form of social memory in so much as it constitutes what is collectively remembered and forgotten' (Billig, 1992, p. 77). People use ideology (collective memory) to think about and discuss the social world, in such a way that ideology determines the nature of the arguments and their rhetorical form. His concept of ideology ('beliefs and practices which assure the reproduction of power relationships', p. 78) implies the existence of contradictions in its realm, and as a result we have confronting points of view which allow argumentation to exist. A practical example of this approach is Billig's study of the memory of events related to the British royal family (Billig, 1989, 1992).

### Social memory and groups

Halbwachs ([1950]1980) stated the importance of the group as a base for social/collective memory. For him, there is only one historical memory, but there are many social memories, and these differ from historical memories in that they never exceed a group's limits. This great importance given to the group as unit of analysis of social memory is also justified by another series of reasons, which we shall now state.

### *Group as 'base or support' for memory*

As Middleton and Edwards (1990a, p. 7) mentioned, one of the problems which has appeared while studying memory is that it has nearly always been seen as just a 'property which the individuals have'. Nevertheless, memory also has other external supports, a group may be considered as a system of information storage (von Cranach, 1992, and chapter 2 this volume). An example of theoretical work which adopts the idea of a group as a memory system are the studies performed by Wegner, and his concept of 'Transactive Memory System' (1986). Wegner states that there are certain types of memory (transactive memory) which cannot be studied in isolated subjects because it is a group property. Transactive memory is a series of individual memory systems in combination with the communication which takes place between the subjects. In a group, every person has his/her own internal memory depot. But, in a group, the other members of the group act as external memory depots. In this way, intercommunication allows an individual's own personal memory to increase and extend itself. Each subject would be a 'trustee' of a portion of the information and would know the location of the other parts of the global information (which would be in the other members of the group). This interdependence produces a *knowledge-holding system* which is more extensive and complex than individual memory systems. The transactive memory system has an impact on the group, stating what a group may remember and how they should remember.

### The reconstruction of memory in conjunction with a group's interests and position

Memory is closely linked to the construction of social identity (Boyarin, 1989). 'Memory . . . describes a characteristical activity of the establishment of the biographical identities of groups and individuals' (Radley, 1990, p. 67). The definition of identity automatically remits us to memory (Lapierre, 1989). Besides constructing its identity, when a group evokes its past it is constructing it in accordance with its own present-day interests. We will now present some studies which have shown this relationship between memory and construction–justification of group identity. We will also mention the social functions of memory and forgetfulness.

In her research on the trial of Klaus Barbie ('the butcher of Lyon') Jodelet (1992, p. 244) studied the close relationship which exists between the reconstruction of the past and identity and group interests. In this trial we were able to see how the revisionists of the Nazi past and the victims of this regime reconstructed in different ways what had happened in the past.

There are also a great number of studies on the social memory of the Holocaust jews. These studies show the significance and importance which this evocation has nowadays as a collective basis for the present day survival of Jewish identity (Stein, 1984; Ertel, 1985; Bar-Tal and Antebi, 1992).

Deyanov (1992) performed a very interesting research on the antagonistic reconstruction of the past in a context of strong intergroup conflict. In this study he analyses how the past is reconstructed in two Bulgarian newspapers (*Douma* and *Demokratsia*) just before the 1991 elections. These newspapers are representatives of two antagonistic political positions, the Social Democrat party founded from the extinct Communist Party, and the UFD, Democratic Forces Union. Even though they hold antagonistic positions, they do show structural analogies in their reconstruction of the past. For example, *Demokratsia* presents Bulgaria as an enormous socialist gulag which has been built on the basis of unknown tombs. On the other hand, *Douma* states that the situation now is beginning to look like it was before 1944, with the country full of unknown tombs. Each newspaper 'brings out of the closet' the other group's corpses while leaving theirs well buried. The newspapers do not refer to a 'specific criminal act but to the violation of all the forbidden codes, it is the *symbology of human corruption* which produces even before conscience has intervened, nausea, and at the same time the desire for vengance' (our italics). Deyanov asks himself, when the discussion loses its intensity after the electoral period, what will have been the consequence of this exhumation? For the author (p. 64) all the events and people which have seen the light again are 'archetypes of public opinion, of public memory censorship. They are *the archetypical sites of memory*, which, once they have disappeared from the newspapers and their reader's conscience, feed the interpretative schemata which are applied to our memory's and opinion's task.'

One of the few studies in the area of social psychology which tries to illustrate the relationship between social identity and memory is Reicher's (1984) study of the St Paul's riots of 2 April 1980, in Bristol, England. In these studies we observe how in an intergroup conflict situation (black community of St Paul's and the police), the reconstruction of the past is different depending on the position of each group in the conflict. This reconstruction has ideological functions of legitimating a group's position. In these studies we find different descriptions of the cause or spark that started the riot. For the police the riots started when police officers, with legal warrant orders, detained a drug pusher and the owner of a pub and also found 372 cans of illegal beer. When they were doing their job confiscating the illegal merchandise, they were surrounded by a group of people who started to insult and throw objects at them; owing to this outburst of violence the police then had to retreat. Moreover, in the process of constructing the past in form of rumours, in the police ranks the news was that a well-known left-wing activist, Tariq Ali, was at the scene of the riots (in fact, he did not arrive until the afternoon of the next day). This last fact may be interpreted as the creation of a 'conspiracy theory' to help explain the events.

On the other hand, the members of the community which participated in the events have a somewhat different version of the facts. Plainclothes police barged into the pub without showing their search warrants, behaving like 'a cross between the Sweeney and Kojak', brutalizing customers. Also, and before all this happened, some plainclothes policemen were involved in a 'ganja business' and smoked marijuana in the pub (see Hewstone and Augoustinos, chapter 4 this volume).

Another example of the point we are trying to make is that presented by Nagata (1990) in which a minority, the American-Japanese citizens, tries to be accepted by the majority which discriminates against them, while also trying to forget those repressive actions of which they have been victims. In this research three generations of American-Japanese were studied. The generation of those who were interned in concentration camps on the west coast of the US after the Japanese attack on Pearl Harbor; the generation of these people's sons and daughters, and finally the grandsons and daughters of the first generation. Nagata shows that in an effort to achieve that their sons and daughters be considered true Americans, those who suffered internment resorted to forgetfulness in order to avoid the differentiation with the rest of the Americans. Nagata (1990, p. 140) reflects in a very precise manner the attitude of those who suffered internment when he quotes one of the descendants as saying: 'it's like a secret or maybe more like a skeleton in the closet, like a relative who is retarded or an alcoholic'.

### Group practices as a source of acquiring knowledge

Memory is always remembrance of knowledge previously acquired. Because of this, any intention of theorizing on social memory implies starting off from some assumption about the mechanisms of acquisition of social knowledge. In this case, the group again may be considered as a unit of analysis which allows us to integrate three types of social phenomena closely linked to one another: social identity, social memory, and the acquisition of social knowledge. An example of this type of theorization integrating these three aspects, which assumes that group activity is a core factor in this integration, is the study by Lave (1991). This author analyses pedagogical problems and 'professional' formation, along with the development of 'professional identities', but if we extrapolate and generalize some of her assumptions we think it could be a very interesting contribution to social psychology. The author defends the idea that 'the acquisition of knowledge, thought and information are relationships between people involved in an activity "in" and "with" a world which is socially and culturally structured' (p. 148). The acquisition of knowledge is a result of a process of ascription to a group which shares common practices. To acquire a social identity and to acquire competence in a certain order (i.e. to become a professional in some kind of job) are two elements of the same process. The first one providing a motivation, the second one an orientation and a meaning. The subject (i.e. 'witch doctor apprentice') acquires knowledge at the same time that he is developing his identity, being recognized by the others and at the same time recognizing himself as a 'witch doctor', and all this is done by participating in socially structured practices. At first, the members of the tribe whose identity is already recognized ('the official witch doctors of the tribe') will allow the apprentice to perform secondary and peripheral aspects and routines of the professional activities. Later on, he will be given more and more responsibilities and take on a more important role in the activities. While the person is involved in these structured activities he is acquiring knowledge (which is associated with its role in the tribe), he starts to develop a socially accepted identity, and allows the group to have a certain continuity in its structure. To acquire a group identity and to acquire competence in a certain instance are two elements of the same process. This social knowledge is perpetuated and prolonged (memory) by means of the ordinary or daily performance of common structured practices.

## Conclusions

In conclusion, we offer a brief synopsis of the argument of this chapter. First, we have seen the eminently social nature of memory, not only in its origin but also in its contents, structure, functions, etc. Middleton and Edwards (1990b) state at least six aspects which mark memory's social role:

1 the importance of the objects which structure the world and are important elements of collective memory;
2 the existence of a socially institutionalized forgetfulness;
3 the sharing of memories leads to the establishment of contexts and contents of what will be remembered and commemorated;
4 commemoration has an enormous social importance – it is a central element in the formation of collective identities;
5 collective memory and commemorations create the context for individual memory;
6 the importance of conversation and discussion in the reconstruction of the past, allowing contradictory versions of a same account.

The importance of these six aspects has already been stressed in previous pages, while it has also been pointed out that these elements have been omitted by the mainstream of current social psychology.

Using again Halbwachs's ([1950]1980) quote, with which we started this chapter, we must remember that memory is more than just a capacity placed into a human being's brain. Memory is social in its *origin*. As many authors have stated, memory is not possible without those tools which we call signs, which, in turn, are the result of a long history of social evolution. As Halbwachs said, the idiosyncratic emergence of individual memory is produced by multiple crossed social influences. Moreover, language and communication are crucial factors in the process of building up and validating what we do and 'must' remember. Memory is also social, owing to the functions which it fulfils. It is also very important to note that there is not only one memory, but several group memories, and that that which is forgotten is of utmost importance in the study of memory owing to the fact that it stresses the importance of a group's position and interests in elaborating and transforming that which should be remembered.

We personally think that the social dimension of memory is so important that it is impossible to understand it if we separate it from the following triad: memory–social identity–social practices.

Finally, it is important to note that the current tendency in social psychology is that of stressing the linguistic aspects of memory, which we think may somewhat obscure the importance of other non-declarative elements of memory and social knowledge. Social practices such as rituals (conmemorations, ceremonies, etc.) allow us better to understand that memory is more than a cognitive capacity. And another factor which merits more study is that of the social space in which things occur and actors interact; we think that this space plays an important part in memory and in remembering.

From all that has been said, we must assume that a purely intrapsychic approach to the study of memory will not help its total comprehension as it does not allow us to study in detail its origins and social functions.

Paraphrasing Gardner (1985) in his definition of cognitive science, we could state that the topic of social memory may lead the way to a multidisciplinary effort which interests not only psychology, but also sociology, sociolinguistics, anthropology, and philosophy.

# 7    Self as social representation

*Daphna Oyserman and Hazel Rose Markus*

## Introduction

A sense of self develops as people find or create answers to the questions of 'who am I' and 'where do I belong.' The psychological literature often focuses attention on the way in which people actively and deliberately pursue these questions in therapy, in solitary travels to the top of mountains, in adolescent rebellions, and in midlife crises. Indeed many of the most obvious answers to these seemingly personal questions are highly idiosyncratic; they are custom-crafted, reflecting fine-grained interpretations of individual experience. Some of the answers, however, are a consequence of one's relative positioning in socio-political and historical context, and they are developed interpersonally and consensually. It is these shared and implicit answers to the 'who am I' and 'where do I belong' questions – the *social representations of selfhood* – that are the focus of this chapter. We will suggest that although making a self appears to be an individual and individualizing pursuit, it is also a collective and collectivizing one.

From a societal perspective, self-construction is too important to be left as a personal project. Social integration and the social order require that individuals of a given group have reasonably similar answers to the 'who am I' and 'where do I belong' questions. Among the commitments of every cultural and social group are those that provide a vision of the 'good' or 'appropriate' or 'moral' person. The philosopher Taylor writes: 'To know who you *are* is to be oriented in moral space, a space in which questions arise about what is good or bad, what is worth doing and what is not, what has meaning and importance for you, and what is trivial and secondary' (1989, p. 28). A cultural group's shared ideas about 'how to be' are reflected in culturally significant stories, sacred texts, proverbs, icons, and institutions, as well as lived in the everyday practices (e.g. language, caretaking, schooling, media, religious, workplace, etc.) of social life.

Our goals in this chapter are to (1) outline the powerful, but often invisible, role of social representations in framing and undergirding the self; (2) provide an example of variation in social representations of selfhood; (3) discuss how individuals come to terms with multiple or conflicting social representations of selfhood; and (4) sketch some consequences of a social representational approach to the self.

We will argue that social representations are critical to the process of framing, developing, and maintaining a sense of self. These representations are the basic building blocks from which the sense of self is constructed. A social representational approach to the self is relatively new in psychology (Farr and Moscovici, 1984; Shweder and LeVine, 1984). For the most part, the socio-cultural embeddedness of the self has been under-explored, and the self as formulated in Western social psychology has been a fundamentally *asocial* entity. Why has this been the case? As suggested by Holland and Quinn (1987), social representations, what they call 'cultural frames', are powerful precisely because they are taken for granted, transparent, and therefore seem logical, necessary, and natural. Social representations provide the form and the language for the 'who am I' or 'who are we' questions, and in so doing structure the nature of the 'right' answer. Thus, in the US, in the course of developing a sense of self, a person typically asks 'How much have I achieved?' and/or 'How happy am I?', and typically does not ask 'Is everything OK in my group?', 'Am I meeting the needs or living up to the expectations of my group?' It is no accident then that American selves are conceptualized and expressed in terms of agency or a lack of it, and happiness or the lack of it. Thus a social representational approach is a useful extension of previous social psychological theorizing on the self because it further highlights the role of culture and the social context.

### Social representations of selfhood – the uniformity in the uniqueness

Replaying some of psychology's and sociology's earliest themes, recent formulations of the self in the social sciences and philosophy stress that it is a necessary social construction. Erez and Earley (1993) claim: 'The self is a universal aspect of humanity and its definition is shaped differentially according to various cultural values and perspectives' (p. vii). One's sense of self, or perhaps more appropriately, one's *senses* of self – self can be considered from a variety of perspectives – develop as people assign meaning or significance to themselves as people (Neisser, 1988). This self-making process is an interpersonal and collective achievement (e.g. Baldwin, 1911; Sullivan, 1940), and depends in large part on the shared ideas of those in one's most significant socio-cultural niches.

According to Vygotsky (1978), children are born into a world of public representations and these representations are eventually internalized through communication and come to form the basis of individual mental representations. As Baldwin writes, 'The knower does not start out in isolation and then come to some sort of agreement with others by "matching" his world of independent sensations and cognitions with theirs. On the contrary, he starts with what he and his neighbors' experiences in common verify, and only partially, and by degrees does he find himself and prove himself to be a relatively competent independent thinker' (1911, p. xx), or, for our purposes, a relatively competent and independent 'self.'

The public representations of selfhood that characterize a given socio-cultural niche function as common denominators – they provide the primary structure of the selves of those who live within these contexts. These shared ideas produce necessary, although often unseen, common-alities in the selves of people within a given context. In defining the nature and role of social representations in constructing the self, we draw on the ideas of Moscovici (1984a) and Farr (1987b) and on the ideas of cultural anthropologists, most notably Holland and Quinn (1987), Hutchins (1980), and D'Andrade (1981), who have developed the idea of cultural schemas (see, e.g., Quinn and Holland, 1987).

Social representations have been described as constructs in the minds of members of a group which allow them to refer to some object for the purpose of communicating and behaving (Farr, 1987b). Individuals are heir to a great deal of knowledge about the world that they do not necessarily draw from first-hand experience (White, 1992; von Hippel, Sekaquaptewa, and Vargas, 1994). This cultural knowledge is trans-mitted and acquired through language and in interaction with others (Holland and Quinn, 1987). There is perhaps no experience, however concrete or novel, that is not informed by shared models which specify what is in the world and how it works (Holland and Quinn, 1987; Strauss and Quinn, 1994). According to Moscovici, social representations refer to a substratum of images and meanings which are essential for societal functioning. They are 'cognitive matrices coordinating ideas, words, images, and perceptions that are all interlinked; they are common sense theories about aspects of the world' (Moscovici and Hewstone, 1983, p. 15).

Collectivities could not operate were it not for a set of theories and ideologies, which they transform into shared realities. Quinn and Holland (1987) refer to these shared commitments and understandings as cultural schemas. They are the 'presupposed, taken for granted models of the world that are widely shared (though not to the exclusion of other alternative models) by the members of a society and that play an enormous role in their understanding of the world and their behaviour in it' (Quinn and Holland, 1987, p. 4).

### Individual and collective representations of the self

To illustrate the role of social representations in shaping the self, we can compare the social representations of selfhood associated with individualism and the social representations of selfhood associated with collectivism (Schwartz, 1990; Triandis, 1990a; Markus and Kitayama, 1991a; Oyserman and Markus, 1993). From a North American perspective, a collective answer to the 'who am I' question is that 'I am a bounded, autonomous whole.' The solution to this question from a Japanese perspective is 'I am a member or a participant of a group.' The two approaches to selfhood are perhaps even more different than this example conveys. The social representation of Americans assume the separate individual as the first fact, the uncontested reality, while for the Japanese it is the interdependent group that is the taken-for-granted, first fact. Both cultural groups must come to terms with the 'who am I' and 'where do I belong' questions. But for Americans these questions are accorded primacy, while for the Japanese they are considered in conjunction with another set of questions about 'Who are we?'

Moscovici (1984a) suggests that all ideas about the social world can be viewed as means of resolving pervading psychic or emotional tensions (cf. Ortner, 1984). The answers to the 'who am I?' and 'where do I belong?' questions are not obvious – there can be a variety of viable solutions and a group's social representations authorize and make 'real' the group's commitment to one solution over others. Individuals need not, perhaps cannot, grapple with such existential issues alone. This would seem to be one of the reasons for which humans have cultures (Carrithers, 1992). As Godelier (1986) asserts, 'human beings, in contrast to other social animals, do not just live in society, they produce society in order to live' (p. 1). Similarly, Shweder (1982) suggests that every group must generate a set of solutions to the questions embedded in what he calls the 'existence themes'. These include 'what is self' (or 'what is me') and also a set of highly related questions such as 'what is good?', 'what is moral?', 'what is male?', 'what is female?', 'what is mature?', 'what is childlike?', 'who is our kind and who is not?', 'what is our way and what is not?', and the question of hierarchy, 'why do people share unequally in the burdens and benefits of life?'.

As the foundation or scaffolding on which the self is constructed, social representations also condition habitual culture-specific patterns of thinking, feeling, and acting (Farr, 1987a; Farr and Moscovici, 1984; Moscovici, 1984a). One can envision two high-achieving high-school students, one American and one Japanese, each of whom imagines themself to be a committed, hardworking student. In many respects the manifest daily experiences of these students may be quite similar. Yet, the American student's view of self is likely to be anchored in a social representational repertoire that includes images and ideas of independence, individual freedom, creativity, uniqueness, and the importance of innate ability, while the Japanese student's view of self may be constructed from social representations which includes images and ideas of interdependence, harmonious group interaction, striving to attain standards or fulfil obligations, and the importance of persistence and endurance. As a consequence, the experience of school, of achievement, and of one's self as a student, may be systematically divergent. Exactly how social representations constrain and afford individual and the collective experience and expression of self and identity is, of course, the remaining theoretical and empirical project.

### Divergence in social representations of the self

*Individualism and collectivism as social representations*

In what ways might social representations of self, person, and society differ? The extensive literature on individualism and collectivism is a useful starting place. Individualism and collectivism can be thought of as different systems of ideas, images, and understandings about people, groups, and society. Thus, individualism focuses attention on the attainment of personal success (Kagitcibasi, 1987; Triandis, 1987; Georgas 1989). Within this world view, the development and maintenance of a separate personal identity is extolled, the importance of striving for self-actualization is highlighted, and the self is viewed as the basic unit of survival (Hui and Villareal, 1989; Markus and Kitayama, 1991a). In this solution to selfhood differences between the group and the individual are clearly delineated, and individuals are supposed to discover and attain their own 'true' selves by reflecting on and attending to themselves (Hsu, 1983).

On the other hand, collectivism focuses attention on maintenance of social norms and performance of social duties as defined by the in-group (e.g. Sinha and Verma, 1987; Triandis, 1990a, 1990b). Within this world view, development and maintenance of a set of common beliefs, attitudes, and practices is extolled, and the importance of cooperation with in-group members is highlighted (Hui and Triandis, 1986; Georgas, 1989;

Markus and Kitayama, 1991a). The group is viewed as the basic unit of survival (Hui and Villareal, 1989) so that attempts to distinguish between the personal and the communal are likely to appear false and be suspect (Triandis, 1990a; 1990b), social responsiveness is valued, and individuals are expected to attain understanding of their place within the in-group by reflecting on and attending to the needs of the group (Cousins, 1989; Markus, and Kitayama, 1991a).

An individualist world view promotes judgement of self and others by the extent of personal success each has achieved (Fiske, 1991). Individual differences are viewed as meaningful and stable, and as coming from the individual and not the context. Coalitions are established for the purpose of maximizing personal gain, and these coalitions change as circumstances change, with each individual seeking relationships with those most able to be of use at any particular point in time (Hsu 1983; Triandis et al., 1988; Waterman, 1984). Alternatively, a collectivist world view promotes judgement of self and others in terms of ascribed group membership. Behavioural or other individual differences are viewed as being due to context differences. Cooperation and co-existence within the in-group is emphasized, and relationships are not described in utilitarian terms but viewed as ends in themselves (Triandis, 1990a, 1990b). Out-group members are viewed with suspicion and hostility (Triandis, 1987; Triandis *et al.*, 1988). In-group membership carries with it a series of ascribed relationships (Triandis, 1987), and culturally prescribed norms dictate which attributes are necessary for meaningful group formation (Hsu, 1983).

### Sources of the social representation of self

The sources of such divergence in social representations of self and society remains a mystery. Recently, Lebra (1992) has sketched a series of ontological differences between North America and Japan, or more broadly between the East and the West. She argues that what it means 'to be' differs quite dramatically within these two regions. Her contention is that much of the East values what she labels the 'Shinto-Buddhist submerged self', while much of the West values a 'Cartesian, split self'. The particular ontological space she describes is defined by two axes – the horizontal anchored by Culture and Nature, and the vertical anchored by Being and Nothingness. Within this space, Lebra (1992) locates two contrasting models of the self. The North American and European self is located in the quadrant defined by Culture and Being. The goal of all existence from this ontological perspective is *self-objectification* – a highlighting of the division between the experiencer and what is experienced. Becoming autonomous, separate, and distinct from others is valued and emphasized, as are words, the head, and processes like ideation and abstraction. The emphasis is on knowing and knowledge and thus on self-knowledge and self-knowing as the goal of existence.

This Cartesian model of the nature of being and the self overlaps, but is importantly different from that model located in the quadrant defined by Nature and Nothingness. The goal of all existence from this latter perspective is not self-objectification but instead *freedom from self* – a downplaying of the division between the experiencer and the object of experience. It is not separation from others and becoming distinct that are to be valued, but connection with others and the surrounding context that are emphasized. Instead of an emphasis on the head there is an emphasis on the body, and a highlighting of feelings and immediacy. Lebra's (1992) analysis is elaborate and detailed and reveals, for example, how a concern with permanence and causation will be important features of a meaning system rooted in self-objectification, whereas a concern with impermanence and co-occurrence will be highlighted in a system rooted in gaining freedom from the constraints or boundaries of an individual self.

The Cartesian ontology gives rise to the Western notion of the self as an entity containing significant dispositional attributes which is detached from the social context. This view has been called the Western, separate, individualist, or independent view of self (Markus and Kitayama, 1991a; Oyserman, 1993; Triandis et al., 1988). It is characteristic of North American and European, but particularly white, urban, middle-class, secularized, contemporary people. The Shinto-Buddhist ontology is associated with a very different model of the self – one that is characteristic of China, Japan, Korea, the Philippines, South America, and Africa. It is typically a collectivist or interdependent view of the self. The self is viewed as interdependent with the surrounding social context, and it is the other or the self or the self-in-relation-to-other that is focal in individual experience. According to this view, people are seen as connected with others, not as separate. The individual is viewed not as an autonomous whole but as a fraction that becomes whole when in interaction with others. The cultural goal is to fit-in with others, to fulfil and create obligation, and, in general, to become part of various interpersonal relationships – to submerge the individual self and to regulate wants and needs in accordance with the wants and needs of others. And it is these cultural imperatives that will be diversely elaborated in a group's stockpile of images, words, schemas, and ideas, and broadly reflected in their modes of thinking, feeling, and being, and their heuristics, scripts, strategies, and ways of living.

The specific psychological consequences of these two contrasting views of the self and the nature of being for behaviour are currently emerging as a focus of much systematic analysis. Ethnographic studies have revealed marked differences in the practices of self and identity (e.g. Marsella, DeVos, and Hsu, 1985; Choi and Choi, 1990; Parish, 1991; Derné, 1992; Kondo, 1992; Rosenberger, 1992), sharp value differences have been established (e.g. Schwartz and Bilsky, 1990), and recent studies (Oyserman, 1993; Oyserman and Markus, 1993; Markus and Kitayama, 1994a; Woike, 1994) are outlining how self-relevant cognition, emotion, and motivation are markedly divergent depending on the view of self that anchors them.

### The example of achievement and control

A clear example of the meaning-making and discourse organizing role of social representations in the US, comes from the social representation of individualism in American society (Oyserman, 1993; Markus and Ki-tayama, 1994b). Within the North American cultural context, people are understood to be independent, bounded, autonomous entities who have an impact on and control over the external world (Hsu, 1985; Farr, 1991). Within this cultural frame, individuals are construed, defined, appraised, and evaluated for their achievement, and for their ability to strive, innovate, and overcome obstacles. People are believed to create themselves and to control actively their environment. A need or desire for control is essentialized as a core feature of personality. While fate, luck, circumstance, and social context are relatively unelaborated in these shared North American theories of social behaviour (Finch et al., 1991; Harter, 1992).

In the United States control becomes a key feature of competence and is viewed as an extremely valuable attribute. This social representation is so centrally implicated in individual functioning in the United States that it is tightly linked to self-esteem, social status, personal security, and mental health (Jones, 1989). As embodied in such concepts as self-efficacy, a control orientation has been related to life satisfaction, persistence, and coping in stressful situations (Finch et al., 1991). Because 'being a self' American style requires maintaining active control, individuals who experience a loss of control are likely to feel powerless, helpless, and therefore depressed and anxious (Fordham, 1988; Finch et al., 1991; Ogbu, 1991). If independence, control, and achievement are the organizing metaphors of personhood, then being a 'good' person, or a

person of value, means being able to embody or 'own' specific instances
or examples of these attributes. Evidence that one is successful in
attaining these standards is sought in one's accomplishments, behaviours,
and interactions with others. Thus the rubric of shared social representations forms the scaffolding of the self and serves as a standard against
which one is assessed and assesses the self.

Within the United States, the sense that a person is a bounded,
autonomous entity, whose abilities and competences allow for mastery of
the environment is a pervasive organizing framework. It is manifest as a
'perception' about individual reality, not as a consequence of one's
particular theory of the person. The ability to control outcomes in a
variety of domains is the basis of competence in this framework. A key
cultural task is to discover the domains in which one is competent and
then to verify and affirm them. The primary role of others is to provide
reflected appraisal or directly to evaluate one's performance. A negative
evaluation suggests a lack of ability in a domain. A positive evaluation
means that one has skill and talent in the domain in question and is
therefore 'good' in terms of that domain. Rather than risk failure, being
'bad', and a loss of self-esteem, individuals are likely to disinvest from
domains in which they have 'failed' or are likely to 'fail' (e.g. James,
1890; Stevenson, Azuma, and Hakuta, 1986; Steele, 1988; Markus, 1990;
Spencer and Steele, 1992).

Jones (1989) suggests that the value placed on control has resulted in a
desire to perceive the self as innately capable rather than as capable by
dint of effort. Consequently, intelligence is valued more than perseverance, and creativity or innovation are valued more than perfecting a
project or carrying through a task. 'Most of us [i.e. Americans] would
rather be a little gifted than a lot dogged, unless we can also convince
ourselves that being dogged is part of a strong character, which is, in
turn, a highly stable – maybe even naturally endowed – attribute' (Jones,
1989, p. 481). Thus, within a social context in which innate ability is
valued above perseverance, failure attributable to a clear lack of effort
may be preferred to expending effort and therefore exposing oneself to
diagnosis of one's competence.

Because the American social representation of personhood makes
achievement and internal control central to one's worth as an individual,
it seems natural that individuals seek out domains in which they can do
well and concentrate effort on these domains, to the exclusion of others.
Thus schoolchildren 'try out' various activities. They are given samplings
of music, language, art, computers, sports, and other activities. Implicit
in this process is that children are to 'discover' which are the domains
they have talent in and focus on those. A consequence of this process is

that children and youths who do not believe they are likely to attain success in school may be likely to disinvest from school and become involved in non-conventional or deviant activities instead (e.g. Steele, 1988; Oyserman and Markus, 1990a, 1990b; Ogbu, 1991; Spencer and Steele, 1992).

Within the American social representation of personhood, dependence on others is assumed to be a negative trait. Thus, 'altruism', or helping without clear, immediate, or concrete personal gain, is viewed with suspicion, and relationships are assumed to be formed in order to attain personal goals rather than being defining in themselves (Hsu, 1983). Parents thus exhort their children to be independent, to stand on their own two feet. Even pre-school teachers provide parents with feedback about their child's leadership capacity as opposed to the child's tendency to 'follow the lead of other children' (Fujita and Sano, 1988; Peak, 1991).

The nature of American social representations of selfhood is placed in high relief when compared with those of Japanese society. Rather than focus on the boundedness of individuals, individual achievement, personal control, and therefore the assessment of skill-based competence, Japanese social representations of personhood focus on interpersonal embeddedness and continuous work at making sense of, and attaining ever closer approximations of, one's roles and responsibilities (Markus and Kitayama, 1991b, 1994a). Thus, while as 'individualists' Americans believe in giving priority to self-interests over those of the groups or contexts to which they belong, Japanese social representations of personhood elaborate participation, interdependence, or collectivity.

Collectivists, it is said, do not distinguish between their own and their group's interests, viewing the self as irrevocably bound to and interconnected to others (Erez and Earley, 1993). While boundedness involves proof of agency, interconnectedness involves continual and ongoing effort to maintain harmony in relationships and to meet the needs and expectations of those with whom one is connected. Persistence as part of the social representation of personhood permeates all of Japanese society (Blinco, 1992). The centrality of persistence is continually reinforced and strengthened throughout development and the educational process. The term 'gambaru' (i.e. 'hold on, don't give up') is a positive one, in which one is exhorted to continue trying to achieve a goal no matter how hard or unattainable it may seem.

Deeply and pervasively embedded in Japanese thinking is the idea it may take many years of intensive training and study to master any worthwhile skill. Any short-cut is seen as potentially harmful because it is the persistence needed to attain the goal that makes the goal worthwhile. The 'truest' experiences of life are believed to occur only through mental training (Rohlen, 1989, 1991). And educators suggest that everyone can achieve if they persevere and endure hardship, especially in the years prior to secondary school. In defining themselves, many Japanese are likely to seek evidence of perseverance, continuous effort toward the socially and interpersonally relevant goals of harmony with one's place, meeting the needs of others in one's role set, as well as the attainment of standards of quality or excellence set out for the group. Rather than seek out and focus on those domains in which one has a sense of expertise, one is to persevere in those tasks set out for one in the social roles that one occupies. Increasing success is assumed to come with steadfast perseverance or concentration on these tasks. Thus, rather than the self-message 'In school some kids can do well at maths and others cannot, what kind of kid am I?', the self-message is 'In school kids are to do well in maths, am I doing well yet?'

Because the social representation of personhood in terms of inter-dependence or collectivism assumes that one's social roles will prescribe much of what one does, one's goals, one's behaviours and therefore who one *is*, individuals are evaluated in terms of the extent that they have met the standards of these social roles. One's task is then to learn these standards and work to attain them because fulfilling one's social place allows others to fulfil theirs.

In the US, boundedness, the ability to control or exert force on the environment, is operationalized as competence. The social representation of competence has to do with the relationship between one's abilities and the effort exerted on the task. Thus, one way of showing competence is to be able to succeed at a task in spite of low effort. Thus, perseverance on task is viewed as the opposite of competence (Jones, 1989). Within the Japanese model, however, ability per se is not valued above effort, and effort is viewed as creating ability. In the US, then, persistence is often understood to be a character trait one has instead of ability, while in Japan it is viewed as a major pathway to ability. The impact of these differing social representations on behaviour is hinted at by findings such as Blinco's (1992), in which over two-thirds of US school students persisted less than the average time on tasks of the Japanese students, while less than 10 per cent of Japanese students persisted at or below the American mean.

We have been describing here a cultural level of reality, one created and maintained by social representations and their supporting practices. Individuals may resist or fail to incorporate these public and mutually constructed ideas of selfhood into their meaning-making systems. Questions of how social representations are transmitted and spread (see Sperber, 1985), of how many individuals in a given socio-cultural niche must share them, and with what level of incorporation and understanding (see Nisbett, 1993; Menon and Shweder, 1994), and of how much resistance or outright negation can be tolerated with a given cultural system constitute a significant research agenda.

## Competing social representations

Social representations are defining features of socio-cultural environments and movement from one social context to another may mean moving from one lexicon, array, or *gestalt* of social representations to another. Because these social representations are the building blocks of self, this movement is likely to result in a disruption or shift in self-conceptualization and self-understanding as one seeks to make sense of oneself in the ideas, images, and language of a new context.

For example, Dympna Ugwu-Oju (1993) describes the process by which an Ibu woman's sense of herself is radically changed when the self-language or frame she uses shifts from the social representations of personhood and 'being a woman' she brings with her from her Nigerian birthplace to the social representations of personhood and 'being a woman' predominant among her New York professional colleagues. This cultural frame switching brings with it a fundamental change in what is viewed as relevant to the self, and in what should be taken into account, resulting in a far-reaching re-evaluation of who she *is*. In Nigeria, self-definition depends on fulfilling one's role as a woman and on meeting the social, interpersonal, and behavioural obligations of wife, mother, daughter, and friend. In the United States, self-definition is typically linked not to duty and obligation but instead to personal happiness.

Although the type of conflict in frames of personhood described by Dympna Ugwu-Oju (1993) is extreme, some tension or discord in the social representational context will be experienced by all people as they move across the life course. Thus, adolescents leaving high school for college may experience a lack of certainty as to 'who they are' because the conceptualizations brought from the high-school context are not isomorphic with those for college. An even larger-scale shift is likely for youth who enter the military or civilian employment after high school (Owens, 1992). New soldiers going through boot camp and then entering the military hierarchy are to learn not simply concrete skills but to experience themselves in terms of a new frame, that of a 'good soldier'. In the US, this process of taking apart and then recreating the individual is part of the lore of boot-camp experience. The process is important because a 'good' soldier is one who will obey commands, and follow procedures because in the process of following procedures and persevering he (or she) will attain proficiency in the behaviours needed to fulfil this social role, and thus act in terms of the good of the group. In the military, as in Japan, identity reconstruction involves framing the self as part of a social unit. Typically, in America, the social unit exists to serve one or another self-goal.

A dramatic shift also occurs for youths entering the job market for full-time employment after high school. These youths must reconceptualize who they are and their worth in terms of the demands and opportunities of the entry-level jobs available to them, rather than in terms of the social context and niche presented by high school. Movement into the world of work involves a transition into the future, from the roles of childhood and student to the roles of parent and wage earner (Oyserman and Markus, 1990a; Jessor, Donovan, and Costa, 1992; Curry et al., 1994). Entry-level jobs may afford relatively few contexts for attaining the possible selves nurtured while in school. What it means to be competent in these new frames can be quite different than what was previously understood, and many youths undergoing social context changes are likely to feel a loss of competence in the transition phases (Owens, 1992). Similarly, the transition to motherhood requires conceptualizations of competence in terms of a new baby, but also shifts in the domains of work, hobbies, and intimate, familial, and social relations.

Life transitions then often are connected to context shifts, which bring changes in the social representational repertoire of personhood used to constructing, defining, evaluating, and bolstering the self. Retirement requires different conceptualizations of how one is to be competent once the domain of work is no longer a ready source of self-definition. Life transitions can highlight and sometimes bring to the fore divergent self-representations. And it is this divergence that often precipitates life crises in America.

The consequences of multiple social representations of personhood are likely to be experienced most directly and extensively by people in industrialized heterogeneous societies who necessarily live in multiple contexts simultaneously. Each of an individual's significant socio-cultural contexts – for example, gender, ethnicity, religion, social class, neighborhood, work-place, birth cohort – can make some claim on the person. Very often, the social representations of a given socio-cultural niche are not just implicit in the surrounding context of images and ideas, but actively invoked and promoted (Felner et al., 1985; Goodnow, 1990; Hutnik, 1991; Spears and Shahinper, 1994). Many contemporary socio-cultural contexts comprise individuals and groups of individuals who are continually providing advice with respect to 'how to be' and 'how not to be' (Oyserman and Markus, 1993).

For some people, the messages will cohere, providing a more or less unified set of ideas about how to be (e.g. I am a good husband, father, and worker because I work hard, am reliable, and provide for my wife and children). In such situations it is relatively difficult to appreciate the importance of social representations and cultural frames. Many people, however, are likely to experience multiple, sometimes independent, and sometimes contradictory representations of what matters in the world, the meaning of personhood and what it means to be a 'good' or 'appropriate' or 'normal' person in the context. Thus, being a woman brings with it one set of social representations concerning femaleness and gender. These representations may overlap significantly with being a mother, but may be independent of, or in significant conflict with, the social representations associated with being a stockbroker (Eagley and Mladinic, 1994).

To the extent that one's social representations are contradictory, grounded in different assumptions, or irrelevant to one another, a person is faced with a more complex and effortful self-construction and main-tenance task (Oyserman and Markus, 1993). Thus, being a parent, worker, spouse, friend, and member of a religious or ethnic group may often involve conflicting representations about how and who to be (e.g. does one invest energies in one's career or work for the good of one's ethnic group?). Within the US, as in other countries, socio-cultural and ethnic groups are likely to differ in their conceptualizations of person-hood (Hutnik, 1991; Julian, McKenry, and McKelvey, 1994). Because of the inherent tension or conflict between these sets of representations, individuals must either find a way to reconcile or fit together ethnically based and larger societal social representations of personhood, or choose one or another conceptualization as one's dominant frame and primary source of self-relevant knowledge (LaFromboise, Coleman, and Gerten, 1993). In the case of minority ethnicity in the US, representations from the in-group have to be connected in some way with the social represen-tations from larger society and these representations of one's group in larger society, are likely to reflect misunderstandings, inaccuracies, and negative or narrow portrayals of one's group's capabilities (McLoyd, 1990).

Social representations held by women, African-Americans, and members of other minority groups about the nature of personhood and themselves as group members are not independent from the larger social contexts in which they are embedded (Jackson et al., 1991). Women come to know themselves via their own representations and in terms of men's representations of them (Oyserman and Markus, 1993). Social representations take into account the larger framework. The organizing framework of the larger society may also provide a yardstick against which one evaluates and values both the self and one's group. For example, Eagley (1993) suggests that both women and men view women as more nurturant than men, and men as more agentic than women. They also view nurturance as not being helpful for success in high-prestige occupations. Nurturance is viewed positively, as a good trait, but it is viewed as incompatible with success in high-prestige occupations. Women may individually choose to self-define as autonomous and agentic, or as not-nurturant, but such an effort will be largely ineffective if others use a different social representational repertoire to interpret their actions. Allen, Thornton, and Watkins (1994) review literature suggesting that, as they are a group over-represented in the lower socio-economic status ranks, social representations about poverty and the self-definitional meaning of poverty are likely to colour the ways in which African-Americans represent themselves as a group. They are likely to mention being poor, unemployed, and doing without in describing African-Americans. Because their options are limited by economic realities, African-Americans of lower socio-economic status are more likely to sharply distinguish themselves from American society in general. They tend to use more distinct positive and negative descriptors than African-Americans of higher socio-economic status. Allen, Thornton, and Watkins (1994) suggest that this may be because African-Americans of higher socio-economic status are afforded more self-definitional options and therefore are not required to view themselves primarily in terms of race. They can therefore see continuities and overlaps between African-Americans and other groups in American society.

When individuals belong to groups with divergent social representations of personhood or when the social representation of their group conflicts with social representations of personhood in larger society, the self-definitional task is two-fold. These individuals must both define what they *are* and also what they are *not*, in spite of expectations that they will be. In America, it is likely that African-Americans interacting with non-African-American others must take race into account in defining themselves because race is defined as important, as having meaning, and providing information in the larger societal context. Judd (1993), in a study of university students, recently found that African-Americans are viewed as athletic, musical, fun loving, religious, violent, loud, uneducated, and irresponsible by whites (Allen, Thornton, and Watkins, 1994, report similar findings). African-Americans may choose to use this vocabulary to self-define or attempt to define in terms of the 'vocabulary' used to define whites (independent, ambitious, intelligent, self-centred, uptight, greedy, racist, and wealthy). In either case, however, the other's template or grid of images, meanings, and language must be taken into account. In other words, the social representation of black-ness produces a vocabulary, a prism, or lens through which the self is viewed (Oyserman, 1994). Spears and Shahinper (1994) also find that minorities describing themselves in majority language describe themselves more in terms of their collective identity than when they utilize their native tongue, suggesting that thinking of themselves in the context of the majority requires group-focused self-definitions.

Generally speaking, Americans of African descent are heir to cultural traditions of communal helping, family aid and connectedness, the legacy of racism (Martin and Martin, 1985; Asante, 1987, 1988); and the Protestant work ethic-based cultural imperatives to be independent, successful, achieving, and self-focused (Katz and Hass, 1988). Embedded as they are in contexts which provide conflicting, contradictory, or negative messages, African-Americans must struggle to find a balance between these messages, some means of creating and sustaining a sense of self that will provide a meaning-making framework, structuring and focusing energies on one's life tasks and productive pursuits, which identities thrust upon the self (Oyserman, 1994).

A social representational approach to the self highlights the need to take into account the interplay between the multiple contexts in which individuals are *simultaneously* embedded. A clear example has to do with ethnicity and gender. Ethnicity-based social representations are inter-woven with gender-based social representations, creating a unique social space which cannot be neatly separated into 'ethnic' and 'gender' component parts (Haw, 1991; Martinez and Dukes, 1991). Social repre-sentations containing gendered and ethnically derived content must be melded with social representations derived from the broader culture as a meaning-making framework critical in making sense of experiences, regulating affect, and controlling behaviour (e.g. Brown, 1990; Hughes and Hertel, 1990; Bilides, 1991; Oyserman, 1994). Some have argued, for example, that being both African-American and female is a 'double' minority status with two sets of negative connotations (e.g. Lewis, 1989). However, it appears that the melding of the two contexts brings a unique set of representations, which is not a simple derivative of either alone (Oyserman 1994).

### Consequences of a social representational approach to the self

It is becoming increasingly critical that we take account of and explore the implications of social contexts as our world and our perspectives becomes more multicultural. To the extent that the motives, behaviours, and emotional experiences of individuals other than those in the majority are of consequence, then, an understanding of the diverse social representations of personhood are critical. Social representations are not merely reflections of reality, they create reality by affording certain perceptions and constraining others. We experience and come to know ourselves and others in terms of the social representations we bring to bear. We do not experience ourselves in terms other than those made available by our social representations.

Given the emphasis in North American psychology on internal attributes, traits, or mental structures as the core elements of the self, it is not surprising that the shared and collective nature of the self have not yet received a great deal of attention. A focus on social representations should allow researchers to ask a variety of new and interesting questions about the foundations and scaffolding of the self-system. Although individuals are highly active in the process of self-making, the materials available for writing one's own story are a function of our public and shared notions of personhood. American accounts of the self, for example, involve a set of culture-confirming ideas and images of success, competence, ability, and the need to 'feel good'. It would be productive to examine how much divergence exists in the nature of the self-structures (self-schemas, possible selves, self-prototypes, life tasks, personal projects, etc.) within and between given groups and systematically to explore the sources of the core cultural ideas about selfhood and the everyday social practices through which individuals live out these core ideas. American notions of 'how to be' appear to be evolving at a rapid rate (i.e. 1990s' men and women are very different people from the 1960s' men and women; see also Kruse, chapter 13 this volume), and many questions arise about how these largely media-driven and negotiated cultural imperatives of selfhood influence the structure and functioning of the self-system. In other cultural contexts, concern focuses on the extent to which collective representations of the self carry within them ethnic divisions, intergroup conflict, mistrust, and rivalry (Mesquita, 1993; Oyserman, 1993).

With respect to changing the self, a social representational approach would involve a careful consideration of the nature and organization of the repertoire of ideas and images and ideologies available in a given socio-cultural context (see also Augoustinos, chapter 10 this volume). Members of various minority and subordinate groups, for example, may confront a social representational environment saturated with images and ideas that are unwanted and undesirable and that cannot be easily individually ignored. Similarly, self-change or self-improvement programmes or therapies of any sort (weight loss, substance abuse, depression) could benefit from an analysis of the nature of the prevalent social representations and cultural frames that characterize an individual's environment. Development of such approaches would do well to heed what are viewed as the 'natural' imperatives of self in a particular context, while dissemination would require that the assumptions on which the approach is built fit the assumptions of the new context.

A social representational framing of the self encourages a broader perspective on the self and explicitly takes the social context into account. It delineates the ways that the self is afforded and constrained by the way personhood, gender, and ethnicity are construed within one's socio-cultural context. This is critical if we are to make sense not only of why certain issues are important to some groups and not to others, but also to appreciate how others make sense of and experience their everyday reality.

On an individual level, social representations are meaning-making structures; at a group level, they are the framework which allows individuals from the same social context to be able to predict or make sense of social interactions with the others. Certain goals, behaviours, and situations are central to the social representations of personhood in any given context. Behaviour in culturally central situations may be carefully scripted, affording little variance in behaviours in these situations and leading to negative construals of others who do not behave according to these scripts. Further, because certain goals are central to our social representation of personhood, we assume their importance and make sense of the other's behaviours in terms of these goals. When both sides to an interaction hold in common these representations, then the other will feel familiar and like the self, and interactions will occur with ease. When individuals with divergent social representations interact, both sides may assume common goals or orientations when they are in fact not held by the other, leading to misinterpretation or misunderstanding of the other. At its most benign, in such circumstances, individuals will understand what the other is doing and what it is intended to convey but will be fundamentally unconvinced by the other's behaviour or rationale because the premises on which it is built are not shared. Often, however, we may be unaware that the other is acting under a different set of premises and simply make sense of his or her behaviour in terms of the premises brought to bear by our own context. Thus, in the classroom Americans will assume that all students are competing to show their own creativity and independence in discussions and assume that the Asian student who is not pushing his own opinion into the fray simply has none. In this way, we are likely to misconstrue the other and not elicit feedback that could correct this misconstrual. Over time, this is likely to lead to mutually held negative appraisals of the other, and a sense of exclusion, particularly on the part of those with less power to impose their representations on interactions.

*Part 2*

# Language and discourse as media for social psychology

*Rom Harré*

## Introduction: two problems

The psychological theory of 'social representations', proposed by Moscovici, expounded by Farr (Farr and Moscovici, 1984) and developed by Jodelet ([1989a]1991, 1991), derives from Durkheim's ([1898]1974) concept of *représentations sociales*. In the course of that development, the concept of social representation has changed in various ways. For me, there are two main problems with the theory as it has been expounded post-Durkheim. The first difficulty can be put in the form of a question: How social are social representations? This seemingly tautologous question comes to the fore when one begins to catalogue the various ways in which the word 'social' is used (see also the contribution of Flick, chapter 3 this volume). One might prefix 'social' to 'representation' to qualify the latter term in one of two main ways. One might want to emphasize that, though each representation is a property or attribute of one and only person, it is nevertheless shared among a group, in the sense that the several individual representations of group members are very similar, identical for practical purposes. But one might have another sense of 'social' in mind. One may want to express the idea that the representation in question is not an attribute of any single individual, but exists in the joint actions (practices) of the people of a certain community or group. The manner of existence and mode of efficacy of a social representation, and the methodology that one should adopt in finding it out, will differ radically depending on which of these meanings one assigns to the term. For the most part Moscovici has used the term in the former sense, that is, to mean a shared representation. Each member of a group has their own representation but in certain important ways it is the same as every other. In a recent book Jodelet ([1989a]1991)[1] uses the term, at least implicitly, in the other sense, since many of the representations of madness and so on in the community she studied have no existence in the minds of individual people but seem to be best construed as attributes of the practices of that community, their ways of talking

129

and acting, particularly the former. Both concepts are useful additions to our technical vocabulary but they are not the same, and not the same in important ways.

The second difficulty can also be put in the form of a question: To what kind of entity do social representations belong? And what is the exact nature of their relationship to the human conduct to which they are relevant? Are they immanent in the conduct or transcendent to it? Are they causative or are they normative?

I propose to use the phrase 'a practice' to mean a category of human action or conduct that is common to many or most members of a community. Driving on the left-hand side of the road in certain countries is a practice, and so is speaking in such a way that noun and adjective agree in number and gender. There are countries where people drive on the right, and there are language communities where noun and adjective do not have to be in grammatical agreement. A practice differs from a causal regularity, in that the attempt to carry out a practice is subject to normative assessment. There is always room for the question as to whether it is done correctly or incorrectly. With the help of this idea we can identify another dimension along which social representations differ. A representation may be transcendent to a *practice,* that is, exist independently of the practice to which it is relevant. It might exist in gossip and comment or in a book of instructions, that is, it might exist discursively. (The way that a representation can be relevant to a *practice* will also have to be addressed.) A representation may, however, have no existence independent of the practice to which it is relevant. I shall then say that it is immanent in the practice. This distinction is important, not only theoretically but methodologically. Representations which are transcendent to practices can, at least in principle, be presented by the members of the community in which they belong independently of the performances to which they are relevant. For example, a social representation of the norms of parenting might be made available to a psychologist in the folklore of the members of the community where it is expressed as a set of rules or sometimes as a collection of exemplary stories. But in those cases in which the representation is immanent in the practice it is only the psychologist who eventually can give an independent presentation of it. Indeed, it might be thought to be the job of the psychologist to do just that (see also Carugati and Selleri, chapter 11 this volume). In the work of Moscovici and his school we find the psychologist sometimes in the one role and sometimes in the other.

'How things are and how they are meant to be' is another distinction that needs to be kept in mind in this context. The social representation of Newtonian mechanics belongs to the former category and the social representation of Freudian psychology in the latter. In general, the reception of academic or religious psychologies in a community follows the principle that people try to be what the best authorities say they already are. It is characteristic of psychologists and of religious teachers alike to present their ideals for human living as the way things are.

Leaving aside for the moment the question of the precise nature of representations, be they social or individual, we need to consider how a representation might be relevant to a practice. One way in which representations appear is in the form of rules. We can usefully consider the question of relevance in the context of the question of how the rules and practices to which they are relevant are related. In the *Philosophical investigations* (Wittgenstein, 1953) Sections 198–240 are devoted to a wide-ranging exploration of this question. The problem can be put as follows: does the adoption or learning of a rule cause the person who has learned it to behave in a certain regular way that can be seen to be in accord with the rule? In series of examples, one of the most famous being that of the schoolboy who after adding *two correctly up* to the number 1,000, thereafter adds four, Wittgenstein demolishes the idea of rules as causes. Yet it is evident that rules play a quite fundamental role in what is most characteristic of the human form of life. Wittgenstein's account of the role of rules in human life is drawn from a close look at particular cases of the use of rules in commonplace examples. Rules, he concludes, tell us what is correct and incorrect. It is obvious that if they caused what happens then the notion of incorrect behaviour, if used in a community in which the rules were well established and systematically taught would be nonsensical. Are social representations meant to be among the causes of certain kinds of conduct or are they to be taken to be of the general nature of rules?

To get closer to these problems and queries I shall try to give a systematic and comprehensive exposition of the ways that Moscovici and his school have used the notion of social representation. I quote from a succinct presentation of the concept in Jodelet ([1989a]1991):

when we concentrate on the positions held by social subjects (individuals or groups) towards objects whose value is socially asserted or contested, representations are treated as *structured fields,* that is to say as contents whose dimensions (information, values, beliefs, opinions, images, etc.) are delimited by an organizing principle (attitude' norms, cultural schemata, cognitive structure etc.) . . . when we concentrate on them [social representations] as modes of knowledge, representations are treated as *structuring nuclei,* that is to say, knowledge structures orchestrating the totality of significations relative to the known object. ([1989a]1991, p. 13)

It is clear, in a very general way, what Jodelet is presenting. Her people are treated as thinking subjects rather than reacting objects. Social representation psychology could hardly be more different from crude behaviourism, and its descendants in American empiricism. Yet I find her presentation very difficult to understand when I begin to focus on the details. The psychological phenomena set between parentheses in the above quote are plainly very diverse in character and severally ambiguous in nature. My first step in comment and development of these ideas, to which in general I am strongly attracted, is to try to work through them from the point of view of the new discursive turn in psychology (see Potter and Wetherell, chapter 9 this volume). How would this presentation of the theory of social representations be transformed when each of its elements is interpreted within the new 'discursive' framework?

To prepare for this work of interpretation I offer a nine-point schema summarizing the writings of Moscovici (1984a, b) which is drawn from McKinlay and Potter (1987):

1  Social representations are partly abstract and partly pictorial.
2  They allow people to make joint sense of an unfamiliar world, and thereby fix the limits of the psychological capacities of a group.
3  People use social representations to make sense of the unfamiliar through 'anchoring' and 'objectification'.
4  Anchoring: relating an object to the prototypical case incorporated in a social representation.
5  Objectification: once an object is anchored an image of it 'joins' the prototype.
6  Objectification determines how a person will see the world.
7  Through social representations past experience influences present.
8  Reality, for us, is determined by social representations.
9  The social scientist must confine his/her analysis to the consensual not the reified universe.

### The discursive turn

I believe that the main difficulties with the concept of 'social representation', which in the end amount to the several ambiguities in the way the concept *has* been used, can be resolved when we reinterpret the theses, definitions, and insights catalogued above in the terms of the concepts and principles of 'discursive psychology' (as, for instance, it is expounded by Edwards and Potter, 1992; Gillett and Harré, 1993; Potter and Wetherell, chapter 9 this volume). Discursive activity is the work we severally and jointly engage in when we make use of a common system of signs for the accomplishment of some task or project. A use of signs is discursive when that use is subject to criteria of correctness and incorrectness. As Wittgenstein has emphasized, normatively constrained sign use cannot be maintained simply by reference to what some individual thinks is correct, but must be referable to concrete and public exemplars of correct use. Sometimes the consensus of a sign-using community can stand in for the public exemplar, but correctness could never be guaranteed by any actual consensus. The fact that in Colombe-les-deux-eglises they agree to use the tape in the *épicerie* for measuring a metre, does not make what they do correct if that consensus does not agree with 'the' standard metre in Paris. Words are amongst the most useful and powerful discursive tools, but they are not the only entities that can meet the above requirements for a role in this or that discursive practice.

How were the social representations that Jodelet ([1989a]1991) records manifested to her enquiring ear? They came to her attention in the course of conversations, manifested in what people said, the rules and conventions they reported and the stories they told, the histories they recounted. It is striking that in these conversations much was concerned with telling what was the correct or proper way of treating the 'lunatics' that were boarded out in the community. Criticism and praise were offered of the practices of this or that village or family. In her story of these conversations Jodelet presents a pattern of two kinds of practices, wordless action and verbal commentary. It is important to see that both kinds of practice fall within the realm of the discursive. When the 'lunatics' are brought their meals in their own rooms, when they have their own places in the cafe and so on, we are seeing normative practices, with which the local category 'lunatic' is immanent. It should also be noted that most of Jodelet's accounts of wordless discursive practices are drawn as stories from stories, though sometimes she reports having seen for herself the events she tells in her story.

### Two kinds of social representations

One major ambiguity in Moscovici's account of social representations is resolved by Jodelet, in the passage quoted above, simply by acknowledging that the term 'social representation' is used in two quite different ways. It is employed to refer to two quite different 'entities'. On the one hand, it is used to refer to 'structured fields' of very diverse kinds of elements whose nature is still to be determined, and, on the other, to 'structuring nuclei', a metaphor for what it is that structures the aforesaid fields. A clue to ways of getting to grips with these somewhat opaque notions is to be found in the previous paragraph of the passage from which I have drawn the quotation. In that passage Jodelet clearly identifies the entities which are thus structured as discursive, including social narratives, material and discursive practices, practical, symbolic, and ideological registers, and speculative systems and ideologies. We should start by distinguishing 'registers', such as internally ordered segments of sign systems, the pronouns of a language for example, from narratives, be they lived or told, and if told concrete or abstract (ideological). Narratives are constructed by the use of registers. What can be said is constrained not only by the structuring norms of what is to count as a proper narrative, but also by what is available in the registers from which the elements of the narrative are drawn. We now have a second duality in the sense of the term 'social representation'. It might be used to refer to what is immanent in the available register or registers, or it might be used to refer to the 'syntactical' or structuring norms which constrain how the elements drawn from this or that register can be put together into narratives.

We can now make sense of the two main cognitive processes proposed by Moscovici and his co-workers, namely anchoring and objectification. According to the principles of discursive psychology all cognitive processes are discursive. To find a proper place for social representations within the discursive point of view it is essential that 'anchoring' and 'objectification' be interpreted as themselves discursive processes. What we will gain by this interpretation is greater clarity about these theoretical concepts and greater efficacy of their use in controlling empirical research.

### Dimensions of social representations

I have pointed out three dimensions along which social representations, as used by Moscovici, Jodelet and others can be located. They may be either individual or collective, immanent or transcendent, concrete or abstract. To find a way to make sense of 'anchoring' and 'objectification' in discursive terms, I shall attempt to explicate their use as sign systems in relating to this three dimensional 'space'.

It is a basic principle of Vygotskian psychology ([1934]1986; see also Moscovici, chapter 14 this volume) that all individual uses of signs including the use of signs to formulate projects for which other signs can be used, are derived from public and collective sign use, that is, practices in which the learner is drawn into an interaction mediated by signs, through the supplementing of nascent skills by the actions of the more mature member of a dyad. This situation is the familiar zone of proximal development. This temporal structure of the individual–collective dimensions is reflected in another way of expressing the same idea, that the use of a sign system is a skill, exercised for the performance of some task, not a reaction to a situation.

But reflecting on the dimension immanent–transcendent, a dimension very much to the fore in Jodelet ([1989a]1991), leads one to add a further level to the discursive treatment of social representations Not only must one take social representation to be a part of a sign system, but one must include the rules and conventions for the use of such signs, that which makes them other than mere objects. What is immanent or transcendent to a use is not the sign system itself, but the rules for its use.

The dimension concrete–abstract takes us back to signs again, now as entities rather than entities in use. This dimension has given philosophers of logic and of language a great deal of trouble to interpret. Berkeley, in criticizing Locke's doctrine of abstract ideas, points out that an entity is a sign only insofar as it used as such. A concrete image can be used as a sign of a general concept, without the need to try to imagine what a general sign might be. The difference between a general sign and a concrete sign is entirely one of how something is used. To use an entity as an abstract sign one simply ignores any unique or concrete characteristics that it has that are irrelevant to the use one wishes to put it. This use, can like all uses, be expressed, if one wishes, in a rule or set of rules. This distinction ought not to be confused with that between pictorial and conventional signs. A drawing of an owl is a pictorial sign of a night-flying bird, but, as a hieroglyph, it is the letter 'x', a conventional sign. When we reflect on the means by which social representations are used in thought these distinctions must be kept in mind. Thinking with a numeral is thinking with a conventional sign, while thinking with an image of people seated at a table, say for the purpose of serving dinner, may also be numerical thinking, but the sign is pictorial.

According to my way of thinking, social representations are systems of signs, with the rules or conventions for their proper use. The psychology of social representations, as it has been developed by Moscovici and others is a form of discursive psychology.

We can turn now to the key processes, objectification and anchoring. In objectification, so far as I understand it, we see a social representation as an ordered set of rules through which a complex of activities, material and symbolic, are produced as an ordered whole. The term 'objectification' draws our attention to the way in which we take, unreflectively, such ordered wholes to be objectively real. A local way of life, the daily workings of an institution, the recurrent pattern of work on a farm, and so on, are taken as real insofar as they are talked about as real, as something which exists beyond the scope of each individual who has a part to play in them, and even more so for an onlooker. In order for this structuring process to be possible the elements that are to play a part in it must become part of the system of signs. To anchor the act 'hitching a horse to a plough' that action must be seen as belonging with other seasonal agricultural actions and so as having a meaning in relation to them. Anchoring, then, is the process by which new items are added to a sign system, while objectification is the process by which the elements of that sign system are produced as an ordered whole according to the rules for their proper use, rules whose existence, be it immanent or transcendent to the action, are what constitutes this or that sign as such.

More can be said about anchoring than appears explicitly in the writings of Moscovici (1984a,b), Jodelet ([1989a]1991, 1991), Herzlich (1973) and others. Above all, human cognition is hierarchical, it makes use of ordered arrays of types, supertypes, and so on. A social representation, interpreted as a sign system, ready for use, cannot be an exception to this ubiquitous practice. The dimension concrete–abstract is also the dimension particular–general. It seems to me that were we to try to state, in a general way, what are the components of a social representation we would find that they were used at different orders of generality. Certainly, in Jodelet's ([1989a] 1991) treatment of the ways that the 'lunatics' are acted towards, talked about, and dealt with, the conversations she reports are strikingly diversified just along this dimension. Indeed, a central point of her expositions is the difference between the way that the general images and definitions of the manner in which the local people present the institution discursively, and their discursive presentation of their actual, particular boarders.

### Social representations in use

Why am I a fellow traveller with Farr and Moscovici and their allies? To explain this I need to say something about the general theory of discursive psychology, the developed form of the old ethogenic approach advocated by Secord and myself (Harré and Secord, 1973). That approach had much in common with symbolic interactionism (Blumer, 1969) and with the original ethnomethodology of Harold Garfinkel (1967). It has little in common with later developments such as positivistic conversation analysis ('CA' – Sacks, 1992). The final step towards a fully realized and reformed psychology is to be able to see that all psychological processes are essentially discursive. There is only one model, in the sense of that term in the physical sciences, namely, life as conversation. To develop this insight properly it is necessary to distinguish between lived and told narratives, since the nub of conversation is the telling of tales. The narratological element in discursive psychology is the realization that one lives tales too. Technically, this step requires one to see all actions, be they verbal or material as falling under the general categories of speech act theory (Austin, 1962), in particular as having illocutionary force and perlocutionary effects. In another idiom, the theory of social representations seems to me to be proposing very much the same approach to the understanding of psychological phenomena, particularly those through which everyday life is managed. Jodelet's 'structured fields' and 'structuring nuclei' are other ways if referring to sign systems and their hierarchical organization, sign systems which we put to use in living out the narratives of everyday life, and providing discursive versions of them when the situation seems to require them.

### Conclusion: two proposals

The key idea we all share is the insight that the episodes of daily life are ordered, and ordered by the skilful action of the people who live them. This does not mean that every action is deliberately and intentionally aimed at some super goal but that immanent in daily practices and transcendently maintained in cited rules and conventions there is a repertoire of social representations through which this orderliness is brought about. Psychological phenomena do not just happen in response to environmental contingencies, they are brought about. I would like to supplement the ideas and methods of my friends with two proposals:

1 that what we are studying when we are 'doing psychology' are discursive practices of various kinds, some of which could exist only in actual or potential interpersonal interactions;
2 that what we ascribe to people on the basis of our studies of their practices are the skills necessary to perform them, and that we bear in mind that it may often be the case that more than one person is needed to bring a skilled activity to fruition.

### Note

1 See also Jodelet (1991) and the short presentation of her study in Flick's introduction to this volume.

# 9　Social representations, discourse analysis, and racism

*Jonathan Potter and Margaret Wetherell*

## Introduction

A minister resigns; an Arab army is attacked in the desert; police officers fight with members of a minority group. These events can be described in various different ways; that is, their nature can be variously formulated in talk and writing. The resignation can be 'honourable' or 'forced by personal animosity'; the attacked army can be 'fleeing', 'retreating', or 'withdrawing'; the police can be 'attacking a legitimate protest' or 'containing a riot'. Such variation in descriptive language is commonplace; as competent cultural members we can 'read' this variation: the politician defends the honour of his own resignation while his competitors stress personal animosity. We expect certain sorts of patterns, and we understand them in terms of the stake or interest of the different individuals and groups involved. We expect minority group members to characterize their actions as a legitimate protest against exploitation; and we are not surprised when a right-wing politician characterizes them as whipped up by people who enjoy confrontation for its own sake. This is a realm of human affairs to which the theories of discourse analysis and social representations can make an important contribution.

Social representations theorists argue that people come to understand events and actions, particularly when they are novel or troubling, by way of simplified images or representations. People do not directly perceive motives for action, or wars, or political demonstrations – they make sense of them by using images. In just the way people might use a simplified diagram of a personal computer to understand it – perhaps coloured boxes representing the memory, the central processing unit, the hard disc, and so on – social representations theorists argue that in everyday life we come to understand a complex social conflict, for instance, using images of formal and informal groupings, of motives and representations of processes of influence. And social representations theory argues that such images are widely shared; indeed, the weave of shared and contrasting social representations in a society is claimed to play a major role in its social organization (Moscovici, 1984a).

Social representations theory has a number of important virtues over more traditional social psychological theories. Three can be picked out as particularly important:

- an emphasis on the *content* or meaning of human life;
- an emphasis on *communication* as a basis for shared social understandings;
- an emphasis on the *constructive* processes through which versions of the world are established.

We will consider these qualities in turn, noting how, in each case, the theoretical perspective of discourse analysis (Potter and Wetherell, 1987; Edwards and Potter, 1992; Wetherell and Potter, 1992) can supplement and strengthen them as well as highlight certain shortcomings. This will serve to flesh out some of the detail of social representations theory as well as introducing some of the central features of discourse analysis.

### Discourse analysis and social representations

*An emphasis on content*

One of the features of much traditional social psychology, particularly that conducted in the predominantly experimental North American tradition, was an emphasis on the production of laws of human social behaviour. The goal was the identification of social processes – features of persuasion, group interaction, aggression, and so on – that would occur in all societies and all times in history. More recently, that goal was refined in the so-called social cognition perspective which tied the understanding of social processes to processes and structures of thinking: such as the way in which information is simplified, processed, and stored (Fiske and Taylor, 1991). In many ways, this cognitivism was a breath of fresh air after the austerity of the behavioural, stimulus/response approach that had been central in much of psychology. However, it suffered from two potentially important difficulties: first, it avoided any engagement with the specifics of a cultural setting, and, second, it encouraged a damaging 'cognitive reductionism', which is the attempt to explain social events and processes entirely by reference to events and structures in the mental processes of individuals.

The theory of social representations marked an important break with this tradition by making the specific contents of culture the centrepiece of analysis. It emphasized the way the world is understood via images or shared mental representations which are present in a particular culture, at a particular time in history, and often only in particular groups in the culture. For example, in Jodelet's ([1989a] 1991) study *Madness and social representations* her concern was to develop an account of a specific set of representations of a particular cultural phenomenon. Jodelet developed a model of people's underlying representation of madness from an analysis of their descriptions and explanations. The contents here were the various ideas about contamination, hygiene, illness, and otherness, as well as the way they are organized together. It is this that made up the specific representation of madness which was the basis of understanding and action for the people in Jodelet's study. Without the content the phenomenon would be lost; and in another culture the content and its organization might been very different. The implications of this are profound, for it requires social psychologists to confront individual cultures in all their richness. It also opens up the exciting possibility of dialogue with other social science disciplines such as anthropology and linguistics.

Although social representations theory has stimulated this important refocusing of psychological interest, it is not free from the reductionism of social cognition. At the centre of the theory is the idea of a shared image: the 'figurative nucleus' (Moscovici, 1984a). It is this that supposedly provides the means for people to make unfamiliar or threatening things familiar: to come to terms with, say, other people's madness by including it within familiar classification schemes. The theory of discourse analysis has rather different roots to social representations theory (Potter and Wetherell, 1987). Nevertheless, it shares the emphasis on the cultural contents rather than underlying psychological laws or abstract generalizations. The way discourse analysts deal with content will be illustrated later. Where discourse analysis parts company with social representations theory is in its conceptualization of cognition.

Discourse analysts have not been against the study of cognitive phenomena, but they have been interested in them as features of people's activities rather than as generative mechanisms lying inside people's heads (Edwards and Potter, 1992). This may seem a rather odd idea; for surely, it will be claimed, the place for cognition is precisely inside people's heads. Without directly denying this, and without going into some of the complex theoretical and philosophical issues at stake here (for which see Coulter, 1979; Harré, 1989a; Edwards, 1991; Harré chapter 8 this volume), it is important to recognize that 'inner objects' like intentions, beliefs, and understandings generally take their significance when they are used to perform actions or convey information. For example, to claim that some action was done intentionally is not to imply that some inner event happened before the action (first there was the intention and then the action); rather it contrasts that action with others which were the result of accident or duress (Austin, 1961).

The discourse analytic perspective on cognition seems even less surprising when we consider that our mental vocabulary did not evolve to assist people in their moments of quiet introspection but to drive communication and interaction in public settings. The important point at stake here is this. Should cultural contents be treated as a set of mental templates that are slotted into place and allow sense to be made of particular phenomena or should they be analysed as elements of inter-action in specific settings: in newspaper articles, in conversations, in political speeches? Social representations theory opts for the former, discourse analysis for the latter (for a range of views on this issue see papers in Conway, 1992).

### An emphasis on communication

Unlike most other recent perspectives in social psychology, social representations theory places communication and, more particularly talk, at centre stage. As Moscovici puts it, 'representations are the outcome of an unceasing babble and a permanent dialogue between individuals' (1984b). This emphasis on mundane, everyday communi-cation meshes closely with the theory's concern with ideas and images specific to a time and place in a culture rather than underlying universal processes. If you are interested in cultural contents then you have to look to the situations where contents are developed and expressed: situations of talk, argument, and gossip. It is for this reason that some of the most profound studies conducted within the social representations framework have used extended, open-ended interviews where the interviewer and interviewee effectively engaged in an unconstrained conversation about a particular topic. Herzlich's (1973) study of health and illness and Jodelet's ([1989a] 1991) study of representations of madness both illus-trate this.

Despite giving everyday communication this pivotal role in the theory, social representations researchers have generally paid very little attention to discourse as such. Even where researchers have used open-ended interviews, the concern has not been with the talk in interaction; rather, the talk has been treated as a pathway to underlying representations. There has been almost no concern with what talk is doing and how it is organised interactionally. For example, when Herzlich interviewed her sample of French people about health and illness she was not concerned with how they were using their discourse to justify particular positions or to display particular identities; her concern was with the representations that, supposedly, lay underneath. Moreover, studies conducted under the rubric of social representations have frequently been little different from the mainstream experimental studies of attitudes, stereotypes and group identity that have dominated social psychology for three decades.

It is here that discourse analysis makes profoundly different theoretical assumptions. Discourse analysis has been influenced by philosophical and sociological traditions which have been concerned with participants' everyday language practices. One of the most important of these is conversation analysis, developed by the sociologist Sacks (1992) and colleagues, which has been one of the most sustained programmes aimed at understanding the way talk forms a central part of social interaction in both everyday and institutional settings (e.g. Atkinson and Heritage, 1984; Drew and Heritage, 1992). This perspective has not looked at talk just for its own sake. Conversation analysts see talk, and particularly unconstrained mundane talk, as the foundation for social life and social structure; it is what opens up one mind to another (Drew, 1986). At the same time, discourse analysis has benefited equally from a rhetorical perspective on language use which emphasizes the way versions and claims tend to be embedded, sometimes implicitly, in arguments and argumentative positions (Billig, 1987). The first thing a rhetorician would ask about any representation is this: what alternative representation is it designed to undermine?

For discourse analysts, the problem is that social representations theory's remaining cognitivist assumptions require a continued and often problematic process of extrapolation from discourse to underlying mental representations. Work in discourse analysis has repeatedly shown the misleading conclusions that can be arrived at if the researcher ignores the complex, subtle, context-sensitive nature of talk and its orientation to ongoing actions and issues of identity (e.g. Edwards and Potter, 1993). Put simply, people do things with their talk; they make accusations, ask questions, flirt, justify their actions – the range is almost infinite. Any theory which attempts to bypass this fact is going to be seriously flawed. The solution is not to abandon a concern with representation, however. Quite the contrary, a discourse approach can reinvigorate the study of representations by conceptualizing them as features of discourse: versions, formulations, characterizations, descriptions. Moreover, this reconceptualization avoids a number of the profound conceptual and analytic problems that have bedevilled social representations research (McKinlay and Potter, 1987).

### An emphasis on construction

Social representations theorists claim that people do not perceive cultural objects directly but deal with them via their construction within shared representations. When we are trying to understand the status of our main political parties, the rise of racism, or why our relationship with another person is failing, our views are ultimately derived from our representations of these things. For example, if the leader of the Christian Democrats acts in a certain way the meaning of his or her actions will be constructed by a range of overlapping representations: of the party itself, of politics in general, of what good leadership is, and so on. Social representations allow people creatively to construct the sense out of what might otherwise be puzzling, incoherent experience, or merely experience that is so complex that it is impossible to grasp. Put another way, meaning does not reside in the world itself; rather the world for any individual is only meaningful insofar as social representations give it meaning (Moscovici, 1984a).

Discourse analysis is also a constructionist theory; however, the two constructionisms are rather different. Social representations is a theory of cognitive construction. It treats sense as constructed in the head through mental processes. These are principally processes of 'anchoring' (in which a novel object or event is assigned to an existing category of thought) and 'objectification' (in which the novel object or event is transformed into a pictorial element in the representation to which it is anchored). By contrast, discourse analysis is a theory of social and discursive construction. It is concerned with the way people collectively construct versions of the world in the course of their practical interactions and the way these versions are established as solid, real, and independent of the speaker. It is also concerned with the sorts of resources that people use to construct versions, or representations. Consider performing a particular activity – for instance, justifying a potentially racist claim about a minority group. We can compare the task to building a bridge. Some of the materials will be relatively pre-formed: the girders, say, although they will need to be cut to shape in various ways; other materials will need to be fabricated on the spot, for example, concrete pillars which are fitted to the contours of the landscape. If we are to analyse the racist activity we will want to look at the equivalent of both the girders and local production of concrete pillars. That is the aim of discourse analysis. Social representations theory has quite a developed view of girders but little to say about pillar production.

It is important to emphasize another difference. Social representations has been largely a theory of people doing their best to understand things.

Ironically, given the emphasis on its being a social theory, it has been a theory of individuals coming to understand and these individuals might as well be entirely isolated from one another. It is their inner representations that bring them to understanding, and this understanding happens to be shared because the representations are, according to the theory at least, shared. However, this misses out something crucial. Representations are often produced in situations of conflict for the accomplishment of particular goals.

### Between report and construction

Consider, for example, the so-called 'Gulf War'. In late February 1991 Iraqi military forces were moving north out of Kuwait while being attacked by planes from a coalition of Western nations. Already this is a highly consequential, not to say politically contentious representation of events. However, we want to concentrate on competing descriptions of what the Iraqi forces were doing, focusing on three contrasting descriptions: the Iraqi forces were variously described as 'withdrawing', 'surrendering' or 'retreating'. Take the following two extracts from the Western media:

not withdrawing . . . simply fleeing . . . [they are] in full retreat. (*CNN International*, 26 February 1991, quoting the US military)

Whether they surrendered or whether they withdrew, Saddam's men were a terrible sight . . . The concentration of killing was unequalled since Hiroshima . . . An American pilot spoke of a 'turkey shoot', a British officer of 'herding sheep'. (*Observer*, 3 March 1991)

From a discourse analytic perspective, the issue is not merely what descriptions people find best make sense of events but what such descriptions would accomplish. *Retreat* and *surrender* were treated as terms with a recognizable military meaning. *Surrender* involves giving up arms and accepting defeat. This was what the coalition wanted. *Retreat* is a strategic move made as part of the war. For the military, a retreat can be legitimately attacked. By contrast, *withdraw* was not treated as having a precise military definition.

The differences in representation had a considerable significance. For during that 'decisive day' of the war there arose important questions about the warranting of the coalition military action. The scale of casualties and the nature of the killing suggested by descriptions such as 'unequalled since Hiroshima' and 'turkey shoot' led to heated debate about the legitimacy of the actions and how far they should be continued. Although the term 'withdraw' did not have a certain military definition it can be seen as precisely fitted to the requirements of this context. In the first case, its military imprecision – neither surrender nor retreat – offered no grounds for enemy reaction. Second, it cited the very terminology of the United Nations resolution that was a pretext for the coalition action:

Last Monday [25 February] . . . Baghdad radio broke into its broadcasting to announce that 'orders have been issued to our armed forces to *withdraw* in an organized manner to the positions they held prior to 1 August . . . as practical compliance with Resolution 660'. (*Observer*, 3 March 1991, our emphasis)

As we have argued in more detail elsewhere (Edwards and Potter, 1992), the representation of this action as withdrawing treated it as following the UN resolution, and countered the implications of terms such as 'surrender' and 'retreat'. It undermines the warrant for continued attacks on the army while keeping future options open and not having to admit defeat. It is important to be cautious here. We are certainly not wanting to suggest that the course of this war was *determined* by these representations; however, we are claiming that a conflict in representations was central in the initiation and realization of the war, and that social researchers need to understand how these representations are oriented to action rather than considering them as simply group-based attempts at making the best possible sense of troubling situations.

So far in this discussion we have explored some of the problems that have been raised with social representations theory from a broadly discourse analytic perspective. They are developed further elsewhere (Litton and Potter, 1985; Potter and Litton, 1985; Parker, 1987; Potter and Wetherell, 1987; Billig, 1988, 1993; Potter and Billig, 1992; McKinlay *et al.*, 1993). For the remainder of this chapter we will take a more positive tack and discuss some of the findings of a discourse analytic study of racism, attempting to demonstrate in a more concrete manner the upshot of this focus on meaning, communication, and construction.

### Discourse analysis and racism

This research we wish to describe was conducted in New Zealand during the mid to late 1980s and it is reported fully in Wetherell and Potter (1992). The 1980s were a period of much debate about race and politics in New Zealand. Important economic changes were accompanied by arguments about the relative status of the two principal communities, the indigenous Maori people and the majority white group, descendants of mainly British colonists. Questions were raised concerning the very origins and legitimacy of the New Zealand state (Kelsey, 1990). Moscovici (1984a) has suggested that periods of crisis and upheaval such as these are particularly revealing when studying representations. These are times when debates about the meaning of different actions and policies become particularly acute.

Our research was based largely on a set of interviews with just over eighty white, majority-group members (mainly middle-class professional people – doctors, farmers, managers, teachers) combined with parliamentary proceedings, and various media materials. In its choice of interview and media materials this research is quite similar to some of the best-known social representations studies (e.g. Moscovici, [1961] 1976). Our goal was to examine the patterns and themes in the representations of one powerful group engaged in an intergroup struggle. The decision to focus on middle-class white people was a deliberate one. This group is often overlooked in psychological studies of racism, which typically concentrate on working-class racism, on obvious authoritarian racists, on examples of overt bigotry or prejudice, or on the minority groups themselves. However, some of the most problematic racism, although often not the most visible, comes from this powerful group: people who control intakes into the professions or who are responsible for implementing policy in areas such as policing, employment, and lawmaking. And these are often the people most able either to disguise their racism or, more simply, to provide articulate justifications for decisions and policies which have racist effects and to cover over injustices and inequalities (Reeves, 1983).

One simple, but analytically fruitful, way to think of our New Zealand participants is as people caught in an ideological dilemma (Billig *et al.*, 1988). On the one hand, such groups often do not want to be heard as racist – particularly by a sympathetic, liberal-seeming social researcher. On the other, they generally do not want to do or support anything that will make their life more complicated, involve abandoning privileges or substantial transfer of power, or potentially threatening social change. One of the tasks of discourse analysis is to show how people manage these kinds of ideological conflicts, legitimating their actions, justifying inequality and exploitative patterns with the range of resources that are provided by their culture. Our analysis of this material followed up a number of dimensions (Potter and Wetherell 1987, 1989; Wetherell and Potter, 1988), but one key concept for organizing our analysis was the notion of *interpretative repertoires* developed in studies of scientific discourse by Gilbert and Mulkay (1984; see also Wetherell and Potter, 1988), combined with some elements of discourse theory from the social theorist Michel Foucault (Potter *et al.*, 1990).

Interpretative repertoires are broadly discernible clusters of terms, descriptions, and figures of speech often assembled around metaphors or vivid images. They can be thought of as the building blocks used for manufacturing versions of actions, self, and social structures in talk. They are the 'preformed girders' we referred to earlier. As such, they are collectively available resources for making evaluations, constructing factual versions, and performing particular actions. They exist because of what they do, not simply as abstract aids to understanding. The notion of interpretative repertoires is designed to address the *content* of discourse and how that content is organized. Although stylistic and grammatical elements are sometimes closely associated with this organization the analytic focus is not a linguistic one; it is concerned with language use and social action: what is achieved by that use, and the nature of the interpretative resources that allow that achievement. In the discussion of some of our findings which follows we hope to illustrate our approach and mark some of the differences with the concept of social representations theory.

### Constructing categories and defining groups

Social representations theorists have been very concerned to link representations to particular social groups. However, they have been less concerned, perhaps because of the difficulties it creates for doing analysis, with social representations *of* groups (Potter and Litton, 1985). By contrast, analysts of discourse and rhetoric have found that an examination of the way groups and social categories are constructed in talk and texts is a particularly fruitful topic (Billig, 1985; Potter and Reicher, 1987; Edwards, 1991). And this is perhaps especially true in studies of racism, since questions of who belongs and who does not, and the substance of group boundaries, are generally crucial to this kind of ideological practice (see Augoustinos chapter 10 this volume). The description of the social landscape as made up of groups X and Y with certain characteristics is never a neutral act but usually part of a complex chain of social actions.

So how did the white New Zealanders we interviewed define, represent, and make sense of themselves and their 'other': Maori people. One important mode of group construction drew on traditional 'race discourse': ideas about innate traits, instincts, blood, skin colour, racial purity, and so on. According to this construction, Maori people were best understood as an 'advanced but still inferior racial group'. Intergroup conflict between white settlers and Maori people was interpreted as a struggle between the 'civilized' and the 'primitive'. The origins of these ideas about group belonging can be traced back to the work of Victorian scientists such as Sir Francis Galton. Despite the historical importance of this mode of accounting in New Zealand and elsewhere, however, these classic racial accounts of groups persist now more as a residue in Western representations. Certain metaphors and images have been retained, such as the concept of 'blood', but the attempt to provide a full and detailed analysis of social relations through racial theories has been largely abandoned in New Zealand as it has in many Western nations. Few people among those we interviewed developed sustained arguments based on race discourse alone.

While traditional race discourse had a low-key presence in this material another set of ideas about group boundaries and group categories were pervasive and widely elaborated. These were ideas clustered around the notion of culture and particularly notions of Maori people as a cultural rather than racial group. When we examined this set of resources for making sense of the position of Maori people it became clear that we were dealing with at least two overlapping but broadly distinct inter-petative repertoires, each making slightly different assumptions and having different uses.

We called the first of these 'Culture-As-Heritage'. In this repertoire the core idea is of Maori culture as a set of traditions, rituals, and values passed down from earlier generations. Culture becomes defined in this repertoire as an archaic heritage, something to be preserved and treas-ured; something to be protected from the rigours of the 'modern world' like great works of art or endangered species. Here is a typical example (the names are pseudonyms to preserve anonymity).

SHELL: I'm quite, I'm certainly in favour of a bit of Maoritanga it is something uniquely New Zealand, and I guess I'm very conservation minded [yes] and in the same way as I don't like seeing a species go out of existence I don't like seeing [yes] a culture and a language [yes] and everything else fade out.

Culture-As-Heritage can be contrasted with a second commonly drawn on repertoire concerning the position of Maori people which we called Culture-As-Therapy. Here culture is constructed as a psychologi-cal need for Maoris, particularly young Maoris who have become estranged and need to rediscover their cultural 'roots' to become 'whole' again. Here is an example.

REED: Well, I think the sort of Maori renaissance, the Maoritanga is important because hh like I was explaining about being at that party on Saturday night, I suddenly didn't know where I was [yes] I had lost my identity in some ways and, I was brought up with the people that were there, I'd known most of them all my life and I couldn't identify with them [yes] and I was completely lost [yes]. Um so when I found my identity again by being able to talk about something that I was really into, then I became a person again . . . and that's what's happening with the Maoris . . . young Maoris were strapped if they spoke Maori at school and we almost succeeded in wiping out a culture, a way of life, an understanding and I don't think it is necessary to do that and I think it is necessary for the people to get it back because there's something deep-rooted inside you.

What is at stake here in the shift from racial repertoires to cultural repertoires? This shift is certainly part of a more general ideological change in Western democracies. The change in representation is tied to changes in social practices and the move from assimilationist policies, for example, to multiculturalist policies. But it also seems clear that repertoires of culture continue to do important ideological work for white New Zealanders.

The Culture-As-Heritage repertoire can be used, for example, to 'freeze' a group into the past, invalidating their contemporary response to their social situation, and separating off a realm of pure 'cultural action' from the modern world of politics. The protests of modern Maoris are thus often interpreted, by white politicians for example, as 'out of tune' with the 'real' foundation of Maori culture. In this case culture becomes part of a system of regulation and control of 'appropriate' and 'inappropriate' behaviour (Cowlishaw, 1988). The Culture-As-Therapy repertoire has similarly been used to represent young urban Maoris as somehow lacking, no longer deficient in comparison to more 'civilized' white society, but now deficient *as* Maoris. The problem becomes defined as a 'lack of culture' rather than possession of the 'wrong type of blood' and with this new representation policies toward the Maori people change accordingly. Cultural repertoires became a resource for reinterpreting Maori protest about sovereignty and land rights as something psychological – something they are doing because of difficulties with their cultural identity rather than as a legitimate protest against continuing injustice.

An important feature of the use of these repertoires is that at this period in New Zealand history as in other Western societies, culture discourse is 'user friendly'. To talk of culture is to be heard as displaying sensitivity and tolerance, respecting difference and appreciating others. So the use of these repertoires does not present the speaker with the sorts of profound identity problems that traditional racist discourse of innate inferiority now tends to invoke (van Dijk, 1992). Indeed, these repertoires of culture have something of the status of a socially accepted cliché. In

Billig's (1987, 1991) terms, they act as 'common-places', sets of taken-for-granted and commonly used value terms. It was very rare to see these culture repertoires explicitly undermined in our materials. Nevertheless, it is a discourse which we suggest is doing some of the same ideological work as traditional racist discourse: it maintains the idea of natural-seeming difference and foregrounds majority-group explanations of inequality rather than minority-group ones. It also keeps much of the traditional notion of group hierarchies and, as we have argued, reworks the concept of the 'white man's burden' (Wetherell and Potter, 1992, ch. 5).

It should be stressed that although these phenomena are, in important ways, representational, they do not fit easily with current versions of social representations theory. Part of the reason for this is that social representations theory has been mainly concerned with linking representations to social categories, while paying less attention to the way categories are constructed *as* representations. In addition, social representations theory does not have a well developed account of the way representations are designed to accomplish particular actions. In this example, we explored the way the members of a powerful white group positioned Maori people using a repertoire of cultural ideas which could be used to sustain a range of ideological claims (see Augoustinos, chapter 10 this volume).

### Stories of conflict and influence

One of the main goals of social psychology is to produce some theory of intergroup relations and processes of social influence. From our perspective, however, what is also interesting is the way the white New Zealanders we interviewed represented these things – their theories of influence and stories of the minority in relation to the majority. In effect, this is the same sort of move as we made with categories. Instead of treating processes as the *technical* resource of the analysts they are treated as a *practical* resource of the participants (cf. Heritage, 1984).

Let us look first at two extracts from our interviews.

SEDGE: Um, a lot of the racial prejudice is brought on, you know, by the Eva Rickards [a Maori 'activist'] that stand up. I've been out time after time and played golf at Raglan [yes] and playing on the golf course there, and I've played with Maori people, and they've said, 'oh, you know, this is the old burial ground, hiya Trevor'. And, you know, nobody minds you playing golf across there, and I said, 'no, no, no, fine'. And it takes Eva Rickard to come down from somewhere else and to stir the whole blooming pot and er, you know, the [inaudible word] government gets in and buys the land. Well they've sorted it all out and given them all a brand new golf course and I mean they [.] I haven't tried the new one.

WOOD: I think we'll end up having Maori wars if they carry on the way they are. I mean no it'll be a Pakeha war [Yes]. Um [.] they're making New Zealand a racist country. Um but you know you usually feel, think, that racism is um [.] putting the, putting the darker people down but really they're doing it the other way around, I feel. Um, everything seems to be to help the Maori people, um, you know. I think at the moment sort of the Europeans sort of they're just sort of watching and putting up with it, but they'll only go so far. Um you know we've got Maori friends out here, uh who we have into the house, you know they're friends, um but when things happen when they suddenly say oh they're going to make Maori language compulsory, um it is, it's antagonizing and the Maori friends that we've got, they don't agree with it. OK you've got your extremists there too, the ones who feel, you know, that everyone should learn it but um I think the average Maori sort of perhaps is worried too.

These two extracts refer to controversial issues – the role of Maori activists such as Eva Richard in a dispute over the ownership of a piece of land (a former golf course) and, in the second extract, to current discussions about the teaching of Maori language in schools. The participants, Sedge and Wood, are arguing their corner; they are engaged in passionate debate, trying to persuade the listening interviewer of the validity of the case. Crucially, they are trying to discredit particular Maori opponents. Here, as always, representations of groups, individuals, and issues are linked to the practice that the speaker is engaged in.

What are the representations of the process of social influence found in these and other New Zealanders' accounts or, in our terms, what are their interpretative repertoires? Take Wood, for example, how does she construct a social landscape? What is her theory of social influence? In effect, she develops a distinction between two groups: 'average Maoris' (Maoris defined as 'friends') and 'extremist Maoris'. The process of influence is portrayed as one where a placid and homogeneous status quo and consensual set of norms is 'stirred up,' 'antagonized', and made turbulent by a small group of protesters defined as extreme. Often in this kind of accounting, the rest of the Maori population (defined here as 'average Maoris') were described as like sheep who mindlessly climb on the bandwagon against their 'best interests'.

This is a particular story of the social influence process which clearly does substantial ideological work for the majority group. It is not a neutral account; it is an interested description, one that is made to work. Our goal was to disentangle the repertoires of social influence process (the girders), show how they are put to work in argument, and to discuss their ideological implications (cf. Wetherell and Potter, 1992, ch. 6). Again, we should emphasize that although social representations theory has developed some subtle analysis of the sorts of resources that people draw on, it has not followed this with equally subtle analyses of the way they are deployed in people's practices. Discourse analysis, by contrast, has taken as a central topic the uses of representations in action.

### Practical politics

As a final theme we want to look at some of the resources for constructing political discourse: the practical politics that was pervasive in our materials. In our reading of the broadly political discourse in the newspaper articles, the interviews, and in the Parliamentary debate itself, we were struck by the small number of arguments that were drawn on over and over again. Indeed, it was possible to formulate them as a brief set of maxims that could be set out as follows.

1 Resources should be used productively and in a cost-effective manner.
2 Nobody should be compelled.
3 Everybody should be treated equally.
4 You can't turn the clock backwards.
5 Present generations cannot be blamed for the mistakes of past generations.
6 Injustices should be righted.
7 Everybody can succeed if they try hard enough.
8 Minority opinion shouldn't carry more weight than majority opinion.
9 We've got to live in the twentieth century.
10 You've got to be practical.

These ten statements are unexceptional and familiar in form – they display the solidity and taken-for-granted feel characteristic of mundane politics. Taking each statement individually, who could disagree that it is important to be practical, that history moves forward, that injustice and inequality are wrong? They can be seen as a summary of a sort of folk wisdom. Moreover, they are undoubtedly not unique to New Zealand. Although this particular list may not be precisely repeated in Germany, the US, or other Western democracies, something similar could be.

As analysts of discourse we were very aware that producing an abstract list like this is not sufficient – indeed, it could be positively misleading. It is well established that rules such as these do not govern their instances of application, that they are open to a wide range of interpretations when used in practice (see Potter and Wetherell, 1987, ch. 3). From a discourse analytic point of view, what happens when these maxims are applied to actual instances is precisely what is interesting. When we examined this list it soon becomes apparent that it embodies some basic tensions (e.g. between individual rights and practical considerations). However, from the perspective of its users this should not be seen as a problem or flaw in the list. Rather, the reverse, for these very tensions provide rhetorical flexibility and argumentative power. Specifically, when dealing with issues of race and racism we could map out the way this set of argumentative maxims provided a wide range of resources which were selectively drawn on in arguments against radical change or Maori advancement.

Take as an example the contentious issue of the teaching of the Maori language in schools. The maxims provide various routes for producing criticisms of this policy justified by the principles of practical politics. It could be attacked on the grounds of principle (nobody should be compelled) and undermined as not suited to the modern world (we've got to live in the twentieth century, you've got to be practical). The advantage of both of these critical routes is that they can avoid an appearance of racist motivation. Moreover, having criticized the policy in this way it was possible to undermine any suggestion of negative feeling toward Maori groups and language by stressing a personal desire to learn the language, or claiming how nice it would be to have it as an optional extra. Here is an example:

WETHERELL: . . . this Taha Maori programme, is it? What is it actually?
RAYMOND KENWOOD: Ah well you know I hope when I retire that I will learn the Maori language, I think it [.] I want to learn it you know because I think I have to learn it, but I'd like to, but I think it's they [.] unfortunate with these Te Kohanga Reo [a Maori-language-teaching programme] situations, is that, you know, they're sort of forcing Maoris and peop [.] forcing Maori children to learn Maori language, well I can see it has no value in our education system. Now they'll straight away say that our system is wrong. But um er er you know as far as the Maori language is concerned, singing and that sort of thing and on the marae, it has its place. But in a Western world it has no place at all.

Teaching the Maori language in schools was just one of a wide range of currently controversial issues for which outcomes which justified the current status quo were justified by calling selectively on this range of resources. Programmes of affirmative action were another example. Here attempts to redress educational disadvantage in minority groups were characterized as unfair, discrimination, or even as a form of apartheid (Potter and Wetherell, 1989; Wetherell and Potter, 1992, ch. 7). Likewise, the issue of historical seizures of Maori land was dealt with using a strong distinction between the rights of the case and what is practical. The Maoris have been swindled out of their land – but what would they do with it if it were returned?

WETHERELL: What do you feel about the sort of land protest generally, things like the Bastion Point issue and eh em Maori land marches and so on? Do you think there's a case there or?

ACKLAND: I can't um I don't think I don't really know what they're protesting about (mm). I think it seems to be uh some of the land they're protesting over is farm land, and other land is land that's been sold years and years ago [mmhm]. You can't turn the clock back really [yes] but they're, historically or even today uh a lot of the Maori-held land isn't utilized to its best, anyway [yes]. A lot of them are very indifferent users of the land

WETHERELL: Mmhm, and so it's just, it should be more productively?

ACKLAND: Yes, I think it's, it would be better if uh if it's productively um used by Europeans that it shouldn't be taken away from them to be given to back to the tribe to just say divide like among many people [mm] and let it deteriorate.

## Conclusions

The point of these examples is that they show the way the practical political resources of a culture can be mobilized in a way that impedes moves for minority-group advancement and the righting of past wrongs. The power of these resources is that they are clothed in the caring ethics of liberalism and common sense. They enable speakers to display themselves as concerned yet aware of the pressures of 'living the modern world'. They are justifiable and, indeed, sayable, in way that traditional forms of racism are not. The point of this discourse analytic study is to show how this justification is put together, assembled from various parts and the procedures for assembly. By doing this we hope to undermine the natural and obvious quality of many of these arguments.

There is a more general conclusion of studies of studies of discourse and rhetoric such as this, whether they are focused on New Zealand race talk, UK talk about the royal family, or everyday explanations of riots.

When we look at the argumentative patterns in such discourse they do not correspond to the neat patterns that might be expected from individuals working from consistent beliefs or attitudes, nor to the organization that would follow from sets of underlying representations shared across social groups. What is striking is the complex and fragmented organization of common-sense reasoning. Billig (1992) calls this the 'kaleidoscope of common sense': a swirling pattern where premises and inferences regularly change places, where shifts are fluidly made between arguments from principle and practice, and where liberal, humanistic, or egalitarian 'values' are drawn on for potentially racist effect or to legitimate inequality.

In some ways it seems incredible, given that this phenomenon was so ordinary and close to home that it has not long been a central topic of social psychological concern. However, it may well have been, in part, a fear that no sense could be made of this apparently buzzing confusion that led social psychologists to deal with everyday discourse only when filtered through experimental manipulations and questionnaire prompts. One of the great virtues of social representations theory is that it refocused psychologists' interest on the content of psychological reasoning. The challenge for social psychologists now is to see the order in the confusion, and discourse analytic work has made a start on this path.

# 10 Social representations and ideology: towards the study of ideological representations

*Martha Augoustinos*

## Introduction

In his critique of mainstream social psychology, Moscovici (1972, p. 55) argues that, 'The central and exclusive object of social psychology should be the study of all that pertains to *ideology* and to *communication* from the point of view of their structure, their genesis and their function.' Moscovici's theory of social representations emerged largely as a result of such concerns. The theory of social representations aims to reintroduce a social focus to the study of social psychology by emphasizing the primacy of collective concepts such as culture and ideology. It seeks to understand individual psychological experience by placing individuals within their social, cultural, and collective milieu. Social representations theory begins with the premise that the individual is primarily and foremost a social being whose own existence and identity are rooted in a collectivity. It therefore attempts to understand how higher-level social processes impinge upon and influence the social psychological functioning of individuals and groups.

Social representations refer to the ideas, thoughts, images, and knowledge which members of a collectivity share: consensual universes of thought which are socially created and socially communicated to form part of a 'common consciousness'. Social representations constitute the stock of common knowledge and information which people share in the form of common-sense theories about the social world. They comprise both conceptual and pictorial elements. Through these, members of a society are able to construct social reality. Moscovici has defined social representations as follows:

Social representations . . . concern the contents of everyday thinking and the stock of ideas that gives coherence to our religious beliefs, political ideas and the connections we create as spontaneously as we breathe. They make it possible for us to classify persons and objects, to compare and explain behaviours and to objectify them as parts of our social setting. While representations are often to be located in the minds of men and women, they can just as often be found 'in the world', and as such examined separately. (Moscovici, 1988a, p. 214)

Just as society can be considered to be an economic and political system, it should also be viewed as a 'thinking system' (Moscovici, 1988a). Social psychology should therefore concern itself with the nature of a 'thinking society' and become a 'psychology of the social'.

While social representations have been defined as internalized social knowledge, such knowledge can reflect the dominant values and widespread beliefs of a society. One of the functions of widespread beliefs and values is that such beliefs may provide legitimacy for the socio-political structure of a society (Gaskell and Fraser, 1990). A number of social theorists have also attributed this functional status to ideology. In this chapter I will be examining the theoretical links between the concepts of social representations and ideology. Clearly, some social representations which are consensual, widespread, and prescriptive may also be seen to contribute to the social cohesion of a society. If certain representations contribute to the support and maintenance of the existing institutional arrangements, power, and social relations within a society, then they can be considered 'ideological' in nature.

### The concept of ideology

Ideology has been described by many as the most contested and elusive concept within the social sciences. Both McLellan (1986) and Larrain (1979) provide thorough historical accounts of this concept. Indeed, McLellan warns that all attempts to define ideology are ideological in themselves.

### *Traditional notion: ideology as coherent beliefs*

The predominant approach in the social sciences is to view ideology as a coherent set of political beliefs and values embraced by formal political parties. The empirical tradition linked with this positivist view has involved large-scale surveys aimed at examining the political, economic, and social attitudes of the mass public. The primary aim has been to determine the underlying structure of these beliefs in terms of a liberal–conservative political framework. This tradition of research culminated in Converse's (1964) work, which concluded that people displayed little internal coherence in their political attitudes. It was argued that the public, unlike the political elite, did not think 'ideologically'. Instead of an overarching belief system that organized large amounts of information, the public were found to have clusters of simple, concrete, and personally relevant ideas which displayed little consistency. The public displayed confusion over the meaning of conservative as opposed to liberal ideological dimensions and did not share with political elites a conservative versus liberal conceptual frame of reference as a means by which to structure and organise their political knowledge.

This inconsistency between beliefs among the public was supported by other empirical research. For example, McClosky (1964) found that although the American public generally endorsed the principles of freedom and democracy in their abstract form, they were inconsistent in their application of these principles to specific instances. Thus, McClosky argued that there existed little ideological consensus among the American electorate, whose knowledge and understanding of politics was, at best, rudimentary.

The notion that the public is politically uninformed and ideologically inconsistent formed the paradigmatic core of American political science during the 1960s and early 1970s. Critics of this research argued that because the public did not structure political beliefs in the same manner as the political elite it did not necessarily follow that the content of lay political beliefs demonstrated little in the way of a substantive ideological orientation. The presence or absence of structure, it was argued, is not synonymous with the presence or absence of ideology (e.g. Marcus, Tabb and Sullivan, 1974; Bennett, 1977).

A more substantial criticism concerns the manner in which ideology has been defined by such research. Equating ideology with political identifications such as 'liberal' or 'conservative' in the American context, or 'Labour' or 'Conservative' in the British context, restricts the concept of ideology to formal political belief systems. This particular conception not only neglects the link between ideology and everyday life – the role which ideology plays in structuring everyday social reality – but also strips the concept of its critical component (Thompson, 1984: McLellan, 1986). From within this perspective ideology is primarily used as a descriptive and neutral concept, which refers to any formal belief system. This also has been the predominant use of the concept of ideology by psychologists (e.g. Eysenck and Wilson, 1978). Restricting the definition of ideology to a coherent system of political beliefs as embodied within the rhetoric of Western democratic political parties focuses only upon superficial political conflicts and the formal processes of political decision-making.

Another positivist approach to the concept of ideology is to equate ideology with political extremism and totalitarianism. The decline of Nazism and Stalinism after the Second World War led to many American political scientists declaring the 'End of Ideology' (e.g. Bell,

1960; Lipset, 1960). Ideology was contrasted with science. Only a rational and positivist approach to the study of society, unfettered by grand political theories such as Marxism, would result in social progress. Indeed, the recent decline of Soviet and east European communism has led to the presumption that capitalism has been vindicated as a rational, value-free, and objective way of organizing society – a social and economic system free from ideology. This view has been argued recently by Fukuyama (1992), who declares liberal democracy to be 'the end of history'. The end of the Cold War has also been characterized as ending one of the most significant ideological battles in history. But does this recent historical event signal the end of the importance of ideology in the way in which people construct and understand their everyday lives? To argue this is to ignore or downplay the inherent ideological currents within liberal-democratic societies themselves and within everyday life outside of formal politics.

### Critical positions: ideology as power and hegemony

So far I have described the dominant ways in which ideology has been defined by mainstream social science. This can be contrasted to a more critical approach, which views ideology as the means by which relations of power, control and dominance are maintained and preserved within any society. In contrast to earlier historical periods, power and control, within Western liberal democracies has been wielded increasingly by covert and subtle means, and less by the use of overt force. Although different in emphasis, social theorists such as Althusser (1970) and Foucault (1977) have identified ideological meaning systems and practices as the central means by which relations of power and dominance are maintained and reproduced within contemporary modern societies.

No discussion of ideological representations would be complete without considering Marxist-influenced accounts of ideology. Such accounts are particularly relevant because they have systematically attempted to explain the role of ideology in contemporary liberal democracies. Whereas Marx's early writings on ideology emphasised the illusory role which ideology plays in portraying society as cohesive and harmonious, his later writings emphasized the role ideology plays in making sense of people's everyday social interactions within a capitalist society. According to Marx, ideology functions to conceal social conflicts by embodying ideas, values, and language which justify existing social and economic inequalities. The ideology of freedom and equality within capitalist society is reinforced by the individual's apparent experience of free exchange in the market place. Marx viewed ideology as concealing the real relations of dominance and inequality which exist in capitalist societies (Larrain, 1983; McLellan, 1986).

But it is in Gramsci's writings on ideology (1971) that links between social representations theory and the study of ideology can most usefully be made. Gramsci emphasized the common-sense nature of ideology, endowing it with an almost 'folklore' quality. Ideology became powerful and pervasive, Gramsci argued, because it was able to make sense of people's everyday lived experience. This is very different from the previously defined concept of ideology as referring to a system of formal political thought. For Gramsci, ideology was intimately linked to the practices of everyday life. This bears strong similarities to Moscovici's (1981, 1984a, chapter 14 this volume) view that social representations form the basis for what is regarded as common sense.

Gramsci also employed the concept of ideological hegemony – the way in which 'a certain way of life and thought is dominant, in which one concept of reality is diffused throughout society in all its institutional and private manifestations, informing with its spirit all taste, morality, customs, religious and political principles, and all social relations, particularly in their intellectual and moral connotations' (Williams, 1960, p. 587). There exists within any society at any given time various conceptions of the world which are not structurally or culturally unified. The hegemonic process can be described as the way in which a particular 'world' view diffuses throughout society, forming the basis of what is described as common-sense knowledge or 'objective truth'. Again, this bears similarities to Moscovici's description of how scientific concepts which originate in the reified universe of science diffuse throughout the rest of society contributing to the stock of common-sense knowledge which people draw upon to make sense of their social world. Gramsci refers to intellectual ideas and scientific knowledge which become a part of everyday common sense as 'organic'. According to Gramsci, an ideology is organic insofar as it informs the practical consciousness of everyday life.

Many factors influence what becomes the dominant ideology. What is particularly important however, is the ability of ideological notions to 'make sense' of the structural organization of society: the dominant social, political, and economic relations. As Mepham (1972, p. 17) suggests, ideology does not simply refer to ideas but is 'firmly grounded in the forms of our social life' and thus has a material reality.

### A dominant ideology: myth or reality?

The question of ideological hegemony has long been debated. The crude version of hegemony has been used to explain almost anything, from the failure of Marxist predictions about the inevitable demise of capitalism, to the acceptance by the masses of capitalist relations of production. The working classes were seen to have failed to recognize their true economic and political interests; worse still, they had internalized the bourgeois values of their oppressors. The German critical theorists such as Adorno, Horkheimer, and Marcuse described the acquiescence of the working classes to capitalism as 'false consciousness' (Agger, 1991). Similarly, cultural analysts emphasize the extent to which contemporary western life is characterised by the conspicuous consumption of goods bought for their symbolic value (Baudrillard, 1983); a preoccupation which some argue undermines the development of critical political awareness (Lash and Urry, 1987).

There is little doubt that some of these analyses are overly simplistic and overly deterministic. Human agency and autonomy disappears and consciousness is determined and directed by powerful structural forces (Thompson, 1984). While Moscovici (1988a) has referred to hegemonic representations, he rejects the view that everyone is always under the sway of a dominant ideology. This crude version fails to acknowledge the constructionist and reflexive capacities of people. Billig (1991; Billig et al., 1988) has also argued against this version of ideological domination which treats people as passive and gullible pawns, duped by an array of ideological managers and institutions which serve the interests of the dominant classes.

Furthermore, empirical studies give only qualified support to the 'dominant ideology' thesis. Rather than a pervasive diffused consensus in people's views about the nature of society, sociological studies have found significant class differences, with the middle classes demonstrating more consensus and cohesion in their views than the working classes (Mann, 1970: Chamberlain, 1983). Indeed, it has been argued that it is this ideological cohesion in the middle to upper classes and ideological disunity amongst the lower classes which helps maintain the stability within liberal democracies. The hegemony of the dominant classes is maintained by the nature of the fragmented and disparate opposition which exists.

### Postmodernism and ideology

One of the central themes emphasized by postmodernist commentators in the last decade is the increasing fragmentation and diversification of modern societies (Lyotard, 1984). Postmodernism celebrates the existence of multiple views and realities, none of which is regarded as being more valid than the other. All perspectives and versions are considered as legitimate points of view. The pluralism embodied in postmodernism renders the notion of a unified and coherent dominant ideology as unrepresentative of modern contemporary culture. Similarly, Moscovici (1988a) has argued that hegemonic representations are more difficult to locate in modern capitalist societies, and are more characteristic of small traditional societies.

So, what are we to make of life in the increasingly diversified 'postmodern' world? Are there no beliefs, values, representations, discourses which bind and unify individuals and groups within the complexity of everyday life? Are there no parameters within which people frame conflicts, questions, and answers, and in so doing legitimate and reproduce the power relations within a society? While many more 'voices' (perspectives) are being heard in contemporary life, do all voices have the same capacity for being heard and the same power to persuade?

While few empirical studies have found evidence of a dominant ideology in modern democracies, there is some evidence of the prevalence of certain ideological themes. The liberal-individualist conception of the person as the centre of cognition, action, and process has been described by various commentators as a shared representation which permeates all aspects of social life within Western industrialized societies (Lukes, 1973). Linked to this conception of the person is one of the few value orientations about which studies do indicate a dominant consensus: individualist values of achievement. For example, Mann's (1970) review indicates that a significant degree of 'dominant consensus' exists between and within classes in both England and the United States concerning statements such as 'it is important to get ahead', and that hard work and ability rather than luck are instrumental for materialistic and occupational success (see also chapter 7 by Oyserman and Markus in this volume). More recent Australian research has found that, among secondary-school students, personal attributions for academic achievement, such as ability and hard work, are significantly more favoured than situational attributions. Furthermore, personal attributions for academic achievement are more dominant among older students (16 to 17 years) than younger students (13 to 14 years) suggesting some kind of socialisation process (Augoustinos, 1990; see also chapter 4 by Hewstone and Augoustinos in this volume).

The development of a cultural emphasis upon individual achievement, the causes of which are primarily located within the indiviudual, has been referred to by some theorists as 'possessive individualism'. Indeed, individualism has been described as the most pervasive ethos characterizing liberal democracies because it has the ability to make sense of the social conditions of a capitalist society. Individual merit and success are largely rewarded in such societies and competition, which forms the cornerstone of economic relations, is heralded as the most effective and efficient means by which to motivate people in most spheres of social life.

### Individualism and liberalism

As a dominant value orientation, individualism is an inherent feature of liberalism; the political creed around which most Western capitalist democracies are structured. Hall (1986) documents the historically dynamic development of liberalism within England since the seventeenth century. So responsive was liberalism to the changing historical and social circumstances within England that a number of variants of liberalism developed, ranging from the conservative to the more pro-gressive and reformist versions. Throughout this century, recurring experiences of economic crises have seriously challenged the classic liberalist emphasis on *laissez-faire* capitalism. Liberalism embraced the necessity for social change by attempting to 'humanize' capitalism. This culminated in increased state intervention in the market economy and the development of the modern capitalist welfare state. Hall argues that liberalism managed to maintain its hegemony because of its ability to accommodate a range of political inflections. While social-democratic parties have embraced the more reformist and progressive versions of liberalism which emphasize the need to redistribute wealth and to protect the casualties of the system, conservative liberalism has continued to stress the importance of free competition and market economics in combination with the rhetoric of tradition and authority. Liberalism's remarkable flexibility has enabled it to become adopted by different political positions and to serve the interests of different social groups.

Despite the differences and contradictions between social-democratic and conservative variants of liberalism, the two strands share a number of core concepts which are fundamental in identifying them as part of a particular ideological discourse. The liberalist conception of the world is premised on the 'sovereign individual'. Liberalism abstracts the indi-vidual from society. All individuals possess certain inalienable rights which are viewed to be consonant with the essential character of human nature. The freedom of individuals to maximize self-interest and to take part in social, political, and religious activities of their own choosing is regarded as most important. The competition and struggle for material resources is viewed as an expression of a natural human drive. An open meritocracy in which individuals are free to compete and maximize self-interest is regarded as a 'natural' society. A market economy which allows all individuals to compete, sell and buy, accumulate wealth, and improve their position in society is regarded as a 'natural' economy. Society and economy organized around market principles are seen to be consistent with the fundamentals of human nature. Indeed, this perspective has gained prevalence since the demise of east European and Soviet communism and the transition to market economies world-wide (Fukuyama, 1992).

Liberalism has been able to maintain its hegemony not only because it forms the basis of philosophical reasoning for many of the major political parties in liberal democracies, but also because it forms the basis of spontaneous everyday thinking by ordinary people. Hall (1986) documents the way in which components of philosophical liberalism have become widely diffused throughout English society, 'informing practical consciousness' and becoming an important component of English common sense:

So much so that, to many of those who constantly think within its limits, it does not appear to be an ideology at all, but simply an obvious way of making sense of things – 'what everybody knows'. However, this 'obviousness' is itself a sign that the ideas do belong to a particular ideological configuration – they are obvious only because their historical and philosophical roots and conditions have somehow been forgotten or suppressed. (p. 35)

While many social theories emphasize the way in which individuals are foremost and primarily social beings, and in some way constituted by society, liberalism abstracts and separates the individual from society. 'Liberalism thus played a role in constructing our prevailing common sense or "spontaneous" awareness of ourselves today as separate, isolable and self-sufficient beings' (Hall, 1986, p. 41).

Billig (1982, 1991) has argued that it is an oversimplification to characterize modern liberal democracies as individualistic, pointing out that both individualist and collectivist values co-exist within contemporary capitalism. Hall also makes this clear in his historical account of variants of liberalism. In a similar vein, the research of Katz and Hass (1988) in the United States has demonstrated the co-existence of two largely independent value systems among American college students: humanitarianism–egalitarianism and the Protestant work ethic. While the former emphasizes the importance of political equality and social justice between individuals and groups, the latter stresses the importance of hard work, individual achievement, self-reliance, and discipline. In practice, these two core values often lead to feelings of ambivalence towards marginalized groups such as black Americans and the poor. Concern for the welfare and justice of these groups is tempered by the belief that individuals in such groups transgress cherished values such as hard work and self-reliance. This is based on the assumption that another person's lower social status within a society is a result of personal shortcomings and failures.

Importantly, Billig has highlighted the contrary nature of ideological themes, pointing to the ways in which people apply these in different contexts. Such inconsistencies and contradictions point to the inherent *dilemmatic* quality of ideological thinking. People do not necessarily accept values uncritically and without conscious deliberation. An empirical issue is to determine the extent to which and the context within which people challenge dominant norms and values and how contradictory themes such as individualism/collectivism find expression in everyday life. As Condor points out (1990), people may not simply endorse or reject dominant views, but rather, develop complex configurations of thought in which some dominant ideological elements find expression in conjunction with individual and group-based understandings. For example, survey research across many Western countries suggest that people in general are very sympathetic and supportive of the provision of welfare and social services for the unemployed, but are less sympathetic of the provision of these services for single parents (Lewis, 1990). Collectivist principles of social justice are therefore tempered by traditional notions of the family.

Despite the rhetoric of postmodernism, liberal individualism continues to exercise ideological constraints on the way people think, live, and behave in modern societies. Consumerism, patriarchy, positivist science, and the domination of nature by technological progress are ideological representations which also have a contemporary relevance. There is no doubt that discourses which challenge and undermine these do exist. The feminist critique of contemporary society has clearly had a discernible impact at all levels of society, from the structural to the personal. Nevertheless, despite changes, women are still under-represented at the highest levels of employment; and are still doing the bulk of the housework and parenting, despite working full-time. Although patriarchy has been significantly challenged, it remains largely intact.

### The study and location of ideological representations

*Ideology as consciousness*

I want now to consider the methods by which we may study ideological representations. Traditionally, ideology has been treated as a cognitive construct which permeates human consciousness. From within this perspective ideology is to be found in the values, beliefs, attitudes and opinions which people hold. Such cognitive concepts and traditional methods of measuring them remain useful in the study of ideological representations. Indeed, it could be argued that research in certain areas of social psychology has 'unwittingly' uncovered ideological components in thinking. For example, the fundamental attribution 'error' or 'bias' demonstrates the dominance of dispositional explanations over situational explanations in Western culture. Increasingly, it has been recognized that this attributional phenomenon is not a universal cognitive bias, but is culture specific, reflecting an underlying ideological representation of the person as the centre of all action and process (Ichheiser, 1949; Bond, 1983; Miller, 1984; see also chapter 4 by Hewstone and Augoustinos this volume).

As argued earlier, individualist values of achievement contribute significantly to the support of a capitalist socio-cultural system. Furthermore, studies have found that as children grow older they are more likely to regard inequalities of wealth and income as inevitable and legitimate (Stacey, 1982; Lewis, 1990). They are also more likely to embrace equity principles of economic distribution rather than principles of equality (Sampson, 1975; Bond, Leung and Wan, 1982). That is, children learn to accept over time that resources within society are (and should be) distributed according to individual inputs (effort, abilities, and skills). As Sampson (1975) argues, equity values encourage and legitimate individual competition and personal advancement at the expense of cooperation, communion, and equality. Indeed, Sampson suggests that the forms of relations which dominate in the economic sphere tend to be adopted in other areas of human relationships.

### Ideology as language

There is little doubt that contemporary social theorists who have concerned themselves with the study of ideology have come increasingly to regard language as *the* location of ideology. The traditional arena for ideology, consciousness, has been replaced by the study of everyday discourse, ranging from the mundane to the more institutional forms. The study of everyday discourse has also been adopted enthusiastically by an increasing number of social psychologists. Potter and Wetherell's (1987) book, *Discourse and social psychology*, reflects the wider paradigmatic shift from the study of 'consciousness' or cognition, to the study of discourse (see Harré, chapter 8 this volume; Potter and Wetherell, chapter 9 this volume). Thompson (1984) describes the current fascination with language thus:

increasingly it has been realised that 'ideas' do not drift through the social world like clouds in a summer sky, occasionally divulging their contents with a clap of thunder and a flash of light. Rather, ideas circulate in the social world as utterances, as expressions, as words which are spoken or inscribed. Hence to study ideology is, in some part and in some way, to study language in the social world (p. 2).

As with social representations theory, everyday communication (the 'unceasing babble' to which Moscovici refers) is viewed as fundamental in producing and transmitting meaning in social life. Language is the medium by which relations of power are communicated and relations of domination are created and sustained.

Ideology is to be located not only in the expression of ideas and values embodied in discourse, but also in the particular types of syntactic structures employed in language. For example, Kress and Hodge (1979) discuss the ways in which certain linguistic transformations can deny the agency and responsibility of actors. A simple sentence like 'South African police have burnt down a black township' can be transformed into a passive and agentless sentence such as 'A black township has burnt down' (Fairclough, 1989). Such transformations simplify information, but, in so doing, suppress, distort, and mystify what is being communicated. Complex social processes can also be objectified – by representing them as 'things', or as persons (personification). For example, a complex economic process such as inflation is often described by the media and in everyday conversation as an adversary that can hurt and harm us: 'inflation has attacked the foundation of our economy'; 'our biggest enemy right now is inflation'; 'the dollar has been destroyed by inflation'. As Lakoff and Johnson (1980, pp. 33–4) explain, the metaphor of 'inflation as an adversary' lends legitimacy to government actions undertaken to deal with an economic process which, in many instances, is the direct result of government policy.

Many researchers have also demonstrated the powerful way in which sexist language such as the use of the generic 'he' in the English language can shape and mould social reality, especially for children who interpret the world as essentially a male domain (Nilsen, 1977). Gendered language not only reflects the prevailing relationships of gender dominance within society but its continued use also serves to sustain those relationships.

Another way in which discourse reflects ideological undercurrents can be found in the kinds of categories people use to communicate about the social world. Categories are important because they communicate something of the 'taken-for-granted' or shared meanings that people have of the world. These shared meanings are likely to differ between different social groups in society so that variations in meaning are contested by different groups with conflicting interests. Categories not only make it easier to communicate by imposing order, but they are also powerful in themselves, being able to define and control conceptions of reality. For example, take the conflicting categories of 'terrorist' or 'freedom fighter'. The label one uses to describe such individuals has clear political and evaluative connotations. As such, categories and systems of classification become the site of struggle between and within different interest groups within society (Thompson, 1984). The categories of 'man' and 'woman' are interesting to consider, for while there is a static, taken-for-granted understanding that these refer to differentiated biological entities, at another level, the meanings, assumptions, and prescriptions associated with these categories are fiercely contested. The way in which the categories of man and woman have been understood has changed markedly throughout history, and is in a constant state of negotiation and struggle (see Kruse, chapter 13 this volume). Ideology can also be located in the process of argumentation. The inconsistencies, contradictions, gaps in knowledge, what is said as opposed to what is never mentioned, are aspects of argumentation which reflect the parameters within which ideology operates.

### *Ideology as behavioural practices*

In addition to cognition and language, ideological representations may be reflected in the social practices that constitute everyday life. Ideological influences may be realized through everyday practices (see Harré, chapter 8 this volume) and rituals within contemporary social institutions such as the family, schools, the legal and political systems. For example, everyday economic practices such as banking, working, selling, and buying may all contribute to legitimating the existing relations of production. Participating in a competitive educational system legitimates meritocracy, while traditional labour arrangements in the home perpetuate and reinforce patriarchal relations. Ideological hegemony may also be exercised in more obvious ways by the dissemination of certain values and ideas by the mass media (see Sommer, chapter 12 this volume). A focus on behavioural practices is akin to Foucault's insistence that modern power is capillary, touching all aspects of social life. Similarly, Althusser (1970) emphasized the materialist base of ideology, grounding it to practices within contemporary institutions such as the family, schools, and legal, political, and state structures. Thus relations of power and dominance are more likely to be maintained and perpetuated by the forms of our everyday micropractices, rather than by our beliefs and cognitions (Fraser, 1989).

### Conclusion

In conclusion, I have argued that some representations embody certain ideological undercurrents. Being widely shared and diffused throughout society, such ideological representations may contribute to the maintenance and reproduction of the existing power and social relations within a society. Asymmetries of power are not only socio-economic in nature but are related also to gender, race, and ethnicity. Social representations theory has the opportunity to develop a social psychological perspective to ideology by understanding the interface between social-structural forces and the social psychological functioning of individuals and groups. This can be contrasted to social cognitive theories which conceptualize thinking as a purely individual phenomenon and also to theories of ideology, which have the tendency to view people as being at the mercy of powerful structural forces. The study of ideological representations needs to be contextualized within a framework which sees the individual as being in a dialectical relationship with society, both as a product of society and an active agent who can effect change in society.

The nature of hegemony or ideological domination is itself problematic. Are certain representations more dominant than others because they are prevalent across most groups in society, or are they dominant because they are held with more conviction by the more powerful groups? Is it the ideological cohesion in certain groups and ideological disunity among others which contributes to the maintainence and reproduction of certain social relations of power and inequity? These are some of the important conceptual and empirical issues social representations research should develop the capacity to confront. In turn, this will require social representations researchers to engage in wider debates about the nature of contemporary Western culture and society (see Oyserman and Markus, chapter 7 this volume). Critical theory, feminist social theory, and postmodernism are intellectual movements which may contribute usefully to the future development of social representations theory. Furthermore, any efforts to study ideological representations must avoid the functionalist trap of simply seeking to explain the stability and reproducibility of social systems. The dynamics of challenge and resistance – the situations in which dominant representations may become undermined or overhauled needs to become an integral conceptual and empirical focus for the study of ideological representations. In this way we can achieve Moscovici's vision of studying 'social life in the making' (1988a, p. 219) and learn more about the 'psychology of the social'.

# 11 Social representations and development: experts' and parents' discourses about a puzzling issue

*Felice F. Carugati and Patrizia Selleri*

### Introduction

From a social constructivist perspective, society is only possible to the extent that the interacting selves share the same underlying symbolic order. Consequently, psychological realities must always refer to the corresponding cultural and historical background upon which they are predicated. This background is manifested in practical activities, rules, norms, normative, and prescriptive ideas. What are the implications of this for theory and empirical findings in research on intelligence and development? The major implication leads to the third point, which is that this research, in order to develop models or theories (both at scientific and at layperson's level) that are 'empirically' testable can only do so by accessing historically and culturally constituted knowledge which people handle, distribute, represent, and communicate in everyday life.

Taking the case of intelligence and child development, we propose to make an overview of what experts spoke about over decades, what they were telling to one of their particular audience, that is to say, to parents, and finally how parents talk about intelligence and development, creating and recreating in original ways the discourses which circulate in society.

### Intelligence as a matter of experts' issue

The 1986 symposium on the definition and measurement of intelligence followed its predecessor (Intelligence and its measurement: a symposium, 1921) by sixty-five years. In 1921 the discussants invited by the prestigious *Journal of Educational Psychology* included, *inter alia*, Terman, Thorndike, and Thurstone. All of these researchers had as their primary affiliation educational psychology, and they published extensively on issues in mental testing. The 1986 symposium was organized by Sternberg and Detterman (1986) on the behalf of *Intelligence*. The two convenors invited a large sample of experts: Anastasi, Baltes, Berry, Baron, Eysenck, Gardner, Goodnow, Jensen, Scarr, Schanck and Ziegler, *inter alia*.

The analysis of the list of main attributes that appeared in the 1986 and 1921 definitions proposed by the experts indicates a moderate overlap: attributes such as adaptation to environment, and higher-order thinking (reasoning, problem-solving, decision-making) are prominent in both listings. Second, certain themes recur in both symposia. The issue of a single or mutliple intelligences continues to be of concern, although no consensus exists upon this matter. As in the earlier symposium, some 1986 experts define intelligence quite narrowly in terms of biological or especially cognitive elements, whereas others include a broader array of elements, including motivation and personality. The issue of the breadth of intelligence, like that of whether it is single or multiple, remains unresolved.

Despite the similarities in views over sixty-five years, some salient differences in the two listings can also be found. Meta-cognition – conceived of as both knowledge about and control of cognition – played a prominent role in the 1986 symposium. A greater emphasis was placed on the role of knowledge and the interaction between this knowledge and mental processes. The change in emphasis is with respect both to functions that occur within the organism and to the role of culture, in defining intelligence, whereas such emphasis was absent in the 1921 symposium. One of the main points to be addressed here is that the overall differences in concerns between the 1921 and 1986 symposia reflect the greater psychometric orientation that predominated in 1921 versus the greater information-processing as well as contextual orienta-tion that predominated around 1986. In this line, the shift of views about intelligence parallels the mainstream shift in metaphors of mind from natural sciences to computer sciences.

Moreover, according to Sigel (1986), psychologists seem nowadays to wallow increasingly in diversity and fragmentation not only of subject matter but also in terms of the way intelligence is studied.

There is thus something of a paradox insofar as experts both agree and disagree about the definition of intelligence on several dimensions: classical, dilemmatic, and across decades; single or multiple; the indi-vidual versus culture. One explanation may be that experts have accen-tuated the diversity and fragmentation of their work, as a consequence of some kind of logic of development of scientific endeavour. A complemen-tary explanation may be that experts tend to disagree among themselves in the course of inventing theories (or even must disagree, in order to produce and maintain professional distinctiveness!), while converging in their views when called upon to present themselves to colleagues in symposia or fair-play-like situations or when they have to diffuse their theories to lay persons or amateurs. A third explanation would be that science is not a unitary discourse, but reflects different general *Weltanschauungen*. The investigation of intelligence as an educational phenomenon has different aims and objectives from the investigation of intelligence as a problem for cognitive science.

An example of the effort to match the aims of education and the perspective of cognitive science is Gardner's (1983) plea in favour of a theory of 'multiple intelligences' that spans the range of previous theories and the claims of the nature–nurture dilemma. Recently, Kornhaber, Krechewsky, and Gardner (1990) assumed that the key features of almost all definitions of intelligence have no less to do with the competences inside one's head than with the values and opportunities afforded by society to engage these competences. For instance, even in a universally developing competence like language, it is only in the interaction of adult and child that such a faculty develops. Societies teach their chidren those bodies of facts, theories, skills, and methods that comprise its various domains of knowledge, ranging from fishing to physics.

Discussing the different views held in Japan and the US, the authors underline that in Japan the development of intelligence is fostered by widely shared values (i.e. school, achievement, and diligent study), which in turn are supported by the institutions of the society. Furthermore, societal values support both schooling and an emphasis on effort and motivation rather than innate abilities. This positive picture of Japan is counterbalanced with respect to the US. America's break with tradition-bound learning coincident with its love for new technologies, may have rendered it especially vulnerable to explanations of intelligence borrowed from hereditarian views and allowed the eugenics movement to take hold in the US. Science, with its paper-and-pencil tests and factor analyses, supported the view that white, Christian, northern Europeans possessed the most intelligence. In the minds of many, these people came from the best genetic stock. Thus America came to believe that intelligence was born and not made. As Gould noted (1981), the rendering of the concept of intelligence into a reified, inherited trait was an 'American invention' (p. 147).

This careful, critical diagnosis of the ways in which intelligence is a matter of the interplay of shared cultural values and the historical vicissitudes of these values is a good example of the central value-laden role intelligence has in present societies, apart from the effort scholars make to describe and explain it in terms of academic language.

## What the experts tell parents about development

If we take as an example the period from 1955 to 1984 (Young, 1990) two trends can be observed in what experts tell (write to) parents. The first trend is research driven as experts have used psychological research of the past thirty years as the basis for the information and advice they present to parents. The results of a thematic content analysis indicate that research-driven advice is most evident in domains that focus on aspects of infant biological development such as perception, cognition, and temperament. Equally powerful is a second trend that in certain areas expert advice is more clearly based on the broader social context and changing demographics. It was particularly seen in the domains of mother–infant relationships, working mothers and child care, feeding practices, and fathers. The parental role was emphasized as psychologists presented information about the infant's perceptual and cognitive abilities. Specifically Piagetian tasks were communicated to parents as activities to do with the infant. Thus, parents were encouraged to provide the infant with, for instance, different-coloured objects, or to allow the infant to explore the environment actively. The experts also spoke of more interactive forms of infant stimulation such as 'pat-a-cake' and 'peek-a-boo' games. In addition, from the mid-1950s, experts stopped giving advice about the centrality of the maternal role and began to write about the quality of the interactions between mother and infant.

Moreover, since 1975, the percentage of articles devoted to working mothers and child care for infants has increased markedly. Concurrently, since the mid-1970s, this topic has been the focus of a significant amount of empirical investigation. Finally, although magazines gave helpful advice, they also stated it was better if mothers did not work when the infant was very young and at times suggested mothers use informal sources of child care. This inconsistent response may be due to the competing ideologies of motherhood, work, and child care. On the one hand, our society considers a full-time mother 'every child's birthright'; on the other, it values the personal growth associated with women successfully combining motherhood and a career. Similarly, within the scientific community there have been conflicting opinions about the effects of early group care on infant development. As a result, differing opinions can be found in both the scientific and the parent literature; moreover, the cultural and historical contexts in which experts find themselves cannot be easily divorced from the information and advice they give parents.

## Development according to parents

The history of research on parents' ideas goes back to parents' expectations and attitudes, went into a decline during an era of insistence on the value of attending only to overt behaviour, and has recently been revived with a marked cognitive emphasis: for example, with reference to ideas, beliefs, concepts, or attributions rather than attitudes (Goodnow, 1988). The revival has been sparked in part by the view that parents' ideas are an interesting form of adult social cognition; extending an area of research that has concentrated on younger subjects and potentially providing evidence of adult development.

The point has now been established that parents do hold a variety of views about children and development, and that these views are not always in agreement with formal psychology or with the characteristics of the children that parents are judging. The content agenda covers starting points and steps in the course of development, the contributions of internal and external conditions, the desirable goals and end-states, optimal and reasonable methods and the particular influence and responsibility of parents in upbringing.

One of the keys of the puzzle connnecting these content areas seems to be the most general issue of hereditary vs. environmental determinants of development. Miller (1988) suggests that most parents adhere to some sort of interactionist matching, in which both factors are afforded a role (p. 265). Neverthless, positions on the heredity vs. environment issue may vary across parents as a function of the amount of their experience with children, and across the different types of ability under scrutiny (e.g. infant achievements are seen as more biologically based than later achievements).

A further key to the puzzle concerns the origins or sources of ideas about development and related topics (Goodnow, 1988). A contrasting pair of models are represented. According to the first model, ideas are self-constructed, built up from an individual's direct experience. This model is to be found in some comparisons of mothers with fathers, parents of younger children with parents of older children, and parents with a varying number of children. In these comparisons, self-construction is seen as the major process underlying the effects of personal experience, giving rise either to complete personal construction or to simple modification after first internalizing the views of others.

Some authors have proposed that it is only in the context of concrete problem-solving or decision-making that parents make use of what they have learned during parenting. On this basis, it is the demand for goal-oriented action, rather than for statements of opinions and knowledge, that allows the effects of experience to emerge. The possibility that direct experiences have only a temporary effect has been already shown (De Grada and Ponzo, 1971): when people are dealing with children of a particular age, their ideas about the competence of children of that age may be fairly accurate. Once the children are beyond that age, however, both parents and teachers may fall back on estimates based on general images of children as 'babies' or starting to grow up, with an accompanying increase in error.

Thus, experiences with children may not be the only critical forms of personal experiences. Information comes from experience with media images, the diffusion of scientific knowledge, and from the form of parents' paid work. Paid work may influence parents' ideas by highlighting the importance of particular qualities such as self-direction or conformity. A Californian study takes the issue of potential conflict between paid work and family (Greenberger and Goldberg, 1988). It asks about the extent to which parents' views of children are influenced by the experience of 'role strain', and by the extent to which they perceive their spouses as supportive. For both fathers and mothers, higher levels of role strain were associated with more negative perceptions of children. For mothers but not for fathers a joint commitment to work and parenting was associated with more positive perceptions of children. For fathers but not for mothers a low commitment to parenting was associated with role strain. Such results are complex; they illustrate, however, that the dialectics between paid work and family often apply to both parents and may have differential effects upon their views of children.

The argument of paid work may well introduce the second model of possible sources of parents' ideas. Many of ideas we hold may be considered as 'social constructions' or 'received knowledge'. If economic or cultural conditions call for restrictions on the size of the paid workforce, for instance, then images will be constructed – vulnerable children who need total care, incompetent older people who should retire – that justify the restriction (Gloger-Tippelt and Tippelt, 1986). In another example, the shift of paid work from a home-base to factories and the restrictions of women to unpaid work at home promotes an image of women and children as forming a unit and sharing a number of similar qualities (Kessen, 1979).

In this sense, these images form 'cultural messages', 'cultural scripts', 'collective wisdom', 'folk models' or 'ethnotheories' (D'Andrade, 1987; Quinn and Holland, 1987; Flick, chapter 3 this volume; Oyserman and Markus, chapter 7 this volume); they are likely to show larger variations across cultural or social groups than within them. This contrasting model underlies several comparisons of cultural groups. The contrasts have sometimes been between mothers in different countries. More often, the contrast has been between groups within a country, sparked by the presence of immigrants. Larger differences than in the first model have yielded a variety of content areas: concepts of infants as vulnerable versus resilient; or as needing a single caretaker versus being able to benefit from several; concepts of children as needing or not needing to be taught language; developmental timetables and the degree of importance attached to obedience.

Summing up theses results, Goodnow and Collins (1990) suggest that the amount of difference in almost every content areas gives rise to the necessity of selecting specific experiences that are likely to be salient to parents. The concept of salience implies several questions. The critical question is where and how salient experiences are to be found. These experiences may not be located in parents' direct experiences with their own chidlren but in experiences outside the family. For instance, the quality of father's paid work may be the main influence on the extent to which parents value conformity in children. In a more insidious fashion, the ideas held about parenting may represent a spread or extension of ideas held about other areas of living. Part of being 'modern', for example, is to consider that everything can be and should be improved, that a better way can and should be found. Such ideas start from the world of economic production and appear to spread to the production of 'good parents' or 'good children'.

Furthermore, a society or a family may present more than one collective wisdom, and individuals or groups may vary in the way they respond to the diversity. There may, in fact, be competing messages. Given this situation, one may begin to ask about the nature of the competition or about the way in which individuals or groups respond to being presented with competing messages.

In fact, we have shown above how 1921 and 1986 experts in intelligence both agree and disagree about some crucial themes which contain conflicting and competing explanations of what intelligence is: single vs. multiple; innate vs. environmental.

### From cultural models to social representations

At this point one may ask the question of the relationship between experts' and laypersons' views of intelligence and development. In other terms, how do parents operate, when forming and sharing ideas on these topics? Do experts start from everyday ideas or prevailing cultural messages of their specific historical period, and try to transform them, allowing them a scientific flavour? As in the case of intelligence, where theories are at any time influenced by the prevailing cultural metaphors of mind or human beings, adults' or parents' views may be best approached by analysing the socio-cultural conditions from which parents have to produce ideas about development.

How to approach this point? The cultural models approach seems at first glance fairly appropriate as far as a cultural model is seen as 'a cognitive schema that is intersubjectively shared by a social group' and is 'a presupposed and taken-for-granted tool for representing some salient themes of the world that are widely shared' (D'Andrade, 1987; Quinn and Holland, 1987). Basically, scholars interested in cultural models emphasize three qualities of information 'out there'. It is social information that is shared with others and comes from others. It often comes with a demand for learning. And it is often not singular in form. In fact, the individuals are likely to encounter a variety of views on the same topic, some contradictory to others. In a sense, people are likely to be told both that 'intelligence is a matter of chance, or providence' and that 'intelligence is mainly a matter of responsibility as a parent' (from both the genes and the quality of the ways of bringing up the child). What we would underline here is the recognition that there is often social pressure to acquire particular items of knowledge. Learning these items is demanded as part of being an adult member of a culture. For instance, in the section entitled 'What the experts tell parents about development' (see p. 173) we illustrated the content and its shifting over time of what experts were telling and advising parents about the infant's skills and methods of bringing up children.

This example also points out that expert knowledge is selectively diffused and changed over time in terms of both the content and the emphasis given to some issues instead of others. Thus the presence of several views both within experts' and everyday knowledge raises the question of what the dynamics are of producing, reproducing, and changing parents' ideas. In other terms: Does plurality matter? One consequence is the feasibility of change. When people hold or have access to double or multiple theories, how do they manage them? They may treat them as resources or tools to be used when suitable and set them aside when not. Thus change may be seen as elements of societal views being shuffled into a different overall pattern with a different weighting of priorities.

Let us take the case of parents. As we have already shown, a tremendous variety of content areas have been illustrated, and the influence of direct experiences, prevailing cultural messages, uncertainty about the future, responsibility, wishes concerning desirable end states have all been reviewed. What clearly emerges is that ideas about intelligence, development, and every kind of content area are by no means simply a matter of the unsolicited gathering of free information. The social cognition approach to these contents underlines a way of interpreting this body of evidence by simply checking how far parents are accurate observers or inference makers, or how far they are biased by short-cuts, handy heuristics, or the extent to which they are simply sloppy in their everyday thinking or problem-solving. This approach seems exceedingly and inappropriately reductionist (Carugati, 1990a, 1990b).

A more parsimonious and ecological approach to the unpaid job of 'being a parent' is to acknowledge that parents have to cope with some salient experiences, from which inescapable questions arise. First, they have daily experiences of the frequency and extent of interindividual difference between children in intelligent behaviour, character, personality, etc. Second, these differences are confronted and evaluated (more often when they concern negative behaviours, negatively considered characteristics, lack of abilities) with some prototypical 'normal' or 'ideal' images of the child. But this comparison is not primarily a matter of information processing as far as it has strong links with the way parents define their identity as a parent, and feel responsible for it.

Thus parents find themseleves daily at the crossroads of salient and socially value-laden experiences of differences, for which both experts and parents have no ultimate exhaustive explanations; moreover, parents may feel themselves provoked by differences, responsible for them and pressed to make decisions, even if they subjectively lack information (explanations) about what they should intervene on. This is a really puzzling (and perhaps uncomfortable) situation, where social identity might play a central organizing role in selecting, accentuating, moulding self-constructed and culturally received general ideas, daily practices, images of bright or mediocre children.

Early studies of social representations considered the unconscious (Moscovici, [1961]1976), illness (Herzlich, 1973), and the mentally ill (Jodelet, [1989a]1991) as puzzling and unfamiliar themes, in the present case it is interindividual differences between children which provoke adults (especially parents or teachers) to think about an unfamiliar theme, which they need to familiarize in order to be able to take responsiblity for it and to make a decision about it. From this point of view, social representations are by no means primarily information processing of strange social stimuli but organizing principles of ideas, normative prototypes, and social practices, which are the rough products of the thinking society.

Two crucial points are prominent in our choice of approaching the issue of ideas concerning children and development through the theory of social representations (Mugny and Carugati, [1985]1989). The first refers to origins: that is to say, the specific conditions under which adults are concerned with intelligence and development as a matter of gift and maturation or in a more interactive perspective. The second point is the investigation of relationships between different contents in social representations. In particular, we described a model which links more general topics such as development, to more specific ones, such as learning processes and even more concretely to the images of the child implied by the degree of perceived influence, which may be considered a mediator between representations and practices (see Doise, Mugny and Pérez, chapter 5 this volume). We also intend to 'throw a stone' into the sea of definitions used when talking about social representations, and try to define in a more explicit way the various steps of our approach. For this purpose, we propose to define (1) *conceptions*, the interconnected set of ideas (like the items of questionnaires) about a specific topic (such as intelligence in general or development of intelligence) – thus the factors emerging from statistical analyses of a set of items may be labelled as conceptions; (2) *theories* are those topics which are linked together and comprise different conceptions, while (3) *social representations* are the set of theories moulded by social dynamics and role conflicts.

In the first study of social representations of intelligence and development (Mugny and Carugati, [1985]1989) we documented the central function of the theory of natural inequalities as an anchoring explanatory principle of the multiple meanings of the phenomena labelled 'intelligence', and more specifically the role played by the intriguing and, to some extent, mysterious question of the unequal distribution of intelligence among individuals.

Why though, after all, should these interindividual differences seem so strange? Our hypothesis maintains that they seem to be so for those people who subjectively do not have an alternative explanatory model at their disposal. We can assume that some individuals may have access to and trust specific information (borrowed, for instance, from scientific disciplines considered as explanations of this topic). At this level, the sophistication of the explanation is fairly unimportant: what matters here is people's belief or confidence in the interpretive power of a given model, which they can adopt if need be, without actually knowing it. Thus the subjective inexplicability and lack of information about alternative explanations ought to give salience to the question of interindividual differences as the topic which may be explained, for instance, by the reference to a 'theory of naturally gifted inequalities'. These theoretically grounded dynamics have been shown in a first study (Mugny and

Carugati, [1985]1989, ch. 4) where adults who acknowledge that they lack information and feel intelligence to be inexplicable are prone to describe it as a gift, flavoured with both cybernetic and social attributes (computer and mathematical subjects at school are the prototype of intelligence, but intelligence is also awareness and respect for rules and social norms, and it should be encouraged by every kind of educational practice!). Moreover, systematic pressures on children, which must be applied through school experiences, are seen as means for intelligence to manifest itself, and clear responsibilities are attributed to teachers and their competences.

Furthermore, social identities can be considerd as steering the socio-cognitive management of the conception of intelligence in terms of natural gift. The main assumption of this identity principle is that specific ways of interconnecting various content areas are produced by social categories for whom intelligence is a salient part of everyday experiences and for whom it constitutes a significant part of their identity. It is primarily in parents (and, for similar reasons, in teachers) that the explanation of interindividual differences in terms of gifted intelligence is a response to their daily experience. Moreover, parents, who do in fact make intellectual differences salient, show more marked divergence between their judgements of bright and mediocre children (particularly in school subjects, such as mathematics vs. drawing, for instance) in terms of gifted intelligence. Reciprocally, non-parents regard bright children in mathematics as fortunate members of bright families of high socio-economic and cultural status. Again, the refusal by parents to 'blame the family' does confirm the role social identities play in producing ideas and judgements.

As well as in these general effects, social identities have also been proved effective, when divergent opinions clash as a result of different identities. The case in point is mothers who also have a job outside the home, compared with full-time mothers (Mugny and Carugati, [1985]1989, ch. 6). The latter category accentuates a maturationist view of intelligence, as well as the importance of socio-emotional equilibrium with adults and between peers, and the image of the gifted child. Working mothers are, to some extent, more defensive against some socially inspired (cf. the earlier discussion of the changing advice experts give mothers!) 'bad conscience' about not being sufficiently involved with their children.

The dynamic of identification in mothers with different professional roles (shown with reference to intelligence and development) was also confirmed in the complementary topic of character (Emiliani and Molinari, 1989). When talking about their own children (aged two–six) mothers (housewives, office workers, teachers) anchor their discourse in character as a way to give meaning to the actual skills of their children and their development. Character is, in mothers' words, a natural property (like a gift, more often in its positive version: 'good character', 'strong character', or 'obstinate') already present at birth, rooted in parental heredity and subject to little influence by family upbringing.

The prominence of the idea of character, and the images of their own children prompted us to expand the general themes of development, and to undertake further empirical inquiries among various groups of mothers about such topics as character, temperament and learning, different images of children and the relationships between ideas and practices. These themes were explored through the analysis of mothers' perceived influence over children's development.

When looking for a logic to the connectedness of women's ideas, we have to acknowledge that these ideas are by no means a site of incoherence or arbitrariness. A systematic pattern of results (Carugati, Emiliani, and Molinari, 1990) confirms as the main source of representations of child development the inexplicability of interindividual differences, at the level both of the subjective acknowledgement that intelligence and character are by no means explicable, and of a subjective lack of information about how much the scientific disciplines may contribute to the explanation of child development. What is worth noting is that as far as mothers (vs. women who are not mothers) do feel intelligence is inexplicable, and subjectively lack information about it, they consider intelligence as a natural gift unequally distributed among children, and that learning is spontaneous maturation. Incidentally, this is the case particularly for mothers of girls!

But this is only one part of the story. Being mothers is not enough, as far as mothers' professional identity plays a significant role in moulding their ideas about child development. The case in point is mothers who are also teachers. What characterizes their discourse (vs. housewives' and office workers') is a conflicting picture of children in general (as autonomous and intelligent), and of their own children in particular, as being dependent upon adults. Where does this conflict come from? Teachers do disagree firmly with the traditional division of housework and parental roles within the family; they demand an active commitment from their partners with their children. Teachers do not seem to be worried about traditional educational practices (toilet training, obedience); on the contrary, they consider that for their own children autonomy, curiosity, and adaptability towards the world are what is important, and this is what they believe they are able to influence. Surprisingly enough, teachers describe their own children in terms of dependency (experienced as painful by both the mother and the child). One may ask here whether some kind of idealized child as 'autonomous and intelligent' will influence some parents' behaviours. A tentative illustration of this point is the correlation between the image of autonomous and intelligent child and the conversational styles teachers use in their daily verbal interactions with children (aged two–six years: cf. Molinari and Emiliani, 1990). In fact, teachers show more frequently a narrative (vs. dialogical) style, in which the speaker takes for granted that the child has the ability to understand the story they are telling them, whithout monitoring the child's comprehension (by, for instance, asking the child to retell some aspects of the story).

### Intelligence, development, learning, and the child: telling more and better than we know

Far from dissolving into a sequence of errors and biases and an absence of a logic, everyday thought seems to have a coherence of its own, and is a type of rationality which actually assumes a cognitive polyphasia, in that it is based on a multiplicity of different orders of reasoning and a diversity of socio-cognitive functions which accounts for the specificity of the way different groups talk about interrelated topics concerning development and the child.

In order to show how rich and original these discourses are, as far as we take into account a specific category of people like mothers, a general model has been outlined in three steps (Molinari, Emiliani, and Carugati, 1992). The first one is concerned with the origins of social representations. Four different sources have been chosen as relevant for the theory of gift and development: the first source is the subjective lack of scientific models of explanations, while the second refers to the relative awareness of inexplicability. Two other sources were added: (1) sharing the idea that biology and mathematics are important for the explanation of children's development (it is assumed that subjects who share such an opinion would agree with a biological perspective); (2) viewing psychology and social psychology as important disciplines would lead to sharing an interactionist view of development.

These four sources were found to be significantly related to only one general conception of children's development shared by our subjects: character as a natural gift expresses the idea that nature unequally distributes several characteristics (in particular, autonomy and firmness) among children. It is worth noting that the dimension of social interaction, which contains items that are viewed as influencing socio-emotional development, was not linked with any of the sources.

Surprisingly enough, despite the fact that some academic psychological models do support the importance of early interaction for the child, from our mother's eyes such disciplines are assimilated to the mainstream natural sciences; thus, consistently, psychology and social psychology are seen as distinct from the conception that children develop through interaction with social agents.

In the second step, these two general conceptions were found to be connected with that of learning processes. On the one hand, character as natural gift with learning as spontaneous maturation; on the other hand, social interaction with learning through social interaction, the latter conception stressing the importance of relationships with teachers and schoolmates.

Finally, how do mothers link these general conceptions with their perceived influence over their own children? This third step should be considered as a crucial one for the understanding of the links between ideas and practices (at least, in terms of perceived influence). In particular, we focused on the perceived influence over two different images of one's own child, that is, the autonomous child and the intelligent and sociable child.

The evidence is fairly clear: those mothers who agree with learning as spontaneous maturation do not feel they can exert much influence over the characteristics of intelligence and autonomy in their own children. On the other hand, those mothers who agree on the importance of social interactions for learning also perceive a fairly high degree of influence over the autonomy and intelligence of their own children.

This general pattern allows us to draw some theoretical considerations. First, among the category of mothers, two theories of children's development are prominent; the theory of gift, however, is grounded on an interconnected set of sources of information, which is not the case for the social interaction theory. This difference is illustrated by considering the specific content of the theory of gift, which is concerned with the question of interindividual differences, a topic particularly salient for those categories of people who daily interact with children; those mothers who do not have any interpretation for interindividual differences or who refer to biological models (or both) are prone to consider development a gift unequally distributed among children. In other words, when directly confronted with interindividual differences, people may feel a gap between the information at their disposal and the information necessary to account for this phenomenon. This gap seems to be filled by a confidence in biology and mathematics as a way to give meaning to the interindividual differences.

It is worth noting the relationships between this couple of disciplines, as far as biology could be seen (from an academic eye) as the cause of human abilities, whereas mathematics could be seen much more as the product or the 'thermometer' of these same abilities: but in the creative realm of social thinking, people assemble both disciplines in a phenomenal causation where effects play the same role as causes. In this amazing form of rationality, which is genuinely social psychological, the theory of naturally gifted inequalities permeates and gives meaning to the whole set of ideas from academic disciplines, through learning processes, to the perceived non-influence on salient child's characteristics.

### Concluding remarks

According to Kagan (1984) the behaviour of the infant is so ambiguous that it is easy for the culture's beliefs about human nature to influence observers' interpretations of what they think they see. Given that observers may be experts and parents, what we wanted to make clear here is that the conceptions both experts and parents share about crucial topics of child development turn around the dilemma of viewing it as natural process much like the growth of an animal or plant, versus the view of development as a matter of interplay between social agents.

About this crucial dilemma, which can be seen as a cornerstone or a cultural stake for both experts and laypeople, a continuing and controversial conversation is produced and consumed over decades both among and between them. In the course of these secular dialogues, people, and particularly children, were being classified and declassified, valorized and devalorized, according to one value, and the multiplicity of discourses concerning intelligence. Any generation of experts or parents can do it without explaining intelligence, development, value-laden images of childhood and educational practices, according to the experience or the social position they occupy in their historical and ecological niches.

In this way, the give and take between experts and parents is a switching melody circling around the surface issue about the nature of intelligence, whether in terms of intelligence as natural gift or as a by-product of social relationships. But viewed more deeply, the ethical issue of parents' responsibility for bringing up children leaps before our eyes as far as parents' ways of organizing a discourse around these issues is by no means arbitrary or cumulative; on the contrary, it depends on their particular socio-cognitive position concerning specific and dilemmatic phenomena for which they have to negotiate explanations compatible with the responsibility society attributes to parents. In fact parents, in some sense, modulate their representations according to the requirements both of their social identities (and parents' responsibility should be seen as a generative part of their own identity!) and of the target (their own children's chracteristics).

The choice of studying the dynamics of creating and recreating images and conceptions in different subcategories of mothers was by no means a matter of finding yet another way of blaming mothers; we decided to question mothers only to make clear the interplay between social responsibility and social identities, on the one hand, and the issue of constructing a discourse about salient topics of the development of children whom mothers have to bring up. If experts have a timeless opportunity to agree, disagree, and circle around the crucial topic of intelligence and development, to the point of identifying themselves with and vigorously defending their own more or less narrow theory, parents (who form part of experts' lay audience!) have neither the freedom nor the time to wait for the ultimately true scientific model to emerge. Thus parents (and mothers after all!) are cognitive prodigals, in the sense that they create and recreate such things as intelligence and development as a matter both of abstract competence and of social conformism; bright and mediocre children as both socially and mathematically gifted; school as the temple of manifestation of intelligent behaviour. It seems to be a creative borrowing from the partial models experts produce and introduce into the wider cultural market of ideas, which they have already drawn from as members of that culture. The art of playing a single theme against itself, mastered by experts, is thus replaced in parents as laypeople, by the art of fugue, an art which is usually based on one theme which is played by several voices in different ways, at different tempi, as inversion or reversed (Moscovici, 1990). But the art of playing the fugue about child development and related topics could be seen as governed by the moral issue of responsibility: an issue that should be given a central position in studies concerned with what a culture, and particularly its institutional representatives for child development (parents and their counterpart, the experts) say about children and children's development.

# 12 Social representations and media communications

*Carlo Michael Sommer*

## Introduction

Any consideration of social representations also means a consideration of communication; social representations originate in communication, they are manifested in it and they influence it. While there is a general acknowledgement or assumption about the relevance of communication for social representations, the specific relationships between them are seldom studied explicitly. This is the case particularly for communication through the mass media. In this contribution, the relationship between TV communication and social representations will be examined more closely.

After a brief presentation of some basic aspects of the theory of social representation, there is an analysis of the role of TV communication in the formation and diffusion of social representations. This is followed by considerations of the role of social representations in the process of media communication. Finally, possible consequences of recent developments in communication technology for the diffusion of social representations will be discussed.

## Social representation

The theory of social representations (cf., e.g., Moscovici, 1981) conceptualizes the cognitive structure and the social dynamics of popular knowledge. Social representations are more or less popular cognitive representations of relevant social phenomena. These phenomena include scientific theories (e.g, psychoanalysis, physics), social roles (woman, child) or such phenomena as 'illness' or 'culture'. The concept of social representations has both structural and dynamic aspects. Structural aspects include representational field (content, hierarchy, and area of validity), knowledge (quantity, quality, and differentiation), and attitude towards the object represented. The central dynamic processes in social representation are objectification and anchoring. Objectification means that particular 'catchy' elements are disconnected from a general inventory of knowledge (for example, the knowledge of psychoanalysis) and joined together in a specific elaboration to make a new coherent 'figurative schema'. The figurative schema of psychoanalysis, for example, consists of the contrast between the conscious and the subconscious, the 'harmful mechanism' of repression in between, and the resulting 'complex'. Another central term in psychoanalysis, however, 'libido', has not entered the figurative schema because it engenders too much societal conflict potential.

This moderated scientific model can then be used as a common pattern for interpretation in everyday life, where a second level of objectification begins to operate. The figurative schema, abstract and hypothetical at first, is increasingly reified and ontologized – in the terminology of social representation, it is 'naturalized'. This means the schema becomes a 'perceivable thing'; 'the subject believes that it "perceives", in the world around it, unhappy unconsciousnesses, rampant repression, and old complexes' (Herzlich, 1972, p. 313). Finally, in the process of anchoring, the social image becomes a functional pattern for interpretation which constitutes social causality, social justification, and social differentiation.

Social representations are not equally distributed within society. One can differentiate between general and group-specific knowledge. For example, all groups in a society have a common core of the representation of psychoanalysis. Around this core, however, there is group-specific variation, so that, for example, psychoanalysis is differently represented by psychoanalysts than by Catholic priests. These differences can be attributed to the specific lifestyles, norms, values, and identities of the different groups. Accordingly, the specific variations of a social representation can be interpreted as manifestations of group membership.

### The role of the media in the process of social representation

The first empirical study of social representations (Moscovici, [1961] 1976) – on the representation of psychoanalysis in France – already employed media analysis. As in later studies, too, the mass media were regarded as an external memory for society-specific or group-specific knowledge. The analysis of this part of 'objective culture' (Mannheim, 1954) provides information on the culture-specific core and the subcultural variations of a social representation, which can then be completed by individual-based data of the 'subjective culture'. The chronological and functional order of these data pools which commonly goes from scientific publications via more or less popular writing to written or oral everyday utterings finally allows conclusions to be drawn about the formation of social representations (see Kruse, chapter 13 this volume). This process, however, is rarely examined as a whole. The majority of studies are 'snapshots' of the process of diffusion which usually analyze verbal communication in print media. Investigations of audiovisual media are rare.

In the following, I will discuss the role of television in the formation and the function of social representations. Of all the mass media, television can be considered particularly relevant for social representations. It has definitely changed fundamentally the diffusion of information in our society both quantitatively and qualitatively. This change has specific consequences for more or less all structural and dynamic aspects of social representations.

Each medium enlarges the opportunities to communicate. However, at the price that the construction of reality is subject to its specific rules. In oral cultures, communication, and the associated construction of reality as well as the authenticity of that construction, is connected to the individual and thus limited in time and space. The culture of literacy made the dissolution of this connection possible, and the diffusion of objectified reality constructions via mass media promoted a standardization of ideas. Television in its classical form, addressing itself to a large and dispersed audience and demanding less qualification than literacy, intensified this effect. In addition, the speed of transmission in TV communication accelerates, as a rule, the diffusion of ideas. The main difference between television and other media, however, is its specific relationship with reality outside media communication:

Of all forms of reconstruction of reality television has the closest resemblance to 'primary' reality. It gives the impression of reproducing, not constructing, reality. The written word always indicates its mediating function, it is a process of abstraction in which the constructive activity of the author remains obvious. Photography produces iconically realistic reproductions, but it always makes evident that these are selected or constructed manifestations of reality. Even the most naturalistic photograph has no sound or motion. Television has got both and therefore gives the impression of something authentic and verifiable by one's own eyes. This is particularly true for the representation of persons; and television as a medium of moving images tends to personalize even abstract information.

Goffmann (1959) has distinguished two types of information that people can communicate about themselves: the information given more or less consciously by a person, and the information given off unconsciously and uncontrolled. The former is mainly conveyed in verbal communication, the latter comes through non-verbal channels like mimickry, or gestures. Since this latter information is commonly not considered as subject to deliberate control, it is regarded as a particularly reliable and authentic kind of information about a person. Television, in contrast to other media, also provides this information, thus reinforcing the effect of authenticity. Moreover, not only live programmes and the increasing number of pre-produced mock 'live' shows but also the typical use of the verbal present tense suggest to viewers that they are direct eye witnesses to the events shown. The specific reception context, too, helps to reinforce the closeness to reality. Watching television, unlike, for example, going to the cinema, is not something that takes place outside normal everyday life, but is rather naturally integrated in the familiar environment of the home.

Paradoxically, this closeness to reality in both presentation and reception is opposed by an extreme degree of construction on the side of production. Shows and programmes, form and content, are meticulously planned and produced. From the vast amount of information available only a small fraction will be selected. 'Merely depicting' an event, for example, in the course of a live transmission actually includes various constructive activities like selecting takes, cutting the material, etc. Additionally, there are a number of other constructive activities, some conscious, some unconscious. So, for example, persons appearing on a television programme will be given explicit instructions about how to conduct themselves, or the protagonists themselves may wilfully or unknowingly manipulate the impressions they 'give' or 'give off'.

Presumably, the protagonists will have a general social representation of how to behave when on television, and they will bring their actual behaviour into line with this idea. This already will most likely result in a standardization of conduct on television. Correspondingly, programmes like the German show *Verzeih mir* ('Forgive me') where people become reconciled in front of the TV audience can be interpreted as normative institutions: the various and mainly private ways to handle interpersonal conflicts are standardized according to the rules of the medium and made public all over the transmission area.

As a rule, the result of televisionary construction is less ambiguous and more schematic than in reality not mediated by television. People on TV programmes appear more stereotypical than in the context of everyday life (Roloff, 1981). It is by no means conclusive that such representations will be transferred into everyday life, for example, onto actually existing persons (cf., e.g., Six, 1989; Winterhoff-Spurk, 1989, p. 94). Such a transfer, however, does seem to take place whenever the recipients do not have personal experience with the objects, concepts, events, or persons in question (cf. Winterhoff-Spurk, 1989, p. 105), i.e. particularly when these are new to the recipients and not yet fully understood and integrated into thinking. If this is the case then personalization and closeness to reality permit an objectification and anchoring of the new representations in everyday life. Especially in the ritual that is exercised in the reconciliation show *Verzeih mir* a feedback into everyday thinking and acting seems very probable. The gap between TV reality and everyday reality seems particularly narrow in 'reality-TV' programmes with their authentic people and authentic fates, with their real tears, and with an outcome decided live in front of the cameras. But this transfer thesis still has to be empirically validated.

There is no doubt that the predominance of TV communication has not only resulted in the televisual adaptation of all kinds of topics, events, and persons, but also in planning and producing more and more events of 'primary reality' according to the rules of TV reality from the start. A German priest who has used the *Verzeih mir*-scenario in his parochial work proves that this not only holds for events aimed at large audiences, such as events in politics, sports, or music.

To sum up, we can draw the following conclusion for the distribution of social representations via television: television accelerates and standardizes the diffusion of social representations; it accentuates the fundamental processes of the elaboration and application of social representations.

The search for new topics typical for this medium, and the large-scale production of realistic and at the same time stereotypic programmes for the greatest possible audience help objectification, that is, first of all, the fast, general elaboration of a sharply contoured figurative schema. The realistic way of representation also supports the naturalization, i.e. the ontologification of the schema into a 'perceivable thing', the transfer of the schema from the reality on screen into everyday reality. Similarity to reality and, even more so, the person-centered form of representation provide suitable models for the anchoring of social representations into the *Lebenswelt* (life world). Here, the representation serves as a self-evident explanation and justification of everyday action. The fact that this action is always guided by group specific interests, values, and attitudes results in specific variations of social representations. Finally, today's predominance of TV communication may also result in a specific selection of social representations: concepts that are especially suited for appropriate processing in the media have the best chance of diffusion.

Two examples can illustrate this process: first, the elaboration of social representations of a social group, and second, the diffusion of a scientific theory.

*The example of 'punk'*

The 'punk' movement started in Great Britain in the late 1970s: Young people dressing in a rebellious and dramatizing manner as the 'trash of society', making loud and unprofessional music and producing unprofessionally pieced-together insider magazines. This movement, in the beginning rather diffuse, was soon discovered by the press, the music industry and also by television. Under the label 'punk', they started the elaboration and objectification of a figurative schema which the first and original punks were surely not aware of to that extent: 'No future', an aggressive demonstration of disrespect for all social and aesthetic norms, found its illustrative manifestation in aggressively coloured spike hair, safety-pins pierced through cheeks, ragged clothes, etc. The worldwide diffusion of this stereotype by means of realistic TV pictures of 'real' punks, together with a typifying commentary facilitated its anchoring in everyday thinking. Viewers all over the world were now able to identify nonconformist youths as punks, to find explanations for their behaviour, and to react accordingly. People visited them – for example in Berlin – like a tourist attraction, but otherwise they were anxious to avoid them and kept them at a distance.

The youths, too, discovered a strongly contoured image in the media which they could use as an explanation, justification, and as a unifying model for their mostly diffuse and contradictory stylings. (For a closer description of this process, see Sommer, 1989; Sommer and Wind, 1991; 1986). The fact that dispersed minorities can identify themselves as belonging to the same group via television has been considered as one of the fundamental effects of this medium (Meyrowitz, 1987).

*The example of 'chaos theory'*

With respect to media communication, the social representation of chaos theory is particularly interesting. It can be said without exaggeration that the social representation of chaos theory is inconceivable without the media – without computers and television, to be precise. This theory, highly popular at present, can be traced back to mathematical phenomena which had already been described at the beginning of this century by French mathematicians. The extraordinary success, however, of chaos theory in almost every scientific field, and even in everyday thinking, required a combination of three elements: computer technology, television, and a specific condition of societal thinking.

Only with computers did it become possible to undertake the extensive calculations that were necessary numerically to verify the hypothesis that slight changes in initial conditions could give rise to strikingly strong effects. (Some critics of chaos theory even say that rounding up or down certain figures in the computerized calculations alone is responsible for these effects.) Additionally, computer graphics facilitated quick, simple, and attractive visualization of these and other aspects of chaos theory. So the theory has already brought along the objectification and material illustration of its figurative schema. This could be described by the paradox 'order within disorder' and its variations 'identity within variety', 'the big in the small', 'predictability of the unpredictable', etc. It is this illustrative vividness that made chaos theory interesting for all visual media. Following what was said above, this is so because, in the age of the media, the concepts which have the best chance of diffusion are those which are best suited for processing in the media.

Personal computers and television facilitated a quick and worldwide diffusion of such images. And television enabled scientists of various origins to demonstrate the ubiquity of 'chaos' in catchy phrases ('butterfly effect', 'owl attractor', 'apple-man'). At the same time it provided the matching 'authentic' pictures of hurricanes, overpopulated continents, or turmoil at the stock exchange. Although some scientists would not accept a transfer on to these and other areas, 'chaos' has become 'visible' everywhere. More than that: every PC (personal computer) user was now able to 'generate' chaos in a 'scientific' way and 'discover' it in their own *Lebenswelt*.

The anchoring of the social representation in everyday life could take its course. Chaos became a functional pattern of interpretation which was readily used for the purposes of social causality, social justification, and social differentiation. At first management consultants, then managers themselves, started to blame out-dated 'linear' and 'chaos-hampering' thinking as the source of economical problems. They fence off inopportune 'chaos killers', justifying their dismissal as well as the reintroduction of only too well-known methods (e.g. brainstorming) with the term 'chaotic management'. Also psychologists, sportsmen, and even the church utilize chaos for their specific purposes: the *Deutsches Pfarrerblatt*, a clerical magazine, certified chaos theory to have 'evangelical power', developed a 'chaos theology' and discovered a 'nonlinearly acting God' (Brügge, 1993, p. 241).

However different the purposes and corresponding variants of 'chaos' may be, they all seem to have in common the figurative core of 'order within disorder'. The extraordinary general interest of so many different social groups might be attributed to this figurative core: the difficulty of orienting oneself in the light of an abundance of choices, on the one hand, and a shortage of reliable standards, on the other, has been called the fundamental problem for the individual in (post-)modern societies (cf., e.g., Schulze, 1992). With that background, the promise of order within disorder should be highly attractive for most of us.

### The role of social representations in the process of media communication

So far it has been argued that media communication, and TV communication in particular, has a constituent impact on the formation and the diffusion of social representations. Conversely, however, social representations also influence the process of media communication. TV communication, for example, contains typical roles, which, because of their institutionalization, are realized by specific groups with their specific norms, values, lifestyles, and social identities: viewers, journalists, actors, etc. All these groups use specific versions of social representations of all kinds; in particular, they use differing social representations of media-specific roles.

TV viewers have specific representations of TV protagonists, and, vice versa. This is of particular interest for (the analysis of) media communication because these mutual representations codetermine the form and content of communication in the form of specific partner hypotheses. If mass communication is regarded as the public, indirect, one-sided, technical, periodical distribution of professionally worked-up, structurally and functionally differentiated communication forms (cf., e.g., Maletzke, 1978), then the formation of partner hypotheses will only be possible within certain restrictions.

To illustrate this, let us take a look at the representation that TV producers have of their communication partner, the audience. Research has shown that particularly TV journalists, who claim that they are mainly working for their audience, have only little contact with their viewers and are rather ignorant about them. When asked who they were making their programmes for, presenters of potential TV magazines, for example, gave answers like 'for the audience' and 'for those who are interested in politics' (Fischer, 1983). Producers of educational programmes were rarely or not at all able to give details about the characteristics of their regular or target audience (Freund, 1990, p. 116). The laconic answers of German TV show hosts asked about their audience can be put into three categories: (1) vague or trivial: 'The audience, like myself, is sometimes in a good mood, sometimes in a bad one' (Joachim Fuchsberger, in Jörg, 1984, p. 152); (2) imagining an ideal audience: 'open-minded, cheerful, ready to let themselves be confronted with varied aspects of entertainment' (Fuchsberger, in Jörg,, 1984, p. 152); (3)

egocentric: 'I think the audience appreciates my naturalness, and the way I see myself' (Harald Juhnke, in Jörg, 1984, 156). Other studies lead to the conclusion that TV producers generally consider the audience dull, incompetent, and ungrateful (Altheide, 1974, p. 59), or that they differentiate four groups of recipients: (1) the interested (like the journalists themselves), (2) the not interested, (3) the rejected (intellectual critics, etc.), and (4) the imagined (different images of recipients meeting the producers' own wishes) (Gans, 1979).

That TV producers have such a blurred image of their audiences can be attributed to the one-sidedness of TV communication and to the fact that the only feedback the producers get from their communication partners comes in the undifferentiated form of ratings and the occasional letter to the editor. So, their picture of the communication partner will be based on vague stereotypes and on ideas that are rooted in their own social identity and *Lebenswelt*. The phenomenon that TV producers are almost 'autistically' (Burns, 1969) 'oriented towards their colleagues' (Donsbach, 1982) may intensify this effect.

An obvious conclusion to be drawn from this seems to imply fatal consequences for media communication: If communicators – despite their claim to be working for the benefit of their audience – have only a vague or egocentrically distorted representation of their recipients then successful communication will be a matter of chance. High ratings do not in principle disprove this conclusion. First, ratings as an undifferentiated and quantitative instrument cannot be used to judge if a communication is appropriate to a qualitatively defined goal, and, second, general approval of a programme does not imply that the quality of communication could not have been increased with a better knowledge of the target group.

### Conclusion

Media communication and social representation are dialectically interwoven. Mass-media communicators have a crucial role in the elaboration of social represenations, but at the same time they are also 'captives' of their own specific representations, for example, of their audience.

Empirical findings from different research fields support these assumptions. Yet, the explicit and empirical investigation of this inter-relation has only just begun. At the same time – with the introduction of interactive television, that is, the combination of television, personal computer, and telephone – new forms of communication are developing that will undoubtedly change the diffusion of social images. Among other things we have to reckon with a considerable fragmentation of programmes and target groups. At the same time the flow of information from the recipient to the sender will increase considerably. Recipients will not only compile their own TV programmes, they will also be able to rearrange single elements like news or feature films. They will be able to send messages, pictures, etc., to other individuals, or to any kind of 'public'. This will at least challenge the traditional opposition of mass-media communication and interpersonal communication. Yet, at present, one can only speculate as to the specific changes in the process of social representation this will bring about.

# 13 The social representation of 'man' in everyday speech

## Lenelis Kruse

### Social representation and speech

The theory of social representations, which was developed from 1961 onward by Serge Moscovici on the basis of Emile Durkheim's *'représentations collectives'* ([1898] 1974), has since been adopted by ever-increasing numbers of researchers (cf., e.g., Farr and Moscovici, 1984; Farr, 1987b; see von Cranach, Doise, and Mugny, 1992; Breakwell and Canter, 1993). This theory holds that every society or speech community possesses common imagery, a stock of knowledge, theories of everyday existence, and systems for interpreting certain facts. Moscovici himself investigated the social representation of psychoanalysis on different levels and in different groups within French society. Since then a plethora of other areas, including health and illness, Aids, working people, women, children, researchers, the human body, etc., have been identified and researched, using a variety of methods (cf. Breakwell and Canter, 1993).

Knowledge of these areas of experience can be very unequally distributed within a society. A large stock of knowledge is shared by most members of society, for example, that the earth is round or that humankind consists of men and women: these are 'unquestioned givens' (Schütz, 1966) and people usually accept them without any conscious thought. In extreme cases, such a stock of knowledge may be equally available to, and equally esteemed by, all members of society. Alongside this *general* or *collective* knowledge – Berger and Luckmann (1966), following Schütz, call it the 'common stock of knowledge' – there is *group-specific knowledge* available only to specific groups within the society – for example, biologists or cyclists or mothers – and such knowledge will be esteemed differently by different groups.

Collective and group-specific knowledge, both of which are super-individual constructs, must be distinguished from individual knowledge (opinions, attitudes, interpretative schemata) which may be elicited from individuals by, for example, opinion polls and which (again in extreme

196

cases) may be idiosyncratic, i.e. valid only for one person (cf. von Cranach, chapter 2 this volume).

Group-specific differentiation of social representations tends to relate to matters over which society disagrees, such as (currently) treatment of refugees, unemployment, ecology versus economics, genetic engineering or legally imposed quotas for numbers of women in politics and the professions. These areas are examples or manifestations of social change, which affects some social groups more, or sooner, than others.

For some time, one of these controversial areas has been the relationship between men and women. Since the 1980s not only public discussion – in the media, in parliament and in the workplace – but also many private communications among friends and family members, have been dominated by various concepts of the 'new man' and the new, more egalitarian relationship between the sexes. Because of the importance and controversial nature of the subject, one would expect all members of society to know at least something about it; but one would also expect a wide variety of opinions and attitudes vis-a-vis such questions as the intellectual and emotional differences between men and women, the emancipation of women and their demands for a greater say in public life, the redistribution of domestic tasks, the diminution of patriarchal structures in private and public life and other dimensions of the relationship between the sexes (see also Augoustinos, chapter 10 this volume).

People draw on this whole stock of knowledge in order to interpret and explain events and to shape their understanding of what is right and wrong, acceptable or 'impossible'; and also in order to typify individuals according to what groups or social categories they seem to belong to ('he's a male chauvinist pig!'). And when we interpret, understand, and also typify people, we do it overwhelmingly through *language*, through our understanding of the language of texts we read and hear – newspaper articles, lectures – and especially through the production of speech in conversation – be it in one-to-one or group discussions, family talk round the dinner-table, or political debates.

Consequently, the different shares which social groups have in a social representation will be reflected in their speech. It follows that social representations are processed – developed, reinforced, or challenged – through oral communication. This can happen either in face-to-face discussion or in the media (radio, television, newspapers and books: cf. Sommer, chapter 12 this volume).

Moscovici himself suggested that speech was a constitutive element and vehicle of social representations when he described the latter as the 'outcome of an unceasing babble' (1984b, p. 950) and sees his theory as a theory of social thinking and interpersonal communication. In the first years (or decades) of work on the theory, however, little attention was given to speech, either as a concept or as the subject of empirical research (cf. Harré, chapter 8 this volume; Potter and Wetherell, chapter 9 this volume).

It was on this basis that the Deutsche Forschungsgemeinschaft decided to support a wide-ranging project, in course of which we attempted some more detailed research into manifestations of the social representation of 'man' and 'relationships between the sexes' (cf., e.g., Kruse, Weimer, and Wagner, 1988; Kruse and Schwarz, 1992).

## The social representation of 'man' as an empirical problem

At the heart of our research project, which aimed to study speech, and more exactly speech about men, were three overarching problems:

- how to analyse collective and group-specific stocks of knowledge independent of individual cognition or speech;
- the role and influence of social representations in the production and understanding of speech;
- the detection of group-specific social representations and their effects, not only (as hitherto) on different social categories and symbolic groups, but also on everyday interaction between social groups.

We undertook a series of studies with the object of throwing light on these three problems. I will summarize some of our results in the following paragraphs. The studies were very various: an extensive analysis of the media, looking closely at magazine articles about 'men'; a questionnaire put to a representative sample of over 2,000 people; experiments to study the recall of texts consistent or inconsistent with representations by members of various groups engaged in day-to-day interaction; and typification research (using, e.g., the Kelly Grid Method) aiming to clarify group-specific use of generally accepted male types, for example, the loan-words *Softi* ('nice' man but with overtones of 'wimp') and *Macho* (with overtones of 'male chauvinist').

Relating this to the structural and dynamic differentiation of social representations, as developed by Moscovici *et al.* (see Figure 13.1), the project covered:

- structural aspects: how much information a person has and how s/he represents and evaluates it (attitude);
- dynamic aspects: anchoring (i.e. social representations as interpretative schemata for persons or events);
- distribution: collective and group-specific knowledge.

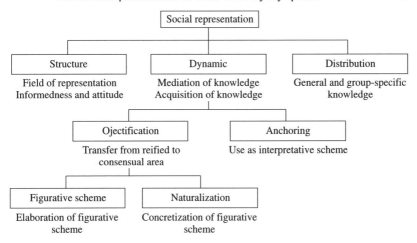

Figure 13.1    Social representations: processes and levels

### Media analysis

In order to test the claim that social representations are structures and contents which can exist over and beyond individual cognition, it was important not to use gleanings from 'subjective culture' (Mannheim, 1954), i.e. the cognition and opinions of individuals, but rather examples of 'objective culture', which could also be seen as concrete traces of, or external storage systems for, knowledge. Examples of 'objective culture' are works of art, films, books, and newspapers which feature typifications of men or the relationship between the sexes: although these have, of course, been inserted by the relevant artist or author, they subsequently assume a quasi-super-individual existence, since they are in principle accessible to all members of society.

We tapped one of these external storage systems by means of a media analysis. Over 7 months we monitored textual material from 72 different magazines with differing target audiences: from 400 actual magazine issues we extracted a total of 515 texts, which were then subjected to comprehensive analysis.

We evaluated the data by analysing the contents according to a number of categories: for example, the typification of men and their presumed attributes; the concept of typical male problem behaviour and the explanations adduced for it (excuse, justification); and the categorizing of the relationship between men and women, and between men and children.

This analysis of gender-typical interactions was particularly important for the progress of the project, and it will therefore be described in more detail. Our analysis of male typification showed that the texts do not always talk about 'new men', *Softis* or *Macho*s, but use a wide range of typifying labels. We found 682 different terms (cf. Schwarz, Weniger, and Kruse, 1989). The commonest term was *Pacha* (literally 'pasha'), meaning a man who expects to be waited on hand and foot, followed by the 'dream man'/'ideal man'. Third came the 'sex maniac', then the 'dud', and the 'ponce'. Of course, these terms correlate with the nature of the magazines in which the kind of man-related texts we were looking for tend to appear. The reason why the *Pacha* featured so often, and was described in comparatively greater detail, was that the articles tended to harp on the subject of the married man who does indeed expect to be waited on hand and foot, has no interest in 'equal rights', exploits or neglects his wife, but feels a bit insecure because of the increasing emancipation of women. His opposite is the ideal man, who is described largely in physical terms but is affectionate, understanding of women, and takes a cheerful view of life. Alongside these two themes is another central feature of the articles: violence against women. The *Softi* appears less often than expected and seems, as a type, contradictory: on the one hand, he shows understanding of women and is affectionate; on the other, he is often described as someone who neglects the (sexual) needs of his partner.

All in all, we found that the media categorize men using a series of positively and negatively valued types. The negative types – the majority – have the same characteristics as appear in discussions of male-role problems: they are violent, neglect women, have old-fashioned notions of gender roles, treat women as objects, are stubbornly inflexible in their notions of male identity and have a negative cast of mind. The positively valued types were always described in terms of attitude, clothes, and cleanliness. They are affectionate and understanding partners, have an altered view of masculinity, accept a new role in family life and are therefore described as 'new men', or often as the (actually non-existent) 'dream/ideal men'. There is also another type, the professionally successful, committed, upwardly mobile man; but he is described less often in terms of his relationships with women. Hence, professional life is an element in the description of men, but is not usually seen as integral to male roles.

Another characteristic which we investigated, using the Allensbach Publicity Analysis, was the social class of the readers addressed by magazines, which also helps to determine the male types presented. In magazines targeting the lower classes there is more discussion of married men; those targeting the middle or upper class pay more attention to the unmarried. This may correlate with the increasing tendency towards single lifestyles, which is more marked in the middle and upper classes. Magazines for the lower classes also have more description and discussion of negative behaviour towards women and negative self-description by men.

This is only a partial and selective presentation of our results. It can also be noted, as a separate conclusion, that the presentation of knowledge of, and attitudes towards, men and male types in a sample of objective culture – widely read German-language magazines – is highly variable and highly evaluative.

### Opinion polls

We had analyzed 'widely read magazines' as an external knowledge store for the subject 'man'. But this analysis could not show us to what degree this storage system was representative of the common stock of knowledge about 'men' in society as a whole, so we also selected one means of access to 'subjective culture', i.e. individual cognitions. To gain a preliminary insight into collective knowledge, which is what a social representation is, we had to question a representative sample of the population so as to retrieve the stock of knowledge which that population actually possessed, and gain some idea of possible group-specific differentiations. This research was performed in collaboration with two polling organizations, ZUMA and GETAS.

The poll, which took the form of structured interviews of 2,127 people, concentrated on the *typification* of men. Some of the questions bore directly on the categories used in the media analysis, for example, typification of men, social relationships among men, men and women, men and children, etc., and typical forms of male problem behaviour. However, we also asked subjects to evaluate each type, for example, was the type 'real man' or 'today's man' felt to be positive or negative?

We found, for example, that there is no consistent picture of 'today's man' current among the population. On the one hand, in his relationships with other men he is often described in terms of attributes like friendliness and trustworthiness, but characteristics such as rivalry and egoism are mentioned just as often. There is more agreement about his relationship to women. He is described as a member of an equal partnership, understanding and affectionate. If we take the different age groups in the sample separately, we find no great differences in the descriptions or evaluations. More significant are the differences between male and female interviewees: asked about the relationship between 'today's men' and other men, women tend to use words such as 'competitive', whereas men say 'cooperative'. Women describe his relationship with women in terms of 'traditional role distribution'; men talk of 'partnership'.

There are similar differences among the sexes with regard to the 'real man'. This type was described much more consistently, and on the whole positively: he is open-minded, active, competent, responsible, reliable, and faithful; however, we find that women describe the 'real man' primarily, and positively, in terms of his relationship to women, as the ideal partner, whereas men prefer to characterize him in terms of personality traits such as self-confidence, and see him as their 'ideal self'.

Both the media analysis and the questionnaire proved to be suitable means of retrieving collective knowledge of the social representation 'man', but less suitable as means of differentiating between group-specific knowledge stocks. There are two methodological reasons for this. First, the fact that we confined our analysis to widely read magazines with a readership larger than 1 per cent of the population automatically excluded certain group-specific print media, for example, feminist journals. For example, at the time of our study, the most widespread feminist magazine in Germany, *Emma*, did not rate inclusion in our collection of magazines.

Second, the high costs of a representative poll (when planning such interviews one learns how to evaluate the potential knowledge gain in crudely monetary terms) and the difficulty of securing sufficient high-quality interviewers made it impossible to cover problem areas and, for example, male types, which were, at the time of the study, familiar only to a small number of the interviewees. This meant, for example, that after preliminary tests for the structured interview we had to drop the label 'ideal man' because – astonishingly – it was unknown to most subjects in our trial sample. Because we had to match our questions to the knowledge of the majority, it proved impossible extensively to explore stocks of group-specific knowledge.

### Frame analysis: the social representation of gender-typical interaction

Part of the media analysis bore on the relationship between the sexes as shown in the magazine articles, i.e. on interaction sequences between a male and a female participant (e.g. 'Hans threatened to leave his mother and never come back'). In order to evaluate such sequences in linguistic terms we developed a multi-level analytical model which would detect the semantic and syntactic structures of utterances (cf. Kruse, Weimer, and Wagner, 1988). The model is based on the concept of cognitive and linguistic *cognitive* structure of an interaction sequence (with defined roles and role-specific behaviour patterns), but also defines the *linguistic* structures which correspond to episodes of the action.

Cognitive and linguistic frames are interrelated. Example: the sentence 'Mary gave Peter a box on the ear' activates the cognitive frame 'marital tiff'. The predicate 'give someone a box on the ear' can be assigned to a verb-set which could be designated 'hit'. 'To hit someone' opens two necessary roles, for a (logical) subject and a (logical) object: 'Mary hits Peter' or alternatively 'Peter hits Mary'. Stereotyped concepts of men (or women) might activate the verb-set 'hit back', which in turn offers two empty semantic slots, which could be filled in a suitably stereotypical way.

On the basis of this frame concept we developed a textual analysis model which we used to distil representations of gender-stereotypical actions and subjective experience from the magazine texts. Actions and subjective experiences were sorted into a hierarchical system of categories on the lowest level of verb-sets and then analysed to see whether the semantic roles of subject and object were filled by a man or a woman. This enabled us to classify particular verb-sets, each encompassing a series of predicates actually used in the text, as typically male or typically female. The verb-sets were then gathered in a subcategory (e.g. *be violent*), and the subcategories assigned to supercategories which can be taken to cover both patterns of action and subjective experiences. We created four supercategories, which we labelled 'associating' (e.g. *help*, *ask for help*), 'dissociating' (e.g. *threaten, defend*), 'evaluating' (e.g. *praise*, *punish*), and 'experiencing' (e.g. *feel hatred, feel joy*).

We analysed a total of 3,090 separate actions from the 515 texts described above. We found, for example, that 60 per cent of the actions in the 'associating' category were initiated by men and only 40 per cent by women. In the 'evaluating' category, only about 25 per cent of actions had women in the subject role, against 75 per cent initiated by men. A still closer analysis showed how often women take the object role when the man is described as subject, and vice versa. We find, for example, that women are more often described as seeking help, while men appear in the complementary role of help-givers.

Our detailed researches into these relationship patterns (cf. Kruse, Weimer, and Wagner, 1988) led to the conclusion that the media texts overwhelmingly stick to traditional role patterns: women are described in terms of positively or negatively valued emotional qualities. Women appear mainly in the role of victims, objects of male intimidation and violence. The woman is the person who seeks help and shows weakness. Complementing this female role, men are characterized as 'persecutors'.

They demand, threaten, and forbid, use force and ignore the wishes and needs of their partners. It is men who advertise themselves, initiate contacts and express their love. Men show empathy, help helpless women, and offer them moral support. Women, on the other hand, tend to appear in media texts as passive, defensive, and resigned.

What about the emancipated women and the new man? In the media culture we examined through our cognitive and linguistic frames they were simply not (yet) to be found. The social representations this culture reflects reproduce traditional clichés. Men act, women react; women ask for help, men give it; men advertise themselves actively to the opposite sex; women are the beneficiaries, or perhaps the victims, of these friendly acts.

### The influence of social representations in the understanding and description of gender-stereotyped behaviour

Using the information gleaned from this analysis of relationships, we then asked what role is played by these – obviously widespread – social representations of male–female relationships in subjective culture, meaning the way individuals perceive, remember, understand, and express gender-typical or gender-untypical actions. How, for example, will an individual perceive, remember, and later describe an episode in which it is not Peter who boxes Mary's ears, but Mary who boxes Peter's?

We did a series of experiments on these lines, relating first to the remembering and reproduction of gender-(un)typical actions and, second, to the oral production of stories which could be elicited using given verb-sets.

In one of our first experiments, for example, we supplied stories of male–female interaction in which the protagonists' behaviour was described as either 'frame-consistent' or 'frame-inconsistent'. The subject of the experiment was asked to reproduce the stories. We tested the assumption that frame-consistent patterns of experience and behaviour would be reproduced more frequently, and therefore that these stories would be retold with fewer mistakes than the frame-inconsistent ones. 'Mistakes' included slips of the tongue, uncertainties, reversal of semantic roles (e.g. 'he made a pass at her' for the correct 'she made a pass at him'), and the removal or substitution of pronouns marked for gender (e.g. 'they yelled at each other' instead of 'she yelled at him'). The substitution, and, even more, the reversal of gender markings can be seen as indicating the influence of frames, some mandatory for all, others distributed in culture-specific ways. This experiment yielded results which clearly confirmed our expectations as far as the substitution of gender markings was concerned. Most subjects remembered, or at least reproduced, not 'Anna mended Peter's bicycle' but 'they mended the bicycle' (cf. Kruse and Schwarz, 1992).

The structure of this experiment meant that imperfect memory might have influenced the reproduction. We corrected this in a further experiment by introducing a second, later occasion for recall: this produced correspondingly greater differences. So as to exclude the memory aspect altogether, we conducted another experiment in which subjects were asked to construct a story using a given verb-set (e.g. 'begin a conversation', 'criticise', 'reconcile'). We knew from the media analysis which verb-sets were likely to be marked for gender, and which were likely to be used in subject or object roles.

We set out to test, in relation to each verb-set, how far the roles of logical object and logical subject would be filled in a frame-consistent way.

These experiments also bore on the social distribution of knowledge (see Figure 13.1) and on the group-specific differentiation of that knowledge and its influence on the verbal construction and reconstruction of the stories. We distinguished between groups which could be expected to have a traditional idea of men and their roles and those which might take a more progressive or unconventional view. By selecting members of traditional male student societies (student fraternities for the men) and members of a Christian group (for the women), together with male and female members of 'green' alternative student groups, we in fact succeeded in detecting such areas of knowledge and their different affects not only with regard to social categories (classes of society with distinguishing traits), but also with regard to groups which engage in everyday interaction. Members of conservative and progressive groups (whom we had also tested on the standardized GRO scale [see Krampen, 1979] to determine their normative gender-role orientation) took a very different approach to the text material. In the story-production experiment we found that members of 'green' alternative groups allotted semantic roles much more inconsistently, in relation to the verb-sets, than did members of the traditional student associations. When retelling the stories, the latter group were much more likely to reverse the semantic gender roles, or at least neutralize them, i.e. they had allocated gender roles according to the patterns we had detected in our media analysis.

We found similar differences when we compared young people doing community service (as an alternative to military service) with students at a military training college.

## Social cognition and language

It can be said that most of what we know about the cognitions which are of primary interest in psychology and social psychology, and their component structures and processes, comes to us from linguistic expressions and linguistic communication. If we want to find out what people know and how they esteem that knowledge, we usually have to ask them. To this end we may set up an interview, lead a discussion, or ask them to fill in a questionnaire. Even when knowledge relates to social phenomena, such as families or our democratic society, it is still an individual's knowledge; in extreme cases we can attach its expression and variation to the single individual involved. That is how 'social cognitions' are perceived and researched in current mainstream social psychology.

In contradistinction to this, and in agreement with the sociology of knowledge, the theory of social representations assumes that the individual is a social being through and through, and that what we describe as knowledge is constituted and handed down basically as a social phenomenon, before it is identifiable as knowledge specific to any particular individual or group: i.e. as socially shared, but also socially distributed, knowledge (cf. Resnick, Levine, and Teasley, 1991). And speech, which is the chief means of access to, and support for, both social and individual knowledge, is also a super-individual construct with its own structures and rules, which is on a higher level than individual speech. In both cognition and speech, therefore, the individual element should be conceived of as a variant of the social element, and should be approached methodologically along those lines.

It was on this assumption that when we attempted to penetrate to the social representation of 'man' via everyday talk about men, we chose a multi-method approach. Only this choice put us in a position to make a more accurate empirical description of what, in a social representation, is common to all members of a speech community, how groups differ with regard to the social representation, and what can be seen as individual cognitive variation.

### Note

The research programme described here was supported by the Deutsche Forschungsgemeinschaft. It was supported as part of the research group and then of the Sonderforschungsbereich 245, 'Sprechen und Sprachverstehen im sozialen Kontext'. The research was conducted with the assistance of R. Kohl, S. Schwarz, F. Wagner, E. Weimer, G. Weniger and others. The chapter was translated from the German by Rosemary Morris.

# Part 3

# Social representations: history and development of a field of research

# 14 The history and actuality of social representations

*Serge Moscovici*

### The scandal of social thought

One often hears that a good science should begin by proposing clear and carefully defined concepts. Actually no science, not even the most exact, proceeds in this way. It begins by assembling, ordering, and distinguishing phenomena which surprise everyone, because they are disturbing, or exotic, or create a scandal. Now, for people living in a culture such as ours, which proclaims science and reason, there are few things as scandalous as the spectacle of beliefs, superstitions, or prejudices which are shared by millions of people. Or, again, of ideologies, those assemblies, according to Marx, of 'chimeras, dogmas, imaginary beings' which obscure the real determinants of the human situation and the authentic motivations of human action. Certainly, we have today become more tolerant towards religious beliefs, which suppose the immortality of the soul, the reincarnation of individuals, the efficacy of prayer, or many other things which our knowledge of humanity and nature excludes. It is enough to glance at popular publications to be surprised by the number of people in our society who read their horoscope, consult faith healers, or consume miraculous remedies. Likewise, one can observe the intensity with which magic is practised in our milieux, in our cities and even our universities. Those who have recourse to these things are not the socially maladapted of the uneducated layers in society, as some would have us believe, but the educated, engineers, and even doctors. Think of those 'high-tech' enterprises which recruit their personnel using graphological or astrological tests. Far from wanting to hide such activities, most of the practitioners of this magic show themselves off on television, and publish books which have a wider readership than any scholarly text.

These things which seem strange and even troubling to us, also have something to teach us about the way in which people think and what they think about. Take, for example, that strange and unfamiliar disease, Aids. Everyday conversations and the media were quick to take possession of it, and immediately catalogued it as the punitive illness of a permissive society. The press represented it as a condemnation of 'degenerate behaviours', the punishment of 'irresponsible sexuality'. The conference of Brazilian bishops spoke out against the campaign for condoms, describing Aids as the 'consequence of moral decadence', the 'punishment of God', and the 'retribution of nature'. There was also a series of publications arguing that the virus was manufactured by the CIA (Central Intelligence Agency) for the extermination of undesirable populations, and so on. This example shows (as others could just as well have done) the frequency with which incredible and alarming ideas or images circulate, which neither good sense nor logic can stop. Needless to say, such a type of mental functionning which clearly confirms this irrationality has generated much research. And this brings us to the heart of the matter.

One can summarize the results of such research by saying that, to our not very great surprise, they show that most individuals prefer popular ideas to scientific ideas, making illusory correlations which objective facts are incapable of correcting. In general, they take no account of the statistics which play such a large role in our decisions and everyday discussions. They distort the information available to them. Moreover, as has repeatedly been said without being contradicted, people accept above all those facts or perceive those behaviours which confirm their habitual beliefs. And they do this even when their experience tells them 'it's wrong' and reason tells them 'it's absurd'. Should we take all of this lightly, arguing that people are the victims of prejudice, deceived by some ideology, or constrained by some power? No, the facts are too widespread for us to be content with such explanations, and that we do not feel an uneasiness at seeing how far *homo sapiens*, the only animal gifted with reason, has proved to be unreasonable.

It is possible to understand these facts, I repeat it, but without ceasing to think that they have consequences for the relations between individuals, for political choices, for attitudes towards other groups, and for everyday experience. I could continue by evoking rascism (see Potter and Wetherell, chapter 9 in this volume), ethnic wars, mass communication (see Sommer, chapter 12 in this volume), and so on. But the most glaring question is this: why do people think in non-logical and non-rational ways? A worrying, very worrying, question. Without a doubt it is a question which belongs to social psychology, and I need to explain briefly why it does.

From the perspective of the individual, it has been agreed, since Descartes I think, that people have the capacity to think correctly about the evidence presented to them by the external world. On the one hand, they are in a position to distinguish the information available, and, on the other, from the ensemble of premises concerning it, they know how to draw a certain conclusion. It should, one supposes, be a matter of following logical rules, of which the most important is that of non-contradiction. Insofar as such reasoning and the conclusion seem correct, one can also consider that the way in which the rules and logical procedures were applied provide the best explanation of persistent beliefs and knowledge. But from the moment that one sees that the reasoning is flawed and the conclusion is wrong, one must look for other causes for the bad application of the rules, non-logical causes which can explain why individuals make mistakes. Among these causes there are, first affective problems, but above all social influences which would submit the psychic apparatus to external pressures. Social influences would incite individuals to yield before habits, or to turn themselves away from the external world so that they succumb to illusions or to the satisfaction of a need to invent.

Thus we uncover a duality which is at the bottom of most explanations in this domain. It can be described in a few words: our individual faculties of perception and observation of the external world are capable of producing true knowledge, whereas social factors provoke distortions and deviations in our beliefs and our knowledge of the world. Let us not pause for the moment over the indetermination of this duality, but examine the three ways in which it is expressed. First, by the idea that one touches the true processes of knowledge when these are considered within the individual, independently of their culture, and, actually, of every culture. In this sense, as Gellner writes, 'culture, a shared set of ideas, held to be valid simply because they constitute the joint conceptual banks of customs of an ongoing community, is spurned. It is spurned *because* it is culture. Its social and customary origin is the *fatal* taint' (1992, p. 18).

Then there is the conviction, expressed particularly in mass psychology, that individuals gathered in a group can be seen to change their psychic qualities, losing some and acquiring others. Or again, more precisely, it is agreed that individuals who behave morally and rationally when isolated, become immoral and irrational when acting in a group (Moscovici, 1985). Lastly, and most recently, in the light of the research I mentioned earlier, the ordinary person, the 'novice', has a tendency to neglect the information given, to think in a stereotyped way, failing to take account of the errors this induces. In other words, the ordinary person is, as they say, a *cognitive miser*.

Here is a very unflattering image of the way in which people think and act when they are brought together in the society to which they belong. I do not believe in a kind of mental infirmity which is invoked and recognized through what appears as an array of habitual beliefs, of deviations or distortions of our knowledge of the world which surprises or scandalizes. But the fact is that it appears as the symptoms of a psychopathology of social origin. I should add that here this is not a metaphor, recalling that social psychology has for a long time been assimilated through this motif to pathological psychology. This is expressed in the very title of a famous American review: *The Journal of Abnormal and Social Psychology*.

This association comes also, and perhaps above all, from the fact that psychologists such as Freud, Jung, and Janet, who all contributed so much to psychopathology, also dedicated important books and articles to collective psychology. Evidently, for them, as for so many others, the normal thought of groups has its counterpart in the mental anomalies of individuals. And this holds for the civilized masses, so-called 'primitive societies', or exotic religions. Although we speak about it less openly, or are less conscious of it, this relation between collective thought and pathological thought is also inscribed in our theories and methods of observation. It signifies that finally reason and society or culture are antithetical. As a consequence, the total self-sufficiency of the individual becomes represented as the reference situation and the norm, whereas the association of individuals in the social unity becomes a derived situation, one of dependence in relation to an environment which modifies this norm in a positive or negative sense.

In the course of this discussion, however, something could not help but strike us, which forces me to make a supplementary remark. We not only accept that it goes without saying that there is a duality between the forms of non-social thought and the forms of common thought and belief. We also presuppose that the concepts and laws of the former serve as the reference for the latter. As Wyer and Srull (1984) observe 'this argument is that the processes involved in dealing cognitively with non-social events are simpler and conceptually more fundamental than the processes involved with social events. The study of cognitive processing in the context of non-social stimuli provides a foundation on which the more complex social cognitive principles can be built' (p. 25). This presupposition, the most constraining and also unfounded, is what we need to try to liberate ourselves from. In any case, it is only in the context of a *different* psychology that we can elucidate the meaning of these forms of common thought and belief.

It is also right to indicate that things are changing. The pre-eminence of the social is more and more recognized in the fields of epistemology, language, and social psychology. Personally I am convinced that this is a tendency which will deepen. Meanwhile, I would not have written this chapter if I was not also convinced that it is not sufficient to recognize the pre-eminence of the social by paying lip service to it, even if in the sense of a general consensus. Above all, we need to recover a theoretical perspective which can illuminate these surprising phenomena as a normal part of our culture and our life in society. All things considered, it is a question of reformulating the polarity of individual–society in clearer and more sharply defined terms.

### An anti-Cartesian notion: collective representations

Nothing in what I have said so far, it seems to me, takes me further away from what is known today as the psychology of the social. The problem is not to choose between the pre-eminence of the individual or of society, it is of a more concrete order. It has to do with the explication of the phenomena of belief, religion, or magic, of ordinary and popular knowledge, of the ideological forms of collective thought and action. To begin with, why does society create such beliefs and ideas, irrespective of whether they are correct? Then, why are they accepted and transmitted from one generation to the next? Even if the social nature of our thought, language, and so on were recognized in psychology, which is not the case today, the problem would be posed in the same terms and those who discuss it and would continue to discuss it would have somehow to resolve it. It is not possible to seek refuge in the trivialities of intersubjectivity or linguistic constructions. And it is because it has not confronted this problem that I think that social cognition is bound to remain less than convincing.

I am therefore led today to acknowledge this simple and evident fact, although it is not without meaning. Leaving psychoanalysis aside, which has related collective psychology and individual psychology through the unconscious, only the line of thought which has developed towards a theory of social representations is seriously dedicated to the solution of this problem. And this is nearly a century after the appearance of its first notions required the autonomy of our psychology for the solution itself. You see that, in an era in which labels change so quickly and where everyone can break as radically as possible with the past, I hesitate to appeal to a line of thought which began with the human sciences themselves and which forms, as it were, a part of their genetic code. But one can also think that the fact it persists, that one can return to this line of thought without being obligated by any tradition of a school, means that it touches something fundamental and precious in the way people live.

The theory of social representations is unique, it seems to me, in that it tends more and more to being a general theory of social phenomena and a special theory of psychic phenomena. This paradox, as we shall see, owes nothing to chance; on the contrary, it comes from the deep nature of things. It is a general theory to the extent that as far as it is concerned society could not be defined by the simple presence of a collective which brought individuals together through a hierarchy of power, for example, or exchanges based on mutual interests. Certainly, power and interests exist, but to be recognized as such in society there must be representations or values which give them meaning. And above all to make the efforts of individuals converge and to unite them through beliefs which ensure their existence in common. This is guided by opinions, symbols, and rituals, by beliefs that is, and not simply by knowledge or technique. They are of a different order: beliefs about life in common, about what it should be, about what should be done; beliefs about the just, the true, and the beautiful; and still others which all have an impact on ways of behaving, of feeling, or of transmitting and exchanging goods.

It is when knowledge and technique are changed into beliefs that they bring people together and become a force which can transform individuals from passive members into active members who participate in collective actions and in everything which brings existence in common alive. Societies break apart if there is only power and diverse interests to unite people, if there is not the sum of ideas and values in which they believe, which binds them to a common passion and which is transmitted from one generation to the next (Moscovici, 1993a). In other words, what societies think of their ways of living, the meanings which they attach to their institutions and the images which they share are a necessary part of their reality, and not simply a reflection of it. As the Polish philosopher Kolakowski has observed, 'the reality of a society depends in part on what is in its representation of itself' (1978, p. 94).

Before continuing, we need to take account of an important but embarrassing fact: there are psychic phenomena which, although of varying complexity, have in common a social origin and are indispensable for life in common. But, as soon as one looks at society from this point of view an enigma surfaces. Indeed, one no longer understands how societies are able to survive while maintaining religious or magical beliefs, and allowing themselves to be guided by illusions, ideologies, and the biases attributed to them. Further, one wonders why people create this hotch-potch of irrationality through which they fool themselves. In speaking of religious beliefs, which interested him above all, Durkheim wrote:

It is unthinkable that systems of ideas like religions, which have held such a large place in history – the well to which peoples in all the ages have come to draw the energy they had to have in order to live – could be mere fabrics of illusion. Today we agree to recognize that law, morals, and scientific thought itself were born in religion, were long confounded with it, and have remained imbued with its spirit. How could a hollow phantasmagoria have been able to mold human consciousness so powerfully and so lastingly? . . . But if the people themselves created those systems of mistaken ideas, and at the same time were duped by them, how could this amazing dupery have perpetuated itself through the whole course of history. ([1912]1995, p. 66)

I suspect that, rightly, it is this abasement of shared beliefs, this contempt for popular ideas and knowledge, for other cultures in general, which offended Durkheim. How to conceive of a society where confidence and solidarity would not only be an illusion? Must we admit that culture has the secular function of furnishing humanity with phantasmagoria and errors? What is the content of the collective consciousness of a society which endeavours to fool itself about its ideas and values? We need to retain the deep sense of these interrogations about things which we manage to slide over so easily, even today in psychology and even in sociology. Whatever they may be, we need to pay less attention to its abnormal character, from the point of the individual and their beliefs and knowledge, and more to their social character, to the mental and psychic life which they express. In order first to describe them and then to explain them as the common being of a group of individuals, we need to take account of three things:

1 We suppose that individuals essentially know both the natural world and the social world (Heider, 1958) by means of sensory perceptions of information which is waiting to be observed and explained by adequate concepts. They are like Adam on the day of his creation, opening his eyes on animals and other things, deprived of tradition, lacking shared concepts with which to coordinate his sensory impressions. This image cannot really be applied to individuals living in society, who have a common way of life which indicates how beings or objects should be classified, how to judge them according to their value, what information is worthy of belief, and so on. One could say of each of us what the English philosopher Cornford said of the philosophers and the scholarly:

Wherever and whenever a professed man of science upholds such an opinion, we may be certain that he is not formulating a description of observed facts, but turning his knowledge to the defence of a belief which he has learnt, not direct from Nature, but at his mother's knee; in other words a collective representation. And this particular representation is not the outcome of long accumulated results of science and philosophy. On the contrary, the further back we trace it the more firmly planted it appears, and the daily contradictions of all experience has not yet uprooted it from the popular mind. (1957, p. 43)

This means that the attempt to understand the complex knowledge and beliefs of a society on the basis of elementary laws of individual knowledge which are, in the last analysis, based on sensory givens or sensory experience, is always a hopeless attempt. Not because any conclusions which might be drawn from it have no value, but because the premises from which it begins are artificial and lack depth.

2 We have no reason to exclude totally individual experience and perceptions. But, in all justice, we must remember that nearly everything which a person knows they have learnt from another, either through their accounts, or through the language which is acquired, or the objects which are used. These are in general the knowledge which is connected with the most ancient knowledge, whose roots are submerged in the way of life and collective practices in which everyone participates and which need to be renewed at each instant. People have always learnt from one another, and have always had knowledge that they do so. This is not exactly a discovery. The importance of this proposition for our theory is that significant knowledge and beliefs have their origin in a mutual interaction, and do not form in any other way.

3 The ideas and beliefs which enable people to live are incarnated in specific structures (clans, churches, social movements, families, clubs, etc.) and adopted by the individuals who are a part of them. The meaning which they communicate and the obligations which they recognize are profoundly incorporated in their actions and exercise a constraint which extends to all the members of a community. It is probably this constraint which obliges us, according to Weber, not to ignore the causal role of collective forms of thought in the orientation of our ordinary activities and those which we expect. Thus he writes:

> These concepts of collective entities which are found both in common sense and in juristic and other technical forms of thought, have a meaning in the minds of individual persons, partly as something actually existing, partly as something with normative authority. This is true not only of judges but of ordinary private individuals as well. Actors thus in part orient their action to them, and in this role such ideas have a powerful, often a decisive, causal influence on the course of action of real individuals. (Weber, [1968]1972, p. 14)

If Weber is right, then forms of collective thought are strongly incorporated in the motivations and expectations of individuals which depend for their efficacy on their action in general. This is precisely what he attempted to show in his study of the spirit of capitalism: rational economic practices were born in the beliefs of Puritan sects and the teachings of the Bible, as in the premeditated hope of their own salvation.

These three things – the primacy of representations or beliefs, the social origin of perceptions and beliefs, and the causal and sometimes constraining role of these representations and beliefs – are the background on which the theory of social representations was developed. I think I have traced their outline sufficiently clearly to justify a remark, which is that this background contributes to the solution of the problem evoked earlier. One can see an outline of it in the work in which Durkheim focused on this problem, *The elementary forms of the religious life* ([1912]1995). The descriptive parts of the book give a large space to the religious beliefs of the indigenous Australians, whereas the explicative parts, in the middle and at the end of the work, are devoted to the creation and the meaning of these beliefs as the cement of society in general. The book exposes with great abundance the peculiarities of human thought, the strange illusions and practices shared by a community, or its ideas, which may be very curious but only weakly scientific.

Thus Durkheim gives a detailed examination of what seems to be the general aspect of the adoration of animals and plants, knuckle-bones, or wood. Or further, the hazy outline of ideas, such as the famous *mana*, and formulas which accompany each ritual. Nothing more is hidden from us, either of the delirious frenzy of the collective dance around the totem in the course of which each individual psyche becomes suggestible, or the licentious character of the ritual ecstasy which suspends the conscious relation with reality. It is in this state of effervescence that beliefs are created and given life in common, inculcated in each of the participants. The morning after the ritual ceremony, the 'savages' awake full of sadness, but they part from one another having made these shared perceptions and values their own. One also sees elsewhere through what prayers and magical manipulations for the propitiation of the spirits, beliefs bring success to hunting or fishing, or provide a remedy for some illness.

The thing which is interesting here is that, through these fantastic and even bizarre elements a universe of sacred, and hence impersonal, things is constituted in these Australian societies, a universe which figures animals as totems, then the objects associated with these totems, and finally even the individuals themselves. Nothing would be easier than to trace the analogy with the religious or political universes of our societies and to show – an opportunity which hasn't been missed – how far their beliefs are founded on symbolic thought, on the displacements of observations, extreme rituals, and intense emotions.

Durkheim acknowledges that such things must appear chimerical or irrational to those who judge them on the basis of their relation to physical reality. But if the reader will excuse me for returning to things I have discussed elsewhere (Moscovici, [1988b]1993), in effect, one arrives at the opposite conclusion as soon as one assumes that behind these illusions, rituals or emotions there are collective representations which are shared and transmitted from one generation to the next without changing. The impression is confirmed and strengthened when one realizes that through totems and rituals society celebrates its own cult by interposed divinities. Their diffuse and impersonal authority over individuals is that of the society itself to which they belong.

It is true that each person, in worshipping a plant or an animal, seems to be the victim of an illusion. But if everyone together recognizes their group in this way, then we are dealing with a social reality. Then they represent not only beings or things, but the symbols of beings and things. It is about them that they think, it is face to face with them that they conduct themselves, as we do when faced with the flag or the flame in the Arc-de-Triomphe. In the same way, ritual behaviours have as their real aim, not so much to make it rain or to mourn a death, as to maintain the community, to reinvigorate the sense of belonging to a group, to inflame belief and faith. I am far from wanting to suggest that this explanation of the religious life is the best, or that it has resisted the criticism of time. But it suffices for me to illustrate the sense in which latent representations are expressed through mental contents and symbolic behaviours. It would be legitimate to ask whether this approach would have yielded what was expected of it, and thereby helped to solve our concrete problem, had the hypothesis been allowed to reach fruition. That is to say, the hypothesis that collective representations are rational, not in spite of being collective, but because they are collective. And even that this is the only way in which we become rational. In fact, according to Durkheim, on the basis of their varied sensations, individuals could neither arrive at general notions, nor establish any regularities. One can no longer see what it is that makes them do so. Criticizing Hume, the sociologist affirms that it is not possible to understand how or why, in our solitude, we could discover an order through our association of ideas or fleeting sensations. And even supposing that an individual were able to do so, it is impossible to grasp how this order could remain stable and impose itself on everyone. On the other hand, one can understand that a representation, which is collective because it is the work of everyone, can become stable through reproduction and transmission from one generation to another. It also becomes impersonal to the extent that it becomes detached from everyone and is shared through the means of the concepts of a common language. 'To think conceptually is not merely to isolate and group the features common to a certain number of objects. It is also to subsume the variable under the permanent and the individual under the social' (Durkheim, [1912]1995, p. 440).

Moreover, the principal categories of representation are social in origin and are bought into play exactly where everyone seems to oppose them. Thus, a mimetic rite, where shouts and movements imitate those of the animal one wishes to see reproduced, brings into play a causal process to the letter. Or again, the magic formula, like attracts like, connects different things and makes some appear as the function of others. But, in this way, an implicit causal power is attributed to one thing to produce its like, and this is what is essential. It is in these ways that a real category of an active causality is formed, as much in the practice of culture as in the practice of magic. Or again, to the extent that each society, as primitive as it may be, divides and classifies its members, it also necessarily tends to classify animate or inanimate beings according to the same criteria. A logic of classifications is thereby instituted which may be crude but is no less rigorous for that. Besides, elementary religions have sketched the essentials of the concepts which, according to Durkheim, have made science and philosophy possible.

Religion made a way for them. It is because religion is a social thing that it could play this role. To make men take control of sense impressions and replace them with a new way of imagining[1] the real, a new kind of thought had to be created: collective thought. If collective thought alone had the power to achieve this, here is the reason: Creating a whole world of ideals, through which the world of sensed realities seemed transfigured, would require a hyperexcitation of intellectual forces that is possible only in and through society. (Durkheim, [1912]1995, p. 239)

Whatever the circumstances, it is clear that the psychic energy created through the participation of individuals in the life of the group and the mental categories which they crystallize allows collective representations to become detached, forming a complex of ideas and inferences which must be called rational. Clearly, I cannot stop at the concept without discussing its justification. It seems to me that Durkheim wished to designate by this term an intellectual content, resembling in some ways Thomas Kuhn's paradigms, and in other ways Cassirer's symbolic forms, which underly religious beliefs, the opinions of a society, and science. Representation has a clearly marked intellectual character, even though the cognitive aspects were not specified by the sociologist (Ansart, 1988).

Durkheim states: 'A man who did not think with concepts would not be a man, for he would not be a social being. Limited to individual perceptions alone, he would not be distinct from an animal' (1995, p. 440). These are strong words. One could not complain that they lack clarity. They trace a clear frontier between individual psychology and social psychology, connecting each to its own reality and to its distinct forms of thought. In these circumstances, and without falling into the banal, one concludes that, according to the sociologist, it is incumbent upon the latter, that is our science, to attain a deeper understanding of public and cultural representations. According to Durkheim, our science needs to study, through comparisons of mythical themes, legends, popular traditions, and languages, how social representations are called and are mutually exclusive, how they merge into one another or differentiate themselves, and so on (cf. Durkheim, [1912]1995).

Durkheim's arguments on this point, the vision he expressed of the collective genesis of our beliefs, our knowledge and what makes us reasonable beings more generally, might be thought to be disputable, out of date even. The same might be said about the influence of latent collective representations on our individual representations. But the fact remains that it is the only sketch of a coherent vision which continues to exist. Such is also the opinion given recently by the English anthropologist Ernst Gellner of the solution to the problem with which we are concerned: 'No better theory is available to answer it. No other theory highlights the problem so well' (1992, p. 37). Besides, the general line of argument matters more than the arguments invoked by Durkheim's critics. And in following the line which is marked out for us, we know at least where we are going.

### Collective representations and cultural development

From all sides we are denied the right to think of a psychology of common representations and to work scientifically on the basis of this hypothesis. And yet it is necessary, since the data of individual psychology are elementary and concern only extremely limited phenomena. As much in the child as in the adult one often sees psychic acts whose explanation implies other acts which do not depend on individual representations. These acts are not only the perceptions of others or attitudes towards ethnic groups. In our least constrained everyday conversations we find ourselves confronted with linguistic images or influences which come to mind without our being the origin of them, and with deductions whose formation cannot be attributed to any of our interlocutors, as is the case with rumours. All of these acts remain incoherent if we claim to deduce them from individual reasoning or expressions. But they can be arranged in a whole whose coherence can be discovered by taking account of the inferred social representations. We find in this better understanding a sufficient motive for going beyond the immediate experience of each person. And if, in another connection, we can show that the psychology of collective representations, contrary to what some people believe, clarifies the mental and linguistic operations of individuals, then our hypothesis will have received a supplementary justification.

In fact, things are like this: above all, Durkheim drew the contours of a research programme by defining a position of principle and the collective background of our mental life. He set forth, as we shall see, the idea of collective representations as the underlying, one could even say unconscious, matrix of our beliefs, our knowledge and our language. Thus, although one could disapprove of this way of speaking, there is no such thing strictly speaking as individual rationality, which is the downfall of one of the most widespread beliefs. As Hocart has written: 'Men of all races and generations are equally convinced that they individually draw their knowledge from reality' (1987, p. 42). By arguing that they draw their categories from the thought of society, Durkheim initiated a radical change in sociology and anthropology. But this is also the reason why still today this idea is contested, or ignored to the point where, even in the clearest biographies of the French sociologist, only a passing allusion is made to it (Giddens, 1985).

Nevertheless, we also need to recognize that, preoccupied with the opposition between the collective and the individual, and with showing the continuity between religion and science, Durkheim gave this idea a sense which is too intellectual and abstract. To approach this issue in the most concrete way, one needs to pay greater attention to the differences than the similarities among collective representations, to connect them to different societies in order to be able to compare them in a sustained way. In this sense, it seems that it was Lévy-Bruhl ([1925]1926) who transformed this general idea into a true concept and proceeded, even if only in a fragmentary way, to make the comparison. This is incontestable from the point of view which concerns us, since, at the same time, he sketched their autonomous social psychology, the significance of which I shall return to later. We know that the premises of his work and of this psychology were, and continue to be, scandalous (Lloyd, 1990). But here I am not concerned with this scandal, or with the confused reasons which led to the rejection of Lévy-Bruhl, since there are too many books and writings on the famous 'prelogical mentality'. One can find a succinct and fair discussion of these disputed questions in a wonderful book by Jahoda (1982).

One can try to grasp the concept quickly by saying that, given the collective background, Lévy-Bruhl ([1925]1926) insisted on four aspects of these representations.

1 They have a character which today we would describe as *holistic*, which is to say that one should not attribute an isolated belief or category to an individual or a group. Thus, every idea or belief assumes a large number of others with which it forms a whole representation. For example, the idea 'This man is German' assumes that the idea of 'man' is available, as well as the idea of 'German', and consequently that of 'kind', 'French', and so on. Thus the belief that 'This man is German' assume beliefs about nations, and implies a belief that 'This man is not a Turk', etc. The holism of a representation means that the semantic content of each idea and of each belief depends on its connections with the other beliefs or ideas. Thus, contrary to what is accepted in social cognition, the error or truth of one of the ideas or beliefs does not entail that the representation shared by the collective has an erroneous or truthful character, or that their way of thinking is erroneous or truthful. Evans Pritchard understood the importance of this aspect when he wrote that Lévy-Bruhl 'was one of the first, if not the first, to emphasize that primitive ideas, which seem so strange to us, and sometimes idiotic, when considered as isolated facts, are meaningful when seen as parts of patterns of ideas and behaviours, each part having an intelligible relationship to others' (1965, p. 86). Now, it is the representation which binds the ideas and behaviour of a collective together, representations which are formed in the course of time and to which people adhere in a public way.

2 We can put an end to all the misunderstandings surrounding the nature of representations if, from now on, in the description of different sorts of beliefs we leave to one side the question of whether to classify them we need to know if they are intellectual or cognitive, and join them together only according to their connection and their adherence to a specific society or culture. For various reasons, this is even more true, according to Lévy-Bruhl, for so-called 'primitive' cultures, since 'what is really "representation" to us is found blended with other elements of an emotional or motor character, coloured and imbued by them, and therefore implying a different attitude with respect to the objects represented' ([1925]1926, p. 36). All the symbols retained and living in a society obey a logic of the intellect as much as a logic of the emotions, even though they might be founded on a different principle. I maintain that this holds for every culture, and not only the so-called primitive cultures. We should not hesitate, therefore, to treat representations as intellectual constructions of thought, while relating them to the collective emotions which accompany them or which they arouse. When you discriminate against a group you not

only express your prejudices about this category, but also the aversion or contempt to which they are indissolubly linked.

3  A German proverb has it that 'the devil is in the detail', and so it is also with collective representations. Evidently, they comprise ideas and beliefs which are general, and relate them to practices or realities which are not. Moreover, it is perhaps legitimate to conceive of them and to present them as a science or a religion. But, nevertheless, it is advisable to search for these representations through the most trivial aspects of language or behaviour, to linger over the most obscure interpretations or the most fleeting metaphors, in order to discover their efficacy and their meaning. If one then examines them as a whole, representations must appear as continuous and internal to both society and reality, and not as their double or their reflection. In this sense, a representation is at once both an image and a texture of the thing imagined, which manifests not only the sense of things which co-exist but also fills the gaps – what is invisible or absent from these things.

Reading the books of Lévy-Bruhl, one is struck by the talent with which he explored religious contents or described rituals. And even more by the minute examination of their ramifications in linguistic expressions, the use of numbers, behaviour towards the sick, or attitudes towards death. In this way an understanding of so-called 'primitive' representations increases progressively as one sees them take root in the concrete life of people. Among contemporary researchers in this domain only Denise Jodelet ([1989a]1991, 1991) shows a similar care.

This, however, does not concern the method, but the concept itself, which takes on a different sense. It is this which Husserl saw clearly when he wrote in a letter to Lévy-Bruhl on 11 March 1935 (the date is important here):

Of course we have long known that each human being has their 'representation of the world', that each nation, each supra-national cultural sphere lives so to speak in another world than that which surrounds them, and we also know that it is the same for each historical epoch. But faced with this empty generality, your work and its excellent theme made us see something so surprising because of its novelty; it is, in effect, possible, and absolutely crucial, to take as a task to 'feel from within' a closed humanity living in an animated and generative sociality, to understand it in so far as it contains a world in its uniformalised social life, and on this basis, that it takes this world not simply as a 'representation of the world', but as the existing world itself. In this way we come to apprehend, identify and think their customs, and hence their logic as much as their ontology, and those of the surrounding world through their corresponding categories.

This is a difficult text, because it goes beyond psychology or anthropology as they existed at the distressing moment when the great German philosopher wrote it. But its author perfectly recognized that a social representation which was only a representation of something, of a common environment or object, would be an 'empty generality'. It has often been thought of in this way, in spite of the precision I have tried to give it. It happens when one does not take sufficient account of its specificity and its 'novelty', which is to be at one and same time the representation of someone, of a collectivity which in this way creates a world for itself.

4  Lastly, one must bear in mind that all collective representations have the same coherence and value. Each has its originality and its own relevance, such that none of them has a privileged relation to the others and could not be their criterion of truth or rationality. Otherwise, as soon as such recognition is given, for example, to a scientific or modern representation, then by inference others appear inferior, incomplete or irrational. If I insist on this point, it is because it is not altogether foreign to contemporary social and cognitive psychology. Everyone can grasp the accuracy of this critique by reading the excellent book by Stephen Stich, *The fragmentation of reason* (1990), which draws up the balance of the research undertaken in this psychology and shows how it has suffered from this misrecognition.

One can think of these four aspects as specifying the concept of knowledge with which we are concerned, and which retains its value even today. But is is above all the fourth aspect which was the source of Lévy-Bruhl's scandalous affirmation, that is to say that it is impossible to propose an absolute criterion of rationality which could be independent of the content of collective representations and their entrenchment in a particular society. Thus he disputed the fundamental proposition maintaining that 'primitive thought' is concerned with the same problems or the same type of problems as advanced thought. Such a view would make the former a rudimentary, even childish, form of the latter. For Lévy-Bruhl, there is a discontinuity, hence a profound difference, between primitive mentality and modern or scientific mentality. It is not that people in traditional cultures have a simpler or more archaic mentality than our own. On the contrary, each is equally complex and developed, and we have no reason for despising one and glorifying the other. Each has its own categories and rules of reasoning which correspond to different collective representations.

We cannot, then, as Durkheim wished, account for the psychology of both 'primitive' and 'civilized' people in terms of the same processes of thought. If one should not reduce the psychology of the group to that of the individual, neither should one reduce the psychology of different groups to a single uniform and undifferentiated entity. As Lévy-Bruhl writes: 'we must then reject beforehand any idea of reducing mental operations to a single type, whatever the peoples we are considering, and accounting for all collective representations by a psychological and mental functioning which is always the same' ([1925]1926, p. 28). It is a wise counsel which authorizes us, in Husserl's phrase, to 'feel from within' how mentality is fashioned and how, in its turn, it fashions, not society in general, but this Melanesian society, or this Indian one, or this European one. This could be shown in detail, but this is not the occasion to do so. Meanwhile, one can grasp the full meaning of the distinction between the two modes of thinking and representing by paying attention to the social psychology which emerges from them. In particular that of the so-called 'primitive' cultures which is founded on three principal ideas.

First, the idea that the non-scientific representations of these cultures are steeped in an emotional ambience which sensitizes people to the existence of invisible, supernatural, in a word 'mystical', entities. These 'mystical' entities colour all their ways of thinking, suggesting pre-liaisons among the things represented. They also render individuals impermeable to the data of immediate experience. Second, there is the idea that memory plays a more important role in these cultures than in ours. This means that the world of mediated and interior perceptions dominates the world of direct and exterior perceptions. Lastly, the third idea is that the people who create these representations and put them into practice are not constrained, as we are, to 'avoiding contradiction' (Lévy-Bruhl, [1925]1926, p. 78). On the contrary, they are enjoined to follow the logic regulated by a law of participation, which allows them to think what is forbidden to us, namely, that a person or a thing can at the same time be both itself and someone or something else.

For example, an animal can participate in a person; or else individuals partake of their names, so they do not disclose them, since an enemy can surprise them and have the owner of the name at their mercy. Further, an individual participates in their child, so that if the child is ill it is the individual who takes the medicine instead of the child. Do we also ever apply the law of participation? Do we not think that an individual is what they eat, suggesting that the qualities of the animal or plant with which they feed themself ends by colouring their qualities? We can see the reason why Lévy-Bruhl qualified the primitives as 'prelogical'. Not because they are illogical or incapable of thinking like the more civilized, but because they follow another law of thinking governed by what is called mystical collective representations.

You are probably struck, as I was, by the resemblance between the psychology of these representations and that of the unconscious set out by Freud in the same epoch. But, while for Lévy-Bruhl this psychology expresses an alternative rationality, for Freud it expresses irrationality itself. To illustrate concretely how the French thinker conceived the difference for which he was so often criticized, one might dream of two fictional cultures. The first would establish, by decree or by vote, psychoanalysis as its public representation, the second cognitive psychology. In the first one may suppose that individuals will think in terms of invisible entities: 'Oedipus complex', 'cathexes', 'superego', and that they will be able to free associate ideas without worrying about contradictions between them. Meanwhile, in the second, they will not take account of anything except measurable information about the frequency of events or perceived behaviours, and they will be constrained to obey the principle of non-contradiction, or any other principle which regulates the calculations of a computer.

Now, this is not to say that individuals in the first culture would be incapable of thinking which respected non-contradiction, nor that those in the second culture could not free associate, but simply that the collective representations of our two imaginary cultures differ, and impose one or the other principle on their members. Further, the inhabitants of the cognitive culture will say, and elsewhere, you can be sure, they have said so (Moscovici, 1993a), that the inhabitants of the psychoanalytic culture are 'prelogical'. But they would be wrong to think, as they do, that this means illogical, since it is only a matter of a different logic. This imaginary example makes us see that it is the content of a representation and the nature of the corresponding group which sets forth the principle of rationality, and not the inverse. To make use of contemporary terms: the criterion of rationality appears as a norm inscribed in the language, institutions, and representations of a specific culture.

A great deal of ink has been poured over this difference between a 'primitive mentality' and a 'civilized' or 'scientific' mentality. In fact, it seems to me to refer to the difference between belief and knowledge, so important but so little understood, as can be established by reading Wittgenstein's (1953) late reflections on belief. In my opinion, a great many misunderstandings would be dispelled if the following suggestion were to be accepted: The difference with which we are concerned takes on a new meaning when we pay attention to the distinction between:

1  common representations whose kernel consists of beliefs which are generally more homogeneous, affective, impermeable to experience or contradiction, and leave little scope for individual variations; and

2  common representations founded on knowledge, which are more fluid,

pragmatic, amenable to the proof of success or failure, and leave a certain latitude to language, experience, and even to the critical faculties of individuals.

Let us sum up. Indifference to contradiction, mobility in the frontiers between inner reality and outer reality, homogeneity of content, these would be the characteristics of the psychology associated with the first culture; abstention from contradiction, distinction between inner reality and outer reality, permeability to experience, these would be the characteristics of the psychology associated with the second culture. But, of course, each culture combines them according to their own aims and history, imposing rules on the relations between them. Whatever the fate of this suggestion might be I have put it forward in order to generalise and throw into relief the psychical sense of the distinction established by the French writer. In return, I hope to expose, if only briefly, what its influence was and how Lévy-Bruhl's concept of collective representations became a model which has been absorbed into contemporary psychology. In fact, almost the whole of the psychology of individual or cultural development is a product of it.

### Piaget, Vygotsky, and social representations

In the 1920s, it was still possible to think in terms of evolution, and more particularly, of an evolution of 'primitive' representations being modified and transformed into 'civilized' representations. Until Lévy-Bruhl it was believed that such evolution could be pursued by virtue of the famous 'psychic unity of mankind'. But after him, it became possible to think that this evolution might consist of a discontinuous change which occurred with the passage from one culture to another. This question might seem abstruse. We need however to recall it if we wish to have a precise idea of the two major influences it exercised, one on Piaget, the other on Vygotsky.

Piaget was, if not the disciple, at least very close to the thought of Lévy-Bruhl in his method as much as in his psychology. Without exaggerating one can say that the psychology of 'primitive' representations established by the French thinker is repeated in the psychology of children's representations (for example, in childhood animism, intellectual realism, etc.) which we owe to the Swiss psychologist. In other words, what one discovered in the public representations of 'exotic' societies, the other rediscovered, in a transposed way, in the supposedly private representations of Swiss children. However, Piaget distanced himself from Lévy-Bruhl (and brought himself closer to Durkheim and Freud) when he envisaged a continuous evolution stretching from these 'prelogical' representations of the young child to the more logical and individual representations of the adolescent.

What we do know is that Vygotsky, Luria, and their school turned towards the same intellectual source. Evidently, their own political inclination and above all the socialist revolution forced them to conceive a psychology which recognized the rightful place of society and culture, that is, a profoundly Marxist psychology which is not content to pay lip service to the primacy of society, as happens in both East and West with the accumulation of declarations and citations while continuing to pursue an individual psychology. Like many Russians of his time, Vygotsky believed in the truth of Marxism, in the coming of a new and better society whose success it was necessary to secure. He and his colleagues did not treat these questions with any ironic detachment, they were committed thinkers.

It was precisely because they took these problems seriously that they went on to a deeper examination of them. They concluded that, aside from the general frame, there was little hope of finding a fundamental concept in Marxism, or a fruitful vision for psychology. They should not be reproached for this; in fact, in the eyes of its founders and the contemporary thinkers of the revolution, Marxism was not the 'science of everything' it has since become. Through a feverish analysis of psychology in the course of these years of creativity and revolution, Vygotsky and Luria discovered the path which allowed them to introduce social phenomena into psychology and to found it upon them. But above all, the introduction of the historical and cultural dimension into psychology was made by default. As one could guess, since I have been speaking about it, it is the path of collective representations and the affirmation that the higher mental processes have their origin in the collective life of people. In particular, the path which led to the concept of these representations was the psychology of Lévy-Bruhl, whose value Piaget and Werner had begun to demonstrate.

You will have no objection if, to confirm this assertion, I appeal to an erudite expert in Soviet psychology, who writes:

Taking into account an overall social orientation of Marxism one might assume that it was Marxist theory that provided an intellectual guideline for Vygotsky. This assumption holds no water, however; as Vygotsky showed in his *Crisis*, Marxist theory in the 1920s failed to develop any concepts required for a psychological study of human behaviour and cognition. The only sufficiently developed theory of human cognition as socially determined was offered by the French sociological school of Emile Durkheim, and was discussed in the related work of Lucien Lévy-Bruhl, Charles Blondel and Maurice Halbwachs. (Kozulin, 1990, p. 122)

Even if this author overestimates the convergence between these different thinkers, he summarizes in precise terms the way in which this connection was established and why it was imposed with such necessity. It is true that one finds in Vygotsky numerous passages which echo this connection and which could be misconstrued if the inspiration behind them is ignored. In any case, as early as these crucial years, the notion of collective representations began to fashion his vision of mental life, its linguistic mediation, and its social content. Vygotsky's encounter with the categories of Lévy-Bruhl gave him a concrete sense and allowed him to set forth a theory of human cultural development. This original theory bears the imprint of Vygotsky, even if personally I am not inclined to give him as much scientific value as others do. Still, this theory proposes, in opposition to that of Piaget, a discontinuous evolution of collective representations.

Be that as it may, once the connection had been established, Vygotsky and Luria were the first to attempt an experimental proof on a true scale, which no one had previously done. As Luria recounts in his memoirs: 'The data relied upon by Lévy-Bruhl as well as by his anthropological and sociological critics – in fact the only data available to anyone at that time – were anecdotes collected by explorers and missionaries who had come in contact with exotic people in the course of their travels' (1979, p. 59). Thus the idea came to them of conceiving the first field study on a relatively large scale into the representations of the Uzbeks in Central Asia at the beginning of the 1930s: 'Although we could have conducted our studies in remote Russian villages, we chose for our research sites the hamlets and nomad camps of Uzbekistan and Khirgizia in Central Asia where great discrepancies between cultural forms promised to maximize the possibility of detecting shifts in the basic forms, as well as in the context of people's thinking' (Luria, 1979, p. 60).

One can see that this vast project sought to explore at the collective level among the nomads what Piaget explored at the individual level among children. They meant to grasp the psychological transformations occurring in a population attached to its religion and living in a traditional way but which had undergone a profound metamorphosis on a social and cultural level as a consequence of the revolution. The old frameworks of life had disintegrated, the hierarchy had disappeared, schools had been opened in numerous villages at the same a time as various technological products had made their appearance, upsetting the traditional economy.

This study, which was only published many years later (Luria, 1976), in my view confirmed Lévy-Bruhl's conjecture and, therefore, gave a solid foundation to Vygotsky's theory of cultural and historical development. But, at a deeper level, Vygotsky and Luria remained more faithful than did Piaget to the canons of individual psychology in the face of the concept of collective representations, and made a less creative use of the psychological analyses of the French thinker. There is here an inversion: Piaget's concept of development is further away from Lévy-Bruhl, although the content of his psychology is closer to him, while with Vygotsky it is the opposite way around. Like rival brothers, they shared the same scientific background while being wholly opposed to each other. I hope that one day epistemologists with more time than I have might take up this interesting relation.

What seems to me important here is that during the years in which his own health declined, as well as the health of the socialist revolution, Vygotsky was attacked because his theory of historical and cultural development, hence his psychology, owed so much to collective representations and to the writings of Durkheim and Lévy-Bruhl which referred to them. In a recent article the Russian psychologist Bruschlinksij (1989) reviewed again these critiques of an approximate value, and defended Rubinstein who had been among those who had made such critiques, since he in his turn had become their victim. But something more surprising is the silence, if not the lightness with which the best specialists of the great Russian psychologist (Wertsch, 1985) pass over his works as if it were a question of an anecdote, and not an essential moment in the history of contemporary psychology. To the point that Vygotsky's ideas and research on historical and cultural development, even on language, appear to have arisen in his mind in the same way as the goddess Athena arose from the brain of Zeus, through a miraculous filiation. A few allusions to Mead or Marx do not render this apparition any the less miraculous, they rather serve to obscure its real genesis. I suspect that this blindness towards the effective historical connection is due to something rather deeper than the simple neglect of the truth.

Such blindness is the result, even in those who are convinced that psychological phenomena should not be reduced to organic or individual phenomena, and those who demonstrate a sympathy for the social, of nevertheless seeing the latter in relation to the individual, or at best as a form of intersubjectivity. Hence they can see clearly neither the limits of Marxism in psychological matters, nor in what sense the opening of a Durkheim or a Lévy-Bruhl was a unique opportunity for the Russian thinkers confronted with an extraordinary historical situation in which they were fully aware of the risks they were taking and for which they paid the consequences. This is still only a partial aspect of the representation (*Darstellung*) which concerns us. What really matters is that as they became a precise concept, social representations inspired a psychology of 'primitives' which was new and non-individualist (Davy, 1931). And this in its turn opened the way for Piaget's psychology of the child and Vygotsky's psychology of the higher psychological functions. One cannot then sustain that there was not here a truly specific notion of the social capable of furnishing the psychology of representation its rightful content. Is this not fundamentally the spirit which should predominate in the human sciences, and in social psychology in particular? Perhaps it is not right to go on and on about positions which have long been overtaken, in order to go further. For evident reasons, I have not evoked the development of which one recognizes the traces in modern episte-mology. But, reading Fleck's ([1935]1979) book, one picks up these traces, mentioned by the author himself. Once again they lead to Lévy-Bruhl, in a significant if not exclusive way. In particular, the concept of collective representation is expressed through the notion of the style of thought of a collective used by Fleck. And we know that Fleck's book found an echo in the theory of Kuhn and in his epistemology of science.

### From collective representations to social representations

The general subject of this chapter is the genesis and fecundity of the idea of social representation. It has served to characterize what is reckoned to be decisive in the processes of thought or the set of beliefs shared by groups or whole societies. It has also served to explain the changes or metamorphoses which these processes and these sets of beliefs have apparently undergone. If we turn towards the contemporary epoch, it is clear that the underlying problem is that of modern rationality. As we know, it implies that the forms of mental and social life conserved by tradition should be replaced by those of science and technology. Our scientific thought elevated to the rank of the norm of all thought, our logic taken as the unique viable logic stigmatise without examining them all different thoughts and beliefs, relegating them to an inferior rank. In this way the diffusion of modern thought supposes *ipso facto* the regression without exception of all others. Of course, one must pay the price: at the limit, if scientific thought imposes its rules and operations on the mind, it serves notice to other forms of thought and dooms them to disappear.

This is the direction in which our processes of thought or sets of belief are changed and transformed. There is therefore nothing surprising if a large part of the work devoted to cultural and individual development strives to elucidate the stages through which societies or individuals reach this point in a necessary way. Today, for all that, our critical conscience is less certain of this evolution. But nevertheless, the postulate of the reducibility of all forms of thought and belief to a unity holds the high ground everywhere, as much in psychology, economics, or sociology as in public discourse.

All of this may strike you as the rehearsal and description of things already well known, and hence without great interest. This would be the case if there were not, however, two consequences which deserve attention:

1 The first consequence is expressed by the fact that a tacit distinction is made between societies without science and those with science. And, consequently, collective representations are studied only in the former, as if they were unrelated to the latter. In such a way that the characteristics, beginning with the beliefs instituted in these traditional or 'exotic' societies, are distinguished as if it were a question of a mental form peculiar to them alone. Further, at a deeper level, these representations are taken as models of 'total' or 'closed' societies in which the symbolic and practical constituents of social relations are perfectly integrated. In such societies every type of behaviour and cognition seems to be fashioned by the mythical and ritual nucleus of the tradition of a people. In this way the greater part of the knowledge brought into play in the subsistence activities, the arts, and everything which is exchanged in the transactions of ordinary life are put to one side. This explains, at least in part, why every representation appears to coincide with the collectivity in its entirety, and to take on a character both uniform and static.

  With this framework in mind it is striking to see a so-called 'primitive' representation compared and contrasted with science, not only as scientists practise it, or as it is diffused in modern societies, but as it is described by the logic of science described in the works of philosophers. For example, the Melanesian rain-maker whose rites are observed and whose magical beliefs are recorded is compared no less a figure than Einstein. But this discussion would take us too far. For now, I prefer simply to state my disagreement with the idea that collective representations should have a meaning in distant societies or in former times, but not in our own, with its deification of scientific beliefs. There is a good reason for that.

2 The second consequence of the postulate of reducibility is what Laudan (1977) called the *arationality assumption*. This is that the social explanations of our intellectual studies fall within sociology only when these studies fail to meet the generally recognized criteria of rationality. Even Mannheim, who in this was faithful to Marxism, invoked this hypothesis when he exempted mathematics and the natural sciences from the domain of the sociology of knowledge. But

this can also be applied to ideology, because it deviates from these criteria, either by being confounded with religion, or because it is a counterfeit of science. It should nevertheless be noted that both Durkheim and Lévy-Bruhl adhered implicitly to this hypothesis. Without doubt they see the universal features of cognition – cause, time, class, or number – as being founded on the features shared by all societies. This does not prevent them from explaining the passage from religious or magical beliefs to modern science as an effect of the passage from the pre-eminence of the collectivity to the pre-eminence of the individual who becomes conscious of her-/himself and 'explicitly differentiates himself from the group of which he feels himself a member' (Lévy-Bruhl, [1925]1926, p. 365).

When we establish a connection between these different aspects, we understand better why following a period of extraordinary interest in collective representations there has been a period of reserve, even abandon. They appeared as explanatory notions only with respect to societies whose beliefs, materialized in institutions, language, and morals, are constraining and centred on the human universe, or, to borrow a term from Piaget, sociocentric. They could not, therefore, as Bergson clearly saw, have validity beyond closed or total societies, such as a nation or a tribe. Further, in the positivist conception which then predominated, the science and rational techniques of modern societies, although derived from religious thought, had an objective and individual character.

It was here that Fleck rightly saw an incongruity, or for that matter a contradiction, insofar as objective properties depend on the particular conditions of a society, just as much as on its models of thinking. And he was not the only one, since Piaget wrote in relation to Durkheim who sustained at the same time both the sociocentric character of collective representations and the individual character of science:

If he was able to maintain two such incompatible positions, it is obviously because, instead of proceeding to the analysis of different types of social interactions, he constantly reverted to the global language of 'totality'. Hence, in order to demonstrate the collective nature of reason, he alternated between two sorts of argument, very different in fact, but used simultaneously under the cover of this undifferentiated notion of the social totality exercising constraint over the individual. (Piaget, [1965]1995, p. 72)

One cannot, then, deny that psychologists and sociologists have had some reasons for distancing themselves from a concept which seemed cut to the measure of a traditional or exotic society and marked by its positivist origins. Or, at the most, to refer to it in a historical way (Farr, 1993). But this is unacceptable when one does not wish to resign oneself to a social psychology both individualistic and deprived of any common framework with the other human sciences, and consequently destined to become fragmented into a multitude of research fields without any links between them and without any historical continuity. Perhaps this can help us to understand why, when one turns toward the collective background of mental life and action, there is no other serious alternative than attempting to give a fresh chance to this line of thought. After all, often in the history of ideas or science a much-debated notion proved useful in a new context, as was the case, for example, of the atom in the nineteenth century.

Be that as it may, through a choice whose motives have little importance here, it seems to me legitimate to suppose that all forms of belief, ideologies, knowledge, including even science, are, in one way or another, *social representations*.[2] It seemed then (Moscovici, [1961]1976), and it seems all the more so today, that neither the opposition of the social to the individual, nor the evolution from the traditional to the modern had, in this regard, the importance which is given to them.

But it seemed right to distinguish those forms according to the way they order their content and represent men, events, and things in a particular universe which society recognizes either as a *consensual* universe or as a *reified* universe. Social representations are marked through and through by the division into these two universes, the former characterized by a relation of trusting appropriation, even implication, and the latter by a distancing, authority, detachment even – or what in German is called *Zugehörigkeit* (affiliation) and *Entfremdung* (alienation). They also correspond to the relations instituted by individuals in society and to the modes of interaction specific to each of them. Without repeating the reasons and descriptions I have given elsewhere (Moscovici, 1984a), I will just recall that this distinction puts popular knowledge, ways of thinking and acting in everyday life, common sense if you like, on one side, and science and ideology on the other. Ideology being, as Ricoeur has described it, 'simplifying and schematic. It is a grid or code for giving an overall view, not only of a group, but also of history and, ultimately, of the world' (1981, p. 226).

One might perhaps try to classify the forms of belief and knowledge according to the place assigned to them in a hierarchy, the reified forms being readily considered as higher in value and power then the consensual forms. Nothing in this would justify placing them where they might be exempted from dependence upon the social. To repeat myself, it is clear that they partake of some social representation. Consequently, the postulate of reducibility, that is to say, the postulate of an elimination of beliefs and common knowledge by science as a *telos* of individual and cultural development, must be renounced. In this sense, in a social sense, science and common sense – beliefs in general – are irreducible to one another insofar as they are ways of understanding the world and relating to it. Although common sense changes its content and ways of reasoning, it is not replaced by scientific theories and logic. It continues to describe the ordinary relations between individuals, it explains their activities and normal behaviour, it shapes their transactions in everyday life. And it resists every attempt at reification which would turn the concepts and images rooted in language into rules and explicit procedures (Farr, 1993).

I believe I was among the first to argue for the irreducibility of common sense to science, which has today become a philosophical position, marking one part of cognitive science. But whereas the reasons invoked by Fodor, Dennett, Putnam, and others are of a logical order, I continue to think that the real reason is of a psychosocial order. In any case one can say that renouncing the myth of total rationalization, that is, of the assimilation of all social representations to scientific representations, of the consensual universe to the reified universe, implies abandoning another idea shared by many of the human sciences, psychology in particular. I mean the idea that one sees an *upgrading* of thought, from perception to reason, from the concrete to the abstract, from the 'primitive' to the 'civilized', from the child to the adult, etc., as our knowledge and our language progressively become more decontextualized. On the contrary, what we see is a *downgrading* of thought, that is, a movement in the opposite direction, as our knowledge and language circulates and becomes contextualized in society. This is completely normal, since, as Maxwell said, the abstract of one century becomes the concrete of another. The changes and transformations take place constantly in both directions, the representations communicate among themselves, they combine and they separate, introducing a quantity of new terms and new practices into everyday and 'spontaneous' usage. In fact, scientific representations daily and 'spontaneously' become common sense, while the representations of common sense change into scientific and autonomous representations. An example of the first kind of transformation is the diffusion of biological ideas and explanations in relation to ecology or to Aids (Herzlich, 1973; Markova and Wilkie, 1987), and of the second kind in theories of personality, or chaos (see Sommer, chapter 12 this volume), and so on.

Let us leave on one side this distinction between the upgrading and downgrading of social representations, and recognize that the popular knowledge of common sense always furnishes the knowledge which people have at their disposal, science and technology themselves do not hesitate to borrow from it when they need an idea, an image, a construction. There is nothing surprising, then, if common knowledge remains at the base of all cognitive processes, which poses a theoretical and empirical problem from the point of knowledge. If a psychologist speaks of an extrovert personality or a prototype, if a biologist evokes information and selection, or again if an economist reasons in terms of the market and competition, each of them, within their own speciality, makes an appeal to concepts drawn from their heritage, from the sources of common knowledge from which it has never been detached. We understand that even the way of naming and communicating these elements of science presupposes and conserves a link with the knowledge of common sense (Moscovici, [1961]1976; Herzlich, 1973; Fleck, [1912]1935; Flick, chapter 3 this volume).

Can one avoid commenting on the profound interest which this phenomenon holds for social psychology? And isn't this precisely the difficulty about collective representations, that they are grasped in practice indirectly through systems of belief and knowledge codified by institutions, morals, and specialized languages? This comes back in some way to isolating them from the flux of social exchanges and to cutting psychic operations without being able to observe how they are articulated in real life. In such conditions it is not surprising that these representations should appear so 'closed', so 'total', and so difficult to apply to our own society. Now the point that I am going to make has led me to a clear decision. Common sense, popular knowledge – what the English call *folk-science* – offer us *direct* access to social representations. It *is*, up to a certain point, social representations which combine our capacity to perceive, infer, understand, which come to our mind to give a sense to things, or to explain the situation of someone. They are so 'natural' and demand so little effort that it is almost impossible to suppress them. Imagine looking at an athletics competition without having the least idea of what the athletes are doing. Or that two people kiss each other in the street without having the least idea that they are in love with each other. These interpretations are so evident that we normally expect everybody to agree to the truth of what passes in front of their eyes.

We have learnt to regard the representations of *folk-physics*, *folk-biology*, or *folk-economics* with some scepticism. But who does not have a representation which allows them to understand why liquids rise in a container, why sugar dissolves, why plants need to be watered, or why the government raises taxes? Thanks to this popular physics we avoid collisions on the roads, thanks to this popular biology we cultivate our garden, and this popular economics helps us to look for a way of paying less tax. The categories of folk-science are so widespread and irresistible that they seem to be 'innate'. We make use of such knowledge and know-how all the time. We exchange them amongst ourselves, we renew them through study or experience in order to explain behaviours confidently – and without being conscious of them – and we pass a good part of our waking life talking about the world, inventing our future, and the future of our children as a function of these representations.

What is the value of *folk-science*? This is a philosophical question which I don't propose to consider here, but, as the philosopher Dennett remarked about it, anyone who ventures on the motorway should judge this science reliable. The vast field of common sense, of popular sciences, allows us to grasp social representations *in vivo*, to grasp how they are generated, communicated, and put to work in everyday life. To make a comparison, we can say that these fields offer prototypical material for exploring the nature of these representations, just as dreams offer an exemplary field to anyone wishing to understand the unconscious. Social representations thus lose the derived and abstract character associated with collective representations to become, in some way, a concrete and observable phenomenon. In spite of a number of critiques (Fraser and Gaskell, 1990), it was and remains my conviction that social psychology is more than ever the science of social representations and can find in them a unifying theme.

In any case, one can see why common sense and popular knowledge offer us this privileged field of exploration.

1  What I have called post-scientific common sense is, like all knowledge shared by society as a whole, interwoven with our language, constitutive of our relations and our skills. It is a structured collection of descriptions and explanations, more or less connected to each other, of personality, illness, feelings, or natural phenomena, which everyone possesses, even if they are not aware of it, and which they use for organizing their experience, taking part in a conversation, or doing business with other people. It is *Umgangsdenken* ('everyday thought') associated with the *Umgangssprache* ('colloquial language'), without which everyday life is inconceivable. Even young children easily grasp – as Freud showed in relation to the sexual theories of children – popular knowledge at an age when they have a limited experience of human activities allowing them to induce such knowledge (Jodelet, 1989b).

One cannot help being struck by the following contrast: on the one hand, we are familiar with a good number of popular sciences, we understand them, use them, renew them easily through conversation, reading newspapers or watching television. On the other, we master hardly a small part of the scientific or technical knowledge which we use for our profession, livelihood, and practice of our whole life. In brief, as Chomsky has written, 'Grammar and common sense are acquired by virtually everyone, effortlessly, rapidly, in uniform manner, merely by living in a community under minimal conditions of interaction, exposure and care. There need be no explicit teaching or training and when the latter takes place, it has only marginal effects on the final state achieved' (1975, p. 144). Individual variations are very limited and, in a given community, everyone acquires a vast and rich store of knowledge, comparable to that of others. Bergson was right when he said that common sense is 'social sense' (1976, p. 110).

2 Contrary to scientific and ideological representations, constructed following the demands of formal logic on the basis of fundamental terms all perfectly defined, distinct even, the representations of common sense are, in one way or another, 'cross-bred'. That is to say that the ideas, linguistic expressions, explanations of different origins are aggregated, combined and regularized more or less like several sciences in a single hybrid science, like several idioms in a créole language. People who share a common knowledge in the course of their ordinary life do not 'reason' about it, and could not place it in front of them like an 'object', or analyze its contents by placing it at a distance to 'observe' it, without themselves being implicated in it. To appropriate it they have to do exactly the opposite, they have to dive into the flux of diverse contents, participate in their concrete implementation, and strive to make them accessible to others. In this way their knowledge thus cross-breeds and their disparate vocabularies have a semantic potential which is not exhausted by any particular usage, but must constantly be refined and determined with the help of the context.

It should be clear for us that these arrangements lead to two results which do not coincide in any way. Common knowledge does not only comprise scientific or religious beliefs. It also transposes them into familiar images, as if the possibility of representing abstract notions dominated the process. Further, social representations of different origins are condensed in common knowledge, in such a way that, according to needs, some can be substituted for others. If we return to the example of Aids suggested earlier, it can be established that religious representations concerning sexual freedom combine with medical representations about the causes of the illness, or political representations about the fabrication of the virus by the CIA in order to eliminate certain populations. This gives an impression of a cognitive and social patchwork. But it is a false impression, since just as our habitual language rests upon the polysemic value of words and a créole language is as rigorous as any other, so popular representations have a their own coherence and rigour. It seems to me that Billig's (1987) work has recently elaborated these aspects and clarified what I thought I had observed and which had been for me only a conjecture.

3 Common sense continues to be conceived of predominantly as an archaic stage of understanding, including a mass of knowledge which has not changed for millennia and which was born in our direct perception of people and things. It thus suits the aims of our everyday life, with an extraordinary success. About the time when I have suggested that social psychologists become interested in common sense, the psychologist Heider (1958) began to argue that, since relations between human beings are a function of their 'naive psychology' we had better study the origin of this naive psychology which gives meaning to our experience. Now, as you know, this has been done starting from the *perception* which individuals have of one another, without taking account of their beliefs, language or the meanings embedded in this language (see Flick, chapter 3 this volume). It is curious that Heider has been taken as supporting this conception, since his analyses begin from literary and philosophical texts, and not from laboratory analyses. However that may be, this dominant conception is acultural and ahistorical. It would be incompatible with my presupposition. Meanwhile, considering it as a form of social representation one not only recognizes that it has cultural traits but also a historical character (Moscovici and Hewstone, 1983; Hewstone and Augoustinos, chapter 4 this volume). In the first study I made in this field (Moscovici, [1961]1976), I attempted to show that folk-science is not the same for everyone and for always. It is modified at the same time that the structures or problems of society with which individuals are confronted themselves change. Further, ideas of a revolutionary scope in the sciences, such as those of Freud or Marx, or artistic movements which sweep away everything in their path, are assimilated by a great many people, leaving a durable impression on their way of thinking, of speaking, of understanding themselves, or of understanding the world in which they live. They can be venerated with impunity, since, used by everyone and incorporated into the very structures of language, the categories and reasoning of popular science are affected by those who have discovered psychoanalysis, physics, etc. They communicate little by little and finally everyone considers them as being independent and forming part of 'reality'.

We ourselves see social representations forming, so to speak, before our eyes, in the media, in public places, through this process of communication which never happens without some transformation.

Whether the change affects the sense, the concepts, the images, or the intensity and association of beliefs, in the bosom of a community, change is always expressed in representations (De Rosa, 1987). Anyone neglecting this fact will never construct a psychosocial theory of thought and action. The French anthropologist Sperber (1990) has formulated an interesting theory of the communication of representations. He sees them as being generated through a process of the epidemiological diffusion of individual representations. This conjecture is hard to admit, given the rule-bound and organized character of such diffusion. On different occasions we have been able to experience the advantage for our science of choosing common knowledge as a field of research and undertaking a serious comparison of one form with another. This assumes that we consider such common knowledge as the kernel of our consensual universe and recognize in it a historical, cultural, and rhetorical character. Failing which, such knowledge is reduced to impoverished traits, to schemas and stereotyypes without meaning. It seems to me important to emphasize the line between popular science, common sense and social representations (see also Flick, chapter 3 this volume), since it justifies at the same time both why I have returned to the tradition of this concept and the way in which it acquires the importance for our science that it has in our society. And it is because representations are a continuous creation, because we can compare them *in statu nascenti* and grasp them directly that we can propose to offer a theory of them. That is to say, not only to articulate a concept of them, but to describe or explain these representations insofar as they are a social phenomenon.

### Representation, communication and the sharing of reality

I must admit that my original intention was not to introduce a concept derived from Durkheim and Lévy-Bruhl into social psychology, nor then to try and distinguish it in order to adapt it to the *Zeitgeist*. On the contrary, it was the problem of the transformation of science in the course of its diffusion and the birth of a post-scientific common sense, hence that of our social psychology, which led me to the concept. To put this clearly, if developmental psychology is concerned with the transformation in the course of children's lives of their 'spontaneous' representations into scientific and rational representations, it seems to me that social psychology must confront the inverse process, that is, to study how scientific representations are changed into ordinary representations. And, like others before me, I discovered that the only line of thought which has known how to articulate beliefs and knowledge with social reality is theirs. For the rest, they must advance with their own means, since the problem of these French thinkers is not the same as ours, and the same holds true for the future. One can add, in another connection, the well-known fact that since the Second World War it has no longer been possible to found society, as had been the case before, on work or belief, but rather on communication or the production of knowledge (Moscovici, 1982). But this is precisely an aspect which most frequently escapes social psychologists, insofar as they limit their interests to interpersonal relations.

Be that as it may, the aspiration of the theory of social representations is clear. By taking as its centre communication and representations, it hopes to elucidate the links which unite human psychology with contemporary social and cultural questions. On this point we can ask ourselves what is the function of shared representations and what they are, from the moment when they are no longer considered indirectly through religion, myths, and so on. In response to this question I have suggested that the reason for forming these representations is the desire to familiarize ourselves with the unfamiliar. Every violation of existing rules, an extraordinary phenomenon or idea such as those produced by science or technology, unusual events which unsettle what appears to be the normal and stable course of things, all of this fascinates us at the same time as it alarms us. Every deviation from the familiar, every rupture of ordinary experience, everything for which the explanation is not obvious creates a supplementary meaning and sets in motion a search for the meaning, and explanation of what strikes us as strange and troubling.

It is, then, not a search for an agreement between our ideas and the reality of an order introduced into the chaos of phenomena or, to simplify, a complex world which is the motivation for elaborating social representations, but the attempt to build a bridge between the strange and the familiar. And this insofar as the strange presupposes a lack of communication within the group in relation to the world which short-circuits the current of exchanges and displaces the references of language. One has the feeling that it no longer fits the matrix of life in common, that it no longer agrees with our relations with others. To master a strange idea or perception one begins by anchoring it (Doise, 1992) in existing social representations, and it is in the course of this anchoring that it becomes modified (Moscovici, 1988a). This observation is corroborated by Bartlett, who writes: 'As has been pointed out, whenever material visually presented purports to be representative of some common object but contains certain features which are unfamiliar in the community to which the material is introduced, these features invariably suffer transformations in the direction of the familiar' (1932, p. 178). The familiar cannot not change in the course of this process and find a certain social and affective satisfaction in rediscovering it, sometimes in an effective and sometimes in an illusory way.

To push our explanation of the formation of these representations further we need to clarify some difficulties. Searching for the familiar in the strange means that these representations tend towards conservatism, towards the confirmation of their significant content. Well, this would then be a pure and simple consequence of their sociocentrism, of the sociomorphic character of their cognitive and linguistic operations. This means that there is a certain distance in relation to the reality not represented by the group. But is this a question of a characteristic peculiar to non-scientific and non-rational representations, as some people maintain? Observation has shown us that scientific representations are also centred, although in a different way, on the scientific community and the society of which it forms a part. I could add that the paradigms of a normal science equally demonstrate a tendency to conservatism in the face of anomalies, up to the point that their resistance becomes impossible (Kuhn, 1962). Thus, I conclude that all representations are sociocentric and that in the familiarization of the strange society is represented in a more implicit way (Mugny and Carugati, [1985]1989).

I have written about these things in more detail elsewhere. Here, I simply want to specify that if we form representations in order to familiarize ourselves with the strange, then we also form them in order to reduce the margin of non-communication. A margin which is acknowledged through the ambiguities of ideas, the fluidity of meanings, the incomprehension of the images and beliefs of the other, in short, through what the American philosopher Peirce spoke of as the 'vague'. What makes relations problematic, and also exchanges between individuals and groups, is the circulation of representations which nevertheless co-exist in the same public space. Existence in common proves to be impossible if this margin of uncertainty persists and becomes important. In that case the members of a group risk remaining as strange in familiar conversations as if they belonged to different groups.

I maintain, therefore, that social representations are first and foremost intended to make communication in a group relatively non-problematic and to reduce the 'vague' through a degree of consensus among its members. Insofar as this is the case, representations cannot be acquired through the study of some explicit belief or knowledge, nor established through some specific deliberation. Rather, they are formed through reciprocal influences, through implicit negotiations in the course of conversations in which people are oriented towards particular symbolic models, images, and shared values. In doing so, they acquire a common repertoire of interpretations and explanations, rules and procedures which they can apply to everyday life, just as linguistic expressions accessible to everyone (Moscovici, 1984a).

I have often been asked what I mean by the sharing of a representation or shared representations. What gives it this character is not the fact that it is autonomous or that it is common, but rather the fact that its elements have been fashioned through communication and are related through communication. The constraints which this exercises, its rules of interaction and influence, determine the particular structure of knowledge and language which results. To simplify we could say that any lone individual could not represent for themselves the result of the communication of thought (Freyd, 1983), of verbal and iconic messages. This is what gives these cognitive and linguistic structures the form which they have, since they must be shared with others in order to be communicated. I speak therefore of shared representations to indicate that the forms of our thought and our language are made compatible with the forms of communication and the constraints which this imposes. I have shown before that there are three forms of public communication which inflect three corresponding forms of thought and public language (Moscovici, [1961]1976).

It seems to me that the notion of sharing expresses the process through which social or public representations appropriate individual or private representations. It seems more apposite than the idea of constraint introduced by Durkheim and Lévy-Bruhl to describe the process through which collective representations fashion the mental life of individuals. For these thinkers, however, representations are formed in relation to reality and not in relation to communication with others, something which they judged to be secondary but which is essential for us.

### A definition of social representations

Now that this point is highlighted, we can ask ourselves what defines a social representation. If this meaning should be pregnant, it must be that it corresponds to a certain recurrent and comprehensive model of images, beliefs, and symbolic behaviours. Envisaged in this way, statically, representations appear similar to theories which order around a theme (mental illnesses are contagious, people are what they eat, etc.) a series of propositions which enable things or persons to be classified, their characters described, their feelings and actions to be explained, and so on. Further, the 'theory' contains a series of examples which illustrate concretely the values which introduce a hierarchy and their corresponding models of action. Here, as everywhere, formulas and clichés are associated in order to recall this 'theory' to distinguish it by its origin and to distinguish it from others (Duveen and Lloyd, 1990; Palmonari, 1980).

For example, doctors' surgeries overflow with people talking about their cholesterol level, their diet, their blood-pressure, explaining that their illness is innate or acquired, and so on, referring to some medical theory. Or again, journalists devote articles to computer viruses, or the ethnic virus, and so on, making allusion to the genetic model. Nothing is more difficult to eradicate than the false idea that the deductions or explanations we draw from common sense are archaic, schematic, and stereotyped. Certainly it cannot be denied that there are a great number of rigidified 'theories'. But, contrary to what is implied, this has nothing to do with their collective nature or the fact that they are shared by a mass of people. Rather, it comes from the flexibility of the group and the speed of communication of knowledge and beliefs at the heart of society.

In fact, from the dynamic point of view social representations appear as a 'network' of ideas, metaphors and images, more or less loosely tied together, and therefore more mobile and fluid than theories. It seems that we cannot get rid of the impression that we have an 'encyclopoedia' of such ideas, metaphors, and images which are connected one to another according to the necessity of the kernels, the core beliefs (Emler and Dickinson, 1985; Abric, 1988; Flament, 1989) stored separately in our collective memory and around which these networks form. I suppose that social representations in movement more closely resemble money than language. Like money they have an existence to the extent that they are useful, circulate, take different forms in memory, perception, works of art, and so on, while nevertheless always being recognized as identical. In the same way that 100 francs can be represented as a bank-note, a traveller's cheque, or an a figure in a bank statement. And their distinctive value varies according to relations of contiguity, as David Hume remarked. If I meet a colleague in the course of a trip to Germany, I represent him to myself as a compatriot, and say to myself, 'Well, a Frenchman'. If I bump into him on a street in Tokyo, I make of him the image of a European. And if, in some extraordinary way, we were to meet each other on Mars I would think, 'Here is a human'.

Like money, in other respects, representations are social, insofar as they are a psychological fact, in three ways: they have an impersonal aspect, in the sense of belonging to everyone; they are the representation of others, belonging to other people or to another group; and they are a personal representation, felt affectively to belong to the ego. Further, we should not forget that representations, like money, are formed with the double aim of acting and evaluating. They would not, then, belong to a separate domain of knowledge, and for this reason are subject to the same rules as other kinds of actions and social evaluations. Contrary to experts, ordinary people do not see themselves separately as a citizen, as someone who goes to church, and so on. Thus social rules are at the same time rules of inference which have a logical sense. For Max Weber's Protestants, 'honesty is the best policy' is not only a religious maxim. It is a rule which they apply when they reason, make judgements about people, and so on. In the opposite way, certain logical rules function as social rules. For example, do not contradict yourself, calculate the probabilities, and many others. This is why mental contents are stronger imperatives than cognitive forms. Briefly, we can say that what people think determines how they think.

Let us go further. All things considered, communication in our society accelerates, the scale of the media (visual, written, audio) in the social space grows ceaselessly. Two things can then be observed which deserve attention. On the one hand, the differences between social representations are blurred, the boundaries between their iconic aspect and their conceptual aspect are obliterated. The disappearance of the differences and boundaries changes them more and more into representations of representations, makes them become more and more symbolic. And this at the expense of the direct reference of each. In this way the question of knowing how to connect representations to realities is no longer a philosophical question but a psychosocial one.

On the other hand, the categories and meanings through which we 'choose' to confer a quality on people or properties on objects become modified. For examples, we 'choose' to describe a food by its taste or by its protein value, according to the culture to which we belong or the use we wish to make of it. To require that all these qualities be reduced to a single 'true' quality is an impossibility. It assumes that there is a once and for all ready-made, given reality for this food, which is imposed on us independently of the representation which we share.

As I argued in the first sketch of our theory, in relation to psycho-analysis ([1961]1976), it is no longer appropriate to consider representations as a replica of the world or a reflection of it. Not only because this positivist conception is the source of numerous difficulties, but also because representations also evoke what is absent from this world, they form it rather more than they simulate it. When we are asked 'what objects is our world made of?' we must in our turn ask 'within what representation?' before answering. That is to say that shared representations, their language, penetrate so profoundly into all the interstices of what we call reality that we can say that they constitute it. They thus constitute identity, the self (Markus and Nurius, 1986; Oyserman and

Markus, chapter 7 this volume), the market, the characteristics of a person or a group, etc. (Mugny and Carugati, [1985]1989). It is incontestable that they have a socially creative or constructive effect, which would have been surprising not long ago but which, today, is commonly recognized (Flick, 1991b). I have the idea that the majority of the research on discourse by Billig (1987), Potter and Litton (1985; see also Harré, chapter 8, and Potter and Wetherell, chapter 9, this volume) does not contradict the theory of social representations. On the contrary, they complement it, and deepen this aspect of it. To ask then, whether language or representation is the better model can have no more psychological meaning than asking the question: 'Does a man walk with the help of his left leg or his right leg?'. But, to realize just how true and deep this contribution is, and to accept it, one would need to begin with a much greater coherence in psychology itself. While waiting for this, I have no hesitation therefore in treating what we have learnt about rhetoric, about linguistic accounts, as being very closely related to social representations.

### Conclusion

To finish, there is one consequence of this perspective about social representations which deserves to be better elaborated, but which I should nevertheless put into words. Each of us accepts without doubt the idea that the contents and meanings represented vary within the same society, the same culture, as do their means of linguistic expression. But we are obliged to assume that these differences in meaning and content should be judged according to differences in the way of thinking and understanding, in short, according to the principles of distinct rationalities. As we have seen, the specificities of the consensual universe and the reified universe, the contexts of the communication in which these representations are elaborated, are responsible for these differences. The contrasts between them are socially marked and reinforced in such a way as to distinguish each form of rationality.

If this is the case, then we must consider that in each society, each culture, there exist at least two types of rationality, two styles of thinking equivalent to the two extreme forms of representing and communicating. It would be impossible to reduce them to a superordinate rationality which would, in this case, be supra-social. Or, in any case, normative, which could not fail to lead to vicious circles. *Mutatis mutandis*, one must assume that individuals share the same capacity to possess many ways of thinking and representing. Here there is what I have earlier called a cognitive polyphasia, which is as inherent in mental life as polysemy is to the life of language. Further, let us not forget that it is of great practical importance for communicating and for adapting to changing social necessities. The whole of our intersubjective relations to social reality depend on this capacity.

The history which leads to a theory is itself a part of that theory. The theory of social representations has developed on this background (Doise and Palmonari, 1986), and on an ever greater number of research studies which contribute to it and deepen it. These are what, justly, allow us better to appreciate retrospectively the choice of precursors and the meaning of their work. It is at least the experience which I came to have in writing this *historische Darstellung* ('historical representation'), which I hope will be useful for others. A great narrative, writes Frank Kermode, is the fusion of the scandalous with the miraculous. My representation began with scandal. If it contains some miracle, I would see it in the longevity and vitality of the theory of social representations.

### Notes

Translated from the French by Gerard Duveen, who is grateful to Marie-Claude Gervais for her advice, and to Alex Schlömmer for her help in tracing quotations in German texts.

1 In her new translation, Karen Fields renders Durkheim's *représenter* here as 'imagining' (translator).
2 In speaking of social representations in place of collective representations, I wanted to break with the associations which the term 'collective' had inherited from the past. But also with the sociological and psychological interpretations which in the classic way determined its nature.

# References

Abelson, R. P. (1981). The psychological status of the script concept. *American Psychologist, 36*, pp. 715–29.

Abric, J. C. (1988). *Cooopération, compétition et représentations sociales.* Cousset: Del Val.

Aebischer, V., Deconchy, J. P., and Lipanski, R. (1991) (eds.). *Idéologies et représentations sociales.* Fribourg: Del Val.

Agger, B. (1991). Critical theory, poststructuralism, postmodernism: their sociological relevance. *Annual Review of Sociology, 17*, pp. 105–31.

Allen, R. L., Thornton, M. C., and Watkins, S. C. (1994). An African American racial belief system and social structural relationships: a test of invariance. *National Journal of Sociology.*

Allen, V. L. (1965). Situational factors in conformity. In L. Berkowitz (ed.), *Advances in experimental social psychology* (Vol. II). New York: Academic Press.

Allport, F. (1924). *Social psychology.* Boston, MA: Houghton Mifflin.

(1961). The contemporary appraisal of an old problem. *Contemporary Psychology, 6*, pp. 195–67.

(1962). A structuronomic conception of behaviour: individual and collective. *Journal of Abnormal and Social Psychology, 1*, pp. 3–30.

Altheide, D. L. (1974). *Creating reality.* London/Beverly Hills, CA: Sage.

Althusser, L. (1970). Ideology and ideological state apparatuses. In L. Athusser (1971), *Lenin and philosophy and other essays.* London: New Left Books.

Ansart, P. (1988). Le concept de représentation en sociologie. In L. Marbeau and F. Audigier (eds.). *Seconde rencontre internationale sur la didactique de l'histoire et de la géographie.* Paris: INRP.

Antaki, C. (1986). Ordinary explanation in conversation: causal structures and their defence. *European Journal of Social Psychology, 15*, pp. 213–30.

Asante, M. K. (1987). *The Afrocentric idea.* Philadelphia, PA: Temple University Press.

(1988). *Afrocentricity.* Trenton, NJ: African World Press.

Asch, S. E. (1956). Studies on independence and conformity: a minority of one against an unanimous majority. *Psychological Monographs, 70*, p. 416.

Atkinson, J. M., and Heritage, J. (eds.) (1984). *Structures of social action: studies in conversation analysis.* Cambridge: Cambridge University Press.

Atkinson, R. C., and Shiffrin, R. M. (1968). Human memory: a proposed system and its control processes. In K. W. Spence and J. T. Spence (eds.). *The psychology of learning and motivation: advances in research and theory*. (Vol. II), pp. 89–195. New York: Academic Press.

Atlan, H., and Morin, E. (1988). Sélection, réjection (dialogue). *Communications*, *49*, pp. 125–36.

Augoustinos, M. (1989). Social representations and causal attributions. In J. Forgas and J. M. Innes (eds.), *Recent advances in social psychology: an interactional perspective*. North Holland: Elsevier.

(1990). The mediating role of representations on causal attributions in the social world. *Social Behaviour*, *5*, pp. 49–62.

Augoustinos, M., and Innes, J. M. (1990). Towards an integration of social representations and social schema theory. *British Journal of Social Psychology*, *29*, pp. 213–31.

Austin, J. L. (1961). *Philosophical papers*. Oxford: Clarendon Press.

(1962). *How to do things with words*. Oxford: Clarendon Press.

Bains, G. (1983). Explanations and the need for control. In M. Hewstone (ed.), *Attribution theory: social and functional extensions*. Oxford: Basil Blackwell.

Bakhurst, D. (1990). Social memory in Soviet thought. In D. Middleton, and D. Edwards (eds.), *Collective remembering*, pp. 203–26. London: Sage.

Baldwin, J. M. (1911). *The individual and society*. Boston, MA: Boston Press.

Bar-Tal, D. (1990). *Group beliefs: a conception for analyzing group structure, process, and behaviour*. New York: Springer.

Bar-Tal, D., and Antebi, D. (1992). Siege mentality in Israel. *Ongoing Productions on Social Representations*, *1* (1), pp. 49–67.

Bartlett, F. C. (1932). *Remembering – a study in experimental and social psychology*. Cambridge: Cambridge University Press.

Baudrillard, J. (1983). *Simulations*. New York: Semiotext(e).

Becker, H. (1986). *Psychoonkologie*. Berlin: Springer.

Bell, D. (1960). *The end of ideology: on the exhaustion of political ideas in the fifties*. New York: Free Press of Glencoe.

Bennett, W. L. (1977). The growth of knowledge in mass belief studies: An epistemological critique. *American Journal of Political Science*, *21*, pp. 465–500.

Berger, P. L., and Luckmann, T. (1966). *The social construction of reality*. Garden City, NY: Doubleday.

Bergson, H. (1976). *Les deux sources de la morale et de la religion*. Paris: Presses Universitaires de France.

Bilides, D. G. (1991). Race, color, ethnicity, and class: issues of biculturalism in school-based adolescent counseling groups. In K. Chau (ed.), *Ethnicity and biculturalism: emerging perspectives of social group work*. New York: Haworth.

Billig, M. (1978). *Fascists: a social psychological view of the National Front*. London: Harcourt Brace Jovanovich.

(1982). *Ideology and social psychology*. Oxford: Basil Blackwell.

(1985). Prejudice, categorization and particularization: from a perceptual to a rhetorical approach. *European Journal of Social Psychology*, *15*, pp. 79–103.

(1987). *Arguing and thinking: a rhetorical approach to social psychology*. Cambridge: Cambridge University Press.

(1988). Social representation, objectification and anchoring: a rhetorical analysis. *Social Behaviour*, *3*, pp. 1–16.

(1989). The argumentative nature of holding strong views: a case study. *European Journal of Social Psychology*, *19* (3), pp. 203–23.

(1990). Collective memory, ideology and the British Royal Familiy. In D. Middleton and D. Edwards (eds.), *Collective remembering*, pp. 60–80. London: Sage.

(1991). *Ideologies and beliefs*. London: Sage.

1992). *Talking about the Royal Family*. London: Routledge.

(1993). Studying the thinking society: social representations, rhetoric and attitudes. In G. Breakwell and D. Canter (eds.), *Empirical approaches to social representations*. Oxford: Oxford University Press.

Billig, M., Condor, S., Edwards, D., Gane, M., Middleton, D., and Radley, A. (1988). *Ideological dilemmas: a social psychology of everyday life*. London: Sage.

Blinco, P. M. A. (1992). A cross-cultural study of task persistence of young children in Japan and the United States. *Journal of Cross-cultural Psychology*, *23*, pp. 407–15.

Blumer, H. (1969). *Symbolic interactionism – perspective and method*. Berkeley and Los Angeles, CA: University of California Press.

Boesch, E. (1991). *Symbolic action theory and cultural psychology*. Berlin: Springer-Verlag.

Bond, M. H. (1983). Cross-cultural studies of attribution. In M. Hewstone (ed.), *Attribution theory: social and functional extensions*. Oxford: Blackwell.

Bond, M., Leung, K., and Wan, K. C. (1982). How does cultural collectivism operate? The impact of task and maintenance on reward distribution. *Journal of Cross-cultural Psychology*, *13*, pp. 186–200.

Boyarin, J. (1989). Un lieu de l'oubli: le lower east side des juifs. *Communications*, *49*, pp. 185–94.

Brandstätter, V., Ellemers, N., Gaviria, E., Giosué, F., Huguet, P., Kroon, M., Morchain, P., Pujal, M., Rubini, M., Mugny, G., and Pérez, J. A. (1991). Indirect majority and minority influence: an exploratory study. *European Journal of Social Psychology*, *21*, pp. 199–211.

Breakwell, G. M. (1993). Social representations and social identity. *Papers on social representations*, *2*, pp. 198–218.

Breakwell, G., and Canter, D. (eds.) (1993). *Empirical approaches to social representations*. Oxford: Clarendon Press.

Brown, P. M. (1990). Biracial identity and social marginality. *Child and Adolescent Social Work*, *7*, pp. p319–37.

Brügge, P. (1993). Der Kult um das Chaos (III). *Der Spiegel*, *41*, pp. 240–52.

Bruner, J. S. (1990). *Acts of meaning*. Cambridge, MA: Harvard University Press.

Bruner, J. S., and Tagiuri, R. (1954). The perception of people. In G. Lindzey (ed.), *Handbook of social psychology* (Vol. II), pp. 634–54. Cambridge, MA: Addison-Wesley.

Bruschlinksij, A. (1989). Sergei Rubinstein. *The Soviet Journal of Psychology*, *10*, pp. 24–42.

Bulman, R. J., and Wortman, C. B. (1977). Attributions of blame and coping in the 'real world': severe accident victims react to their lot. *Journal of Personality and Social Psychology*, *35*, pp. 351–63.

Burns, T. (1969). Public service and private world. In P. Halmos (ed.), *The sociology of mass media communicators*, pp. 53–73. Keele: University of Keele.

Butera, F., and Mugny, G. (1992). Influence minoritaire et falsification: a propos de 'Quelques réflexions psycho-sociologiques sur une controverse scientifique' de B. Matalon. *Revue Internationale de Psychologie Sociale*, *5*(2), pp. 115–32.

Butera F., Huguet P., Mugny G., and Pérez J. A. (1994). Socio-epistemic conflict and constructivism. *Swiss Journal of Psychology*, 53, pp. 229–39.

Butera, F., Legrenzi, P., Mugny, and G., Pérez, J. A. (1991–2). Influence sociale et raisonnement. *Bulletin de Psychologie*, *45*, pp. 144–54.

Butera, F., Mugny, G., Legrenzi, P., and Pérez, J. A. (1996). Majority and minority influence, task representation, and inductive reasoning. *British Journal of Social Psychology, 35,* pp. 123–36.

Caplan, N., and Nelson, S. D. (1973). On being useful: the nature and consequences of psychological research on social problems. *American Psychologist, 28*, pp. 199–211.

Carrithers, M. (1992). *Why humans have cultures: explaining anthropology and social diversity*. Oxford: Oxford University Press.

Carugati, F. (1990a). From social cognition to social representations in the study of intelligence. In G. Duveen and B. Lloyd (eds.), *Social representations and the development of knowledge*. Cambridge: Cambridge University Press.

(1990b). Everyday ideas, theoretical models and social representations: the case of intelligence and its development. In G. R. Semin and K. J. Gergen (eds.), *Everyday understanding*. London: Sage.

Carugati, F., Emiliani, F., and Molinari, L. (1990). Being a mother is not enough: theories and images in the social representations of childhood. *Revue internationale de psychologie sociale*, *3*(3), pp. 289–306.

Chamberlain, C. (1983). *Class consciousness in Australia*. Sydney: George Allen & Unwin.

Choi, S. C., and Choi, S. H. (1990). *We-ness: a Korean discourse of collectivism*. Paper presented at the 1st International Conference on Individualism and Collectivism: Psychocultural Perspectives from East and West.

Chomsky, N. (1975). *Reflections on language*. New York: Pantheon Books.

Cohn, N. (1966). *Warrant for genocide: the myth of the Jewish world conspiracy and the Protocol of the Elders of Zion*. New York/Evanston, Il: Harper & Row.

Condor, S. (1990). Social stereotypes and social identity. In D. Abrams and M. Hogg (eds.), *Social identity theory: constructive and critical advances*. London: Harvester Wheatsheaf.

Converse, P. E. (1964). The nature of belief systems in mass publics. In D. E. Apter (ed.), *Ideology and discontent*. New York: The Free Press.

Conway, M. A. (ed.) (1992). Developments and debates in the study of memory. *The Psychologist*, *5*, pp. 439–55.

Cornford, F. M. (1957). *From religion to philosophy*. New York: Harper.

Coulter, J. (1979). *The social construction of mind*. London: Macmillan.

(1985). Two concepts of the mental. In K. Gergen and K. Davis (eds.), *The social construction of the person*. New York: Springer.

Cousins, S. (1989). Culture and selfhood in Japan and the US. *Journal of Personality and Social Psychology*, 56, pp. 124–31.

Cowlishaw, G. (1988). Australian Aboriginal Studies: the anthropologists' accounts. In M. de Lepervanche and G. Bottomley (eds.), *The cultural construction of race*. Sydney: University of Sydney Press.

Cranach, M. von (1990). Eigenaktivität, Geschichtlichkeit und Mehrstufigkeit. In E. H. Witte (ed.), *Sozialpsychologie und Systemtheorie*, pp. 13–49. Braunschweiger Studien zur Erziehungs – und Sozialwissenschaft, 26.

(1992). The multi-level organization of knowledge and action: An integration of complexity. In M. von Cranach, W. Doise, and G. Mugny (eds.), *Social representations and the social bases of knowledge*, pp. 10–23. Lewinston, NY: Hogrefe & Huber.

(1993). Die Unterscheidung von Handlungstypen. In B. Bergmann, and P. Richter (eds.), *Von der Praxis einer Theorie – Ziele, Tätigkeit und Persönlichkeit*. Göttingen: Hogrefe.

Cranach, M. von, and Kalbermatten, U. (1987). Soziales Handeln. In D. Frey and S. Greif (eds.), *Sozialpsychologie. Ein Handbuch in Schlüsselbegriffen*, pp. 321–25. Munich/Weinheim: PsychologieVerlagsUnion.

Cranach, M. von, and Tschan, F. (1990). Mehrstufigkeit im zielgerichteten Verhalten von Organisationen. In F. Frei, and I. Udris (eds.), *Das Bild der Arbeit*. Berne: Huber.

Cranach, M. von, Doise, W., and Mugny, G. (eds.) (1992). *Social representations and the social bases of knowledge*. Lewiston, NY: Hogrefe & Huber.

Cranach, M. von, Ochsenbein, G., and Valach, L. (1986). The group as a self-active system (outline of a theory of group action). *European Journal of Social Psychology*, 16, pp. 193–229.

Curry, C., Trew, K., Turner, I., and Hunter, J. (1994). The effect of life domains on girls' possible selves. *Adolescence.*, 29, pp. 133–50.

D'Andrade, R. (1981). The cultural part of cognition. *Cognitive Science*, 5, pp. 179–195.

(1987). A folk model of the mind. In D. Holland and N. Quin (eds.), *Cultural models in language and thought*, pp. 112–49. Cambridge: Cambridge University Press.

(1990). Some Propositions about the relations between culture and human cognition. In J. Stigler, R. Shweder and G. Herdt (eds.), *Cultural psychology – essays on comparative human development*, pp. 65–129. Cambridge: Cambridge University Press.

Dann, H. D. (1990). Subjective theories: a new approach to psychological research and educational practice. In G. R. Semin and K. J. Gergen (eds), *Everyday understanding: social and scientific implications*, pp. 204–26. London/Newbury Park, CA/New Dehli: Sage.

Davy, G. (1931). *Sociologues d'hier et d'aujourd'hui*. Paris: Alcan.

De Grada, E. and Ponzo, E. (1971). *La normalità del bambino come pregiudizio dell'adulto*. Rome: Bulzoni.

De Paolis, P., Doise, W., and Mugny, G. (1987). Social marking in cognitive operations. In W. Doise and S. Moscovici (eds.), *Current issues in European social psychology* (Vol. II). Cambridge: Cambridge University Press.

De Rosa, A. M. (1987). The social representations of mental illness in children and adults. In W. Doise and S. Moscovici (eds.), *Current issues in European social psychology* (Vol. II), pp. 47–138. Cambridge: Cambridge University Press.

Derné, S. (1992). Beyond institutional and impulsive conceptions of self: family structure and the socially anchored real self. *Ethos, 20*, pp. 259–88.

Deutsch, M., and Gerard, H. B. (1955). A study of normative and informational social influence upon individual judgement. *Journal of Abnormal and Social Psychology, 51*, pp. 629–36.

Deyanov, D. (1992). La guerre des interpretations symboliques. *Communications, 55*, pp. 55–66.

Doise, W. (1986). *Levels of explanation in social psychology*. Cambridge: Cambridge University Press.

   (1989). Attitudes et représentations sociales. In D. Jodelet (ed.), *Les Représentations sociales*. Paris: Presses Universitaires de France.

   (1992). L'ancrage dans les études sur les représentations sociales. *Bulletin de psychologie, 45*, pp. 189–95.

Doise, W., and Hanselmann, C. (1990). Conflict and social marking in the acquisition of operational thinking. *Learning and Instruction, 1*, pp. 119–27.

Doise, W., and Mugny, G. (1984). *The social development of the intellect*. Oxford: Pergamon Press.

   (1997). *Psychologie sociale et développement cognitif*. Paris: Armand Colin.

Doise, W., and Palmonari, A. (1984). *Social interaction in individual development*. Cambridge: Cambridge University Press.

   (eds.) (1986). *L'étude des représentations sociales*. Paris: Delachaux et Niestle.

Doise, W., Dionnet, S., and Mugny, G. (1978). Conflit socio-cognitif, marquage social et dévelopment cognitif. *Cahiers de psychologie, 27*, pp. 231–43.

Donaldson, M. (1978). *Children's minds*. Glasgow: Fontana-Collins.

Donsbach, W. (1982). *Legitimationsprobleme des Journalismus: Gesellschaftliche Rolle der Massenmedien und berufliche Einstellung von Journalisten*. Freiburg: Alber.

Dörner, D. (1988). Wissen und Verhaltensregulation: Versuch einer Integration. In H. Mandl and H. Spada (eds.), *Wissenspsychologie*, pp. 264–82. Munich/ Weinheim: PsychologieVerlagsUnion.

   (1989). *Die Logik des Mißlingens: Strategisches Denken in komplexen Situationen*. Reinbek: Rowohlt.

Drew, P. (1986). A comment on Taylor and Johnson. *British Journal of Social Psychology, 25*, pp. 197–8.

Drew, P., and Heritage, J. (eds.) (1992), *Talk at work: interaction in institutional settings*. Cambridge: Cambridge University Press.

Durkheim, E. ([1893]1984). *The division of labour in society*. London: Macmillan.

   ([1897]1952). *Suicide*. London: Routledge & Kegan Paul.

   ([1898]1974). Individual and collective representations. In *Sociology and philosophy*. New York: The Free Press.

([1912]1995). *The elementary forms of the religious life.* New York: The Free Press.

([1895]1982). *The rules of sociological method.* London: Macmillan.

Duveen, G., and Lloyd, B. (eds.) (1990). *Social representations and development of knowledge.* Cambridge: Cambridge University Press.

Duvignud, J. (1968). Preface. In M. Halbwachs, *La mémoire collective.* Paris: Presses Universitaires de France.

Eagley, A. H. (1993). Are people prejudiced against women? Paper presented at the University of Michigan, Ann Arbor, Michigan, MS.

Eagley, A. H., and Mladinic, A. (1994). Are people prejudiced against women? Some answers from research on attitudes, gender stereotypes, and judgements of competence. In W. Stroebe and M. Hewstone (eds.), *European review of social psychology* (Vol. V). Chichester: Wiley.

Edwards, D. (1991). Categories are for talking: on the cognitive and discursive bases of categorization. *Theory & psychology, 1*, pp. 515–42.

Edwards, D., and Potter, J. (1992). *Discursive psychology.* London: Sage.

(1993). Language and causation: a discursive action model of description and attribution. *Psychological Review, 100*, pp. 23–41.

Emiliani, F., and Molinari, L. (1989). Mothers' social representations of their children's learning and development. *International Journal of Educational Research, 13*(6), pp. 657–70.

Emler, N., and Dickinson, J. (1985). Children's representations of economic inequalities. *British Journal of Developmental Psychology, 3*, pp. 191–8.

Engels, F. ([1876]1968). The part played by labour in the transition from ape to man. In *Marx and Engels: selected works.* London: Lawrence & Wishart.

Erez, M., and Earley, P. C. (1993). *Culture, self-identity, and work.* New York: Oxford University Press.

Ertel, R. (1985). Jeux et enjeux de la mémoire et de l'histoire. *Revue française de Psychanalyse, 49* (4), pp. 1029–52.

Evans-Pritchard, E. E. (1965). *Theories of primitive religion.* Oxford: Oxford University Press.

(1976). *Witchcraft, oracles, and magic among the Azande.* Oxford: Clarendon Press.

Eysenck, H. J., and Wilson, G. D. (eds.) (1978). *The psychological basis of ideology.* Lancaster: MTP Press.

Fairclough, N. (1989). *Language and power,* London: Longman.

Farr, R. M. (1987a). Social representations – a French tradition of research. *Journal for the Theory of Social Behaviour, 17*, pp. 346–69.

(1987b). Social representations. *Journal for the Theory of Social Behavior, 17* (4) (Special Issue).

(1991). Individualism as a collective representation. In V. Aebischer, and J. Deconchy, *et al.* (eds.), *Idéologies et représentations sociales.* Cousset: Delvad.

(1993). Common sense, science and social representations. *Public Understanding of Science, 7*, pp. 189–204.

Farr, R., and Anderson, A. (1983). Beyond actor/observer differences in perspective: extensions and applications. In M. Hewstone (ed.), *Attribution theory: social and functional extensions.* Oxford: Blackwell.

Farr, R. M., and Moscovici, S. (eds.) (1984). *Social representations*. Cambridge: Cambridge University Press.

Fauconnet, P. (1928). *La responsabilité*. Paris: Alcan.

Feagin, J. R. (1972). Poverty: we still believe that God helps those who help themselves. *Psychology Today*, *6*, pp. 101–29.

Feather, N. T. (1974). Explanations of poverty in Australian and American samples: the person, society of fate? *Australian Journal of Psychology*, *26*, pp. 199–216.

(1985). Attitudes, values and attributions: explanations of unemployment. *Journal of Personality and Social Psychology*, *98*, pp. 876–89.

Felner, R. D., Aber, M. S., Primavera, J., and Cauce, A. M. (1985). Adaptation and vulnerability in high-risk adolescents: an examination of environmental mediators. *American Journal of Community Psychology*, *13*, pp. 365–79.

Fillmore, C. J. (1976). Frame semantics and the nature of language. In S. R. Harnad, *et al.* (eds.), *Origins and evolution of language and speech* (Annals of the New York Academy of Sciences, Vol. CCLXXX), pp. 20–32. New York.

(1977). Scenes-and-frame semantics. In A. Zampoli (ed.), *Linguistic structures processing*, pp. 55–82. Amsterdam: North-Holland.

Finch, M. D., Shanahan, M. J., Mortimer, J. T., and Ryu, S. (1991). Work experience and control orientation in adolescence. *American Sociological Review*, *56*, pp. 597–611.

Finn, G. P. T. (1979). *Social context, social interaction and children's interpretation of class inclusion and related problems*. St Andrew's University, PhD thesis.

Fischer, H.-D. (1983). *Fernsehmoderatoren in der BRD*. Munich: TR-Verlagsunion.

Fiske, A. P. (1991). *Making up society: the four basic relational studies*. New York: Free Press.

Fiske, S., and Taylor, S. (1991). *Social Cognition*, 2nd edn. New York: McGraw-Hill.

Flament, C. (1989). Structure et dynamique des représentations sociales. In D. Jodelet (ed.), *Les représentations sociales*, pp. 204–19. Paris: Presses Universitaires de France.

Fleck, L. ([1935]1979). *Genesis and development of a scientific fact*. Chicago: University of Chicago Press.

Flick, U. (1987). Das Subjekt als Theoretiker? – Zur Subjektivität subjektiver Theorien. In J. B. Bergold and U. Flick (eds.), *Ein-sichten: Zugänge zur Sicht des Subjekts mittels qualitativer Forschung*. Tübingen: DGVT.

(1989). *Vertrauen, Verwalten, Einweisen – Subjektive Vertrauenstheorien in sozialpsychiatrischer Beratung*. Wiesbaden: Deutscher Universitätsverlag.

(1990). Fallanalysen: Geltungsbegründung durch Systematische Perspektiven-Triangulation. In G. Jüttemann (ed.), *Komparative Kasuistik*, pp. 184–203. Heidelberg: Ansanger.

(ed.) (1991a). *Alltagswissen über Gesundheit und Krankheit – Subjektive Theorien und Soziale Repräsentationen*. Heidelberg: Asanger (French translation: *La perception quotidienne de la Santé et la Maladie: théories subjectives et représentations sociales*. Paris: L'Harmattan).

(1991b). *Zwischen Repräsentation und Konstruktion – Alltagswissen als Ansatzpunkt sozialpsychologischer Forschung. Beitrag zur 3. Tagung der Fachgruppe Sozialpsychologie der Dt. Ges. für Psychologie.* Unpublished Ms.

(ed.) (1993). *La perception quotidienne de la Santé et la Maladie. Théories Subjectives et Représentations sociales.* Paris: L'Hamattan.

(1996). *Psychologie des technisierten Alltags – Soziale Konstruktion und Repräsentation technischen Wandels in verschiedenen kulturellen Kontexten.* Opladen: Westdeutscher Verlag.

Fordham, S. (1988). Racelessness as a factor in Black students' school success: Pragmatic strategy or pyrrhic victory? *Harvard Educational Review, 58,* pp. 54–84.

Foucault, M. (1977). *Discipline and punish: the birth of the prison.* London: Allen Lane.

Fraser, C., and Gaskell, G. (eds.) (1990). *The social psychological study of widespread beliefs.* Oxford: Clarendon Press.

Fraser, N. (1989). *Unruly practices: power, discourse and gender in contemporary social theory.* Minnesota: University of Minnesota Press.

Freund, B. (1990). Verständlichkeit und Attraktivität von Wissenschaftssendungen im Fernsehen: Die subjektiven Theorien der Macher. In D. Meutsch and B. Freund (eds.), *Fernsehjournalismus und die Wissenschaften,* pp. 89–123. Opladen: Westdeutscher Verlag.

Frey, D., and Greif, S. (eds.) (1987). *Sozialpsychologie: Ein Handbuch in Schlüsselbegriffen (2. erweiterte Auflage).* Munich: PsychologieVerlagsUnion.

Freyd, J. J. (1983). Shareability: the social psychology of epistemology. *Cognitive science, 7,* pp. 191–210.

Fujita, M., and Sano, T. (1988). Children in American and Japanese day-care centers: ethnography and reflective cross-cultural interviewing. In H. T. Trueba and C. Delgado-Gaitan, C. (eds.), *School and society: learning content through culture.* New York: Praeger.

Fukuyama, F. (1992). *The end of history and the last man.* London: Hamish Hamilton.

Furnham, A. (1982a). Why are the poor always with us? Explanations for poverty in Britain. *British Journal of Social Psychology, 21,* pp. 311–22.

(1982b). The perception of poverty amongst adolescents. *Journal of Adolescence, 5,* pp. 135–47.

(1982c). Explanations for unemployment in Britain. *European Journal of Social Psychology, 12,* pp. 335–52.

Galli, I., and Nigro, G. (1987). The social representation of radioactivity among italian children. *Social Science Information, 25,* pp. 535–49.

Gans, H. J. (1979). *Deciding what's news.* New York: Vintage Books.

Gardner, H. (1983). *Frames of mind: the theory of multiple intelligences.* New York: Basic Books.

(1985). *The mind's new science.* New York: Basic Books.

Garfinkel, H. (1967). *Studies in ethnomethodology.* Englewood Cliffs, NJ: Prentice-Hall.

Gaskell, G., and Fraser, C. (1990). The social psychological study of widespread beliefs. In C. Fraser and G. Gaskell (eds.), *The social psychological study of widespread beliefs*, pp. 3–24. Oxford: Clarendon Press.

Gaskell, G., and Smith, P. (1985). An investigation of youth's attributions for unemployment and their political attitudes. *Journal of Economic Psychology*, 6, pp. 65–80.

Geertz, C. (1975). On the nature of anthropological understanding. *American Scientist*, 63, pp. 47–53.

Gellner, E. (1992). *Reason and Culture*. Oxford: Blackwell.

Georgas, J. (1989). Changing family values in Greece: from collectivist to individualist. *Journal of Cross-Cultural Psychology*, 20, pp. 80–91.

Gergen, K. (1973). Social psychology as history. *Journal of Personality and Social Psychology*, 26, pp. 309–320.

(1985). Social constructionist inquiry: context and implications. In K. Gergen and K. Davis (eds.), *The social construction of the person*, pp. 3–18. New York: Springer.

(1987). Toward a self as a relationship. In K. Yardley and T. Honess (eds.), *Self and identity: psychological perspectives*. New York: John Wiley and Sons.

(1994). *Towards transformation in social knowledge*. (2nd edn) London: Sage.

Gergen, K., and Gergen, M. (1983). Narratives of the self. In T. Sarbin and K. Scheibe (eds.), *Studies on social identity*. New York: Praeger.

(1988). Narrative and the self as relationship. In L. Berkowitz (ed.), *Advances in experimental social psychology* (Vol. XXI), pp. 17–56.

Giddens, A. (1985). *Durkheim*. London: Fontana Press.

Gilbert, G. N., and Mulkay, M. (1984). *Opening Pandora's Box: a sociological analysis of scientists' discourse*. Cambridge: Cambridge University Press.

Gillett, G. and Harré, R. (1993). *The discursive mind*. Los Angeles and London: Sage.

Gloger-Tippelt, G. and Tippelt, R. (1986). Kindheit und kindliche Entwicklung als soziale Konstruktion. *Bildung und Erziehung*, 2, pp. 149–64.

Godelier, M. (1986). *The mental and the material*. London: Verso.

Goffman, E. (1959). *The presentation of self in everyday life*. Garden City, NY: Doubleday.

Goodman, N. (1978). *Ways of worldmaking*. Indianapolis: Hackett.

Goodnow, J. J. (1988). Parents' ideas, actions, and feelings: models and methods from developmental and social psychology. *Child Development*, 59, pp. 286–320.

(1990). The socialization of cognition: what's involved? In J. W. Stigler, R. A. Shweder and G. Herdt (eds.), *Cultural psychology: essays on comparative human development*, pp. 259–286. Cambridge: Cambridge University Press.

Goodnow, J. J., and W. A. Collins (1990). *Development according to parents*. Hillsdale, NJ: Laurence Erlbaum Associates.

Gould, S. (1981). *The mismeasure of man* New York: Norton.

Gramsci, A. (1971). *Selections from the prison notebooks*. London: Lawrence & Wishart.

Graumann, C. F. (1988). Der Kognitivismus in der Sozialpsychologie – die Kehrseite der 'Wende'. *Psychologische Rundschau*, 39, pp. 83–90.

Greenberger, E., and Goldberg, W. A. (1988). Work, parenting, and the socialisation of children. *Developmental Psychology*, *25*, pp. 22–35.

Groeben, N. (1990). Subjective Theories and the Explanation of Human Action. In Semin, G, Gergen, K. J. (eds.), *Everyday understanding – social and scientific implication*, pp. 19–44. London, Dehli/Newbury Park: Sage.

Groeben, N., and Scheele, B. (1982). Einige Sprachregelungsvorschläge für die Erforschung subjektiver Theorien. In H.-D.Dann et al. (eds.), *Analyse und Modifikation subjektiver Theorien von Lehrern*, pp. 13–39. Konstanz: Universitätsverlag.

Guimelli, C. (1993). A propos de la structure des représentations sociales. *Papers on Social Representations*, *2*, pp. 85–93.

Hacker, W. (1986). *Arbeitspsychiologie: Psychische Regulation von Arbeitstätigkeiten*. Berne: Huber.

Halbwachs, M. ([1950]1980). *The collective memory*. New York: Harper Colophon.

Hall, S. (1986). Variants of liberalism. In J. Donald and S. Hall (eds.), *Politics and ideology*. Milton Keynes: Open University Press.

Harré, R. (1989a). Language games and the texts of identity. In J. Shotter and K. Gergen (eds.), *Texts of identity*. London: Sage.

(1989b). Metaphysics and methodology: some prescriptions for a social psychological approach. *European Journal of Social Psychology*, *19*(5), pp. 439–53.

Harré, R., and Secord. P. F. (1973). *The explanation of social behaviour*. Oxford: Basil Blackwell.

Harter, S. (1992). *Visions of the self: beyond the me in the mirror*. Paper, Nebraska Symposium on Motivation.

Harvey, J. H., Town, J. P. and Yarkin, K. L. (1981). How fundamental is 'the fundamental attribution error'? *Journal of Personality and Social Psychology*, *40*, pp. 346–9.

Haw, K. (1991). Interactions of gender and race – a problem for teachers? A review of the emerging literature. *Educational Research*, *33*, pp. 12–21.

Heider, F. (1958). *The psychology of interpersonal relations*. New York: Wiley.

Heritage, J. (1984). *Garfinkel and ethnomethodology*. Cambridge: Polity.

Herrman, D., and Chaffin, R. (1988). *Memory in historical perspective: the literature before Ebbinghaus*. New York: Springer.

Herzlich, C. (1972). La représentation sociale. In S. Moscovici (ed.), *Introduction à la psychologie sociale*. Paris: Librairie Larousse.

Herzlich, C. (1973). *Health and illness: a social psychological analysis*. London: Academic Press.

(1991). Soziale Repräsentation von Gesundheit und Krankheit und ihre Dynamik im sozialen Feld. In U. Flick (ed.), *Alltagswissen über Gesundheit und Krankheit – Subjektive Theorien und soziale Repräsentationen*, pp. 293–302. Heidelberg: Asanger. (French translation: Représentations sociales de la maladie et de la santé et leur dynamique dans le champ social. In U. Flick (ed.), *La perception quotidienne de la Santé et la Maladie. Théories subjectives et Représentations sociales*, pp. 347–57. Paris: L'Harmattan).

Hewstone, M. (ed.) (1983). *Attribution theory: social and functional extensions*. Oxford: Blackwell.

(1989a). *Causal attribution: from cognitive processes to collective beliefs.* Oxford: Basil Blackwell.

(1989b). Représentations sociales et causalité. In D. Jodelet (ed.), *Les Représentations sociales.* Paris: Presses Universitaires de France.

Hewstone, M., Stroebe, W., and Stephenson G. M. (eds.) (1995). *Introduction to social psychology.* Oxford: Blackwell.

Hippel, W. von, Sekaquaptewa, D., and Vargas, P. (1994). *On the role of encoding processes in stereotype maintenance.* Unpublished ms.

Hocart, A. M. (1987). *Imagination and proof.* Tucson: University of Arizona Press.

Holland, D., and Quinn, N. (eds.) (1987). *Cultural models in language and thought.* Cambridge: Cambridge University Press.

Hsu, F. L. K. (1983). *Rugged individualism reconsidered.* Knoxville: University of Tennessee Press.

(1985). The self in cross-cultural perspective. In A. J. Marsella, G. De Vos and F. L. K. Hsu (eds.), *Culture and self*, pp. 24–55. London: Tavistock.

Hughes, M., and Hertel, B. R. (1990). The significance of color remains: a study of life chances, mate selection, and ethnic consciousness among Black Americans. *Social Forces, 68*, pp. 1105–20.

Hui, C., and Triandis, H. C. (1986). Individualism–collectivism: a study of cross-cultural researchers. *Journal of Cross-cultural Psychology, 17*, pp. 225–48.

Hui, C., and Villareal, M. (1989). Individualism–collectivism and psychological needs. *Journal of Cross-cultural Psychology, 20*, pp. 310–23.

Hutchins, E. (1980). *Culture and inference: a Trobriand case study.* Cambridge, MA: Harvard University Press.

Hutnik, N. (1991). *Ethnic minority identity: a social psychological perspective.* Oxford: Oxford University Press.

Ichheiser, G. (1949). *Misunderstandings in human relations: a study in false social perception.* Chicago: University of Chicago Press.

Intelligence and its measurement: a symposium (1921). *Journal of Educational Psychology, 12*, pp. 123–47, pp. 195–216, pp. 271–5.

Israel, J., and Tajfel, H. (eds.) (1972). *The context of social psychology: a critical assessment.* London: Academic Press.

Jackson, J. S., McCullough, W. R., Gurin, G., and Broman, C. L. (1991). Race identity. In J. S. Jackson (eds.), *Life in Black America: findings from a national survey*, pp. 238–95. Beverly Hills, CA: Sage.

Jahoda, G. (1982). *Psychology and anthropology.* London: Academic Press.

(1992). *Crossroads between culture and mind.* New York: Harvester Wheatsheaf.

James, W. (1890). *Principles of psychology.* New York: Holt.

Jantsch, E. (1980). *The self-organizing universe.* Oxford: Pergamon.

Jennings, M. K., and Markus, G. B. (1984). Partisan orientations over the long haul: results from the three wave political socialization panel study. *American Political Science Review, 78*, pp. 1000–18.

Jessor, R., Donovan, J. E., and Costa, F. M. (1992). *Beyond adolescence.* New York: Cambridge University Press.

Jeudy, H. (1986). *Mémoires du social.* Paris: Presses Universitaires de France.

Jodelet, D. (1984). Représentations sociales: phénomènes, concepts et théorie. In

S. Moscovici (ed.), Psychologie sociale, pp. 357–79. Paris: Presses Universitaires de France.

([1989a]1991). *Madness and scial representations.* Hemel Hempstead: Harvester/Wheatsheaf.

(1989b). Représentations sociales: un domaine en expansion. In D. Jodelet (ed.), *Représentations sociales*, pp. 20–39. Paris: Presses Universitaires de France.

(1991). Soziale Repräsentationen psychischer Krankheit in einem ländlichen Milieu in Frankreich: Entstehung, Struktur, Funktionen. In U. Flick (ed.), *Alltagswissen über Gesundheit und Krankheit – Subjektive Theorien und soziale Repräsentationen*, pp. 269–92. Heidelberg: Asanger. (French translation: Les Représentations sociales de la maladie mentale dans un milieu rural: genèse, structure, fonction. In U. Flick (ed.), *La perception quotidienne de la Santé et la Maladie: théories subjectives et représentations sociales.* Paris: L'Harmattan, pp. 321–46).

(1992). Mémoire de masse le cote moral et affectif de l'histoire. *Bulletin de Psychologie, 45* (405). pp. 239–59.

Jones, E. E. (1989). The framing of competence. *Personality and Social Psychology Bulletin, 15*, pp. 477–92.

Jones, E. E., and Davis, K. E. (1965). From acts to dispositions: the attribution process in person perception. In L. Berkowitz (ed.), *Advances in experimental social psychology.* New York: Academic Press.

Jörg, S. (1984). *Unterhaltung im Fernsehen. Show-Master im Urteil der Zuschauer (Schriftenreihe Internationales Zentralinstitut für das Jugend – und Bildungsfernsehen, Nr. 18).* Munich: Saur.

Judd, C. M. (1993). *Perceived variability and ethnocentrism: moving beyond the laboratory.* Paper presented at the Institute for Social Research, Ann Arbor, University of Michigan.

Julian, T. W., McKenry, P. C., and McKelvey, M. W. (1994). Cultural variations in parenting: perceptions of Caucasian, African-American, Hispanic, and Asian-American parents. *Family Relations, 43*, pp. 30–7.

Kagan, J. (1984). *The nature of the child.* New York: Basic Books.

Kagitcibasi, C. (1987). Individual and group loyalties: are they compatible? In C. Kagitcibasi (ed.), *Growth and progress in cross-cultural psychology.* Lisse: Swets & Zeitlingler.

Katz, I., and Hass, R. G. (1988). Racial ambivalence and American value conflict: correlational and priming studies of dual cognitive structures. *Journal of Personality & Social Psychology, 55*, pp. 893–905.

Katz, D., and Kahn, R. L. (1978). *The social psychology of organizations.* New York: Wiley.

Kelley, H. H. (1967). Attribution theory in social psychology. In D. Levine (ed.), *Nebraska symposium on motivation.* Lincoln: University of Nebraska Press.

Kelly, G. A. (1955). *The psychology of personal constructs* (Vol. I, II). New York: Norton.

Kelsey, J. (1990). *A question of honour?: labour and the treaty 1984–1989.* Wellington: Allen & Unwin.

Kelvin, P. (1984). The historical dimension of social psychology: The case of unemployment. In H. Tajfel (ed.), *The social dimensions: European develop-*

*ments in social psychology* (Vol. II). Cambridge/Paris: Cambridge University Press/Maison des Sciences de l'Homme.

Kessen, W. (1979). The american child and other cultural inventions. *American Psychologist*, *15*, pp. 815–820.

Kleinman, A. (1980). *Patients and healers in the context of culture.* Berkeley: University of California Press.

Klix, F. (1992). *Die Natur des Verstandes.* Göttingen: Hogrefe.

Kluwe, R. H. (1990). Gedächtnis und Wissen. In H. Spada (ed.), *Allgemeine Psychologie*, pp. 264–82. Berne: Huber.

Kolakowski, L. (1978). *La Pologne: une société en dissidence.* Paris: Maspero.

Kondo, D. (1992). Multiple selves: the aesthetics and politics of artisanal identities. In N. Rosenberger (ed.), *Japanese sense of self*, pp. 40–66. Cambridge: Cambridge University Press.

Kornhaber, M., Krechewsky, M., and Gardner, H. (1990). Engaging intelligence. *Educational Psychologist*, *25* (3 and 4), pp. 177–99.

Kozulin, A. (1990). *Vygotsky's psychology.* Hemel Hempstead: Harvester Wheatsheaf.

Krampen, G. (1979). Eine Skala zur Messung der normativen Geschlechtsrollen-Orientierung (GRO-Skala). *Zeitschrift für Soziologie*, *2*, pp. 152–6.

Kress, G., and Hodge, R. (1979). *Language as ideology.* London: Routledge & Kegan Paul.

Kruglanski, A. W., and Ajzen, I. (1983). Bias and error in human judgement. *European Journal of Social Psychology*, *13*, pp. 1–44.

Kruse, L., and Schwarz, S. (1992). Who pays the bill? The language of social representation. In M. von Cranach, W. Doise and G. Mugny (eds.), *Social representations and the social bases of knowledge* (Swiss Monographs in Psychology, Vol. I), pp. 23–9. Berne: Huber.

Kruse, L., Weimer, E., and Wagner, F. (1988). What men and women are said to be: social representation and language. *Journal of Language and Social Psychology*, *7*, pp. 243–62.

Kuhn, T. (1962). *The structure of scientific revolutions.* Chicago: University of Chicago Press.

LaFromboise, T., Coleman, H. L. K., and Gerton, J. (1993). Psychological impact of biculturalism: Evidence and theory. *Psychological Bulletin*, *114*, pp. 395–412.

Lakoff, G., and Johnson, M. (1980). *Metaphors we live by.* Chicago: University of Chicago Press.

Lalljee, M., and Abelson, R. P. (1983). The organization of explanations. In M. Hewstone (ed.), *Attribution theory: social and functional extensions.* Oxford: Blackwell.

Lang, A. (1992). On the knowledge in things and places. In M. von Cranach, W. Doise and G. Mugny (eds.), *Social representations and the social bases of knowledge* (Swiss Monographs in Psychology, Vol. I), pp. 112–19. Berne: Huber.

Lapierre, N. (1989). Dialectique de la mémoire et de l'oubli. *Communications*, *49*, pp. 5–10.

Larrain, J. (1979). *The concept of ideology.* London: Hutchinson.

(1983). *Marxism and ideology.* London: Macmillan Press.

Lash, S., and Urry, J. (1987). *The end of organised capitalism*. Cambridge: Polity.

Lau, R. R., and Hartman, K. A. (1983). Common sense representations of common illnesses. *Health Psychology*, 2, pp. 167–85.

Lau, R. R., Bernard, T. M., and Hartman, K. A. (1989). Further explorations of common-sense representations of common illness. *Health Psychology*, 8, pp. 195–219.

Laucken, U. (1974). *Naive Verhaltenstheorie*. Stuttgart: Klett.

Laudan, L. (1977). *Progress and its problems*. Berkeley: University of California Press.

Lave, J. (1991). Acquisition des savoirs et practiques de group. *Sociologie et societés*, 23 (1), pp. 145–62.

Le Bon, G. ([1895]1947). *The crowd: a study of the popular mind*. London: Ernest Benn.

Lebra, T. S. (1992). *Culture, self, and communication*. Ann Arbor: University of Michigan.

Legrenzi, P., Butera, F., Mugny, G., and Pérez, J. A. (1991). Majority and minority influence in inductive reasoning: a preliminary study. *European Journal of Social Psychology*, 21, pp. 359–63.

Lévy-Bruhl, L. ([1925]1926). *How natives think*. London: George Allen & Unwin.

Lewis, A. (1990). Shared economic beliefs. In C. Fraser and G. Gaskell (eds.), *The social psychological study of widespread beliefs*. Oxford: Clarendon Press.

Lewis, E. A. (1989). Role strain in African-American women: the efficacy of support networks. *Journal of Black Studies*, 20, pp. 155–69.

Lieury, A. (1978). *La memoria*. Barcelona: Herber.

Lipset, S. (1960). *Political man*. London: Heinemann.

Little, B. R. (1983). Personal projects: a rationale and method for investigation. *Environment and Behavior*, 15, pp. 273–309.

Litton, I., and Potter, J. (1985). Social representations in the ordinary explanation of a 'riot'. *European Journal of Social Psychology*, 15, pp. 371–88.

Lloyd, G. E. R. (1990). *Demystifying mentalities*. Cambridge: Cambridge University Press.

Luhmann, N. ([1984]1995). *Social systems*. Stanford, CA: Stanford University Press.

Lukes, S. (1973). *Individualism*. Oxford: Basil Blackwell.

Luria, A. R. (1976). *Cognitive development*. Cambridge, MA: Harvard University Press.

(1979). *The making of mind*. Cambridge, MA: Harvard University Press.

Lyotard, J.-F. (1984). *The postmodern condition: a report on knowledge*. Manchester: Manchester University Press.

Mackie, J. L. (1965). Causes and conditions. *American Philosophical Quarterly*, 2, pp. 245–64.

(1974). *The cement of the universe: a study of causation*. Oxford: Clarendon Press.

Macpherson, C. B. (1962). *The political theory of possessive individualism: Hobbes to Locke*. Oxford: Clarendon Press.

De Madariaga, M. R. (1988). L'imáge et le retour du maure dans le mémoire collective du people Espagnol et la guerre civile de 1936. *L'Homme et la société*, 63, pp. 63–79.

Maletzke, G. (1978). *Psychologie der Massenkommunikation*. Hamburg: Hans Bredow Institut.

Mandl, H., and Spada, H. (eds.) (1988). *Wissenspsychologie*. Munich/Weinheim: PsychologieVerlagsUnion.

Mann, M. (1970). The social cohesion of liberal democracy. Reprinted in A. Giddens and D. Held (eds.), *Classes, power and conflict: classical and contemporary debates*. London: Macmillan Press.

Mannheim, K. (1954). *Ideology and utopia*. London: Routledge & Kegan Paul.

Marcus, G. E., Tabb, D., and Sullivan, J. L. (1974). The application of individual differences scaling to the measurement of political ideologies. *American Journal of Political Science, 18*, pp. 405–20.

Markova, I. (1982). *Paradigms, thought and language*. New York: Wiley.

Markova, I. and Wilkie, P. (1987). Representations, concepts and social change: the phenomen of Aids. *Journal for the Theory of Social Behavior, 17*, pp. 389–401.

Markus, H. (1990). On splitting the universe. *Psychological Science, 1*, pp. 1–5.

Markus, H. and Nurius, P. (1986). Posssible selves. *American Psychologist, 41*, pp. 954–69.

Markus, H. R., and Kitayama, S. (1991a). Culture and the self: implications for cognition, emotion, and motivation. *Psychological Review, 98*, pp. 224–53.

(1991b). Cultural variation in the self-concept. In J. Strauss and G. R. Goethals (eds.), *The self: interdisciplinary approaches*, pp. 18–48. New York: Springer.

(1994a). The cultural construction of self and emotion: implications for social behaviour. In S. Kitayama and H. R. Markus (eds.), *Emotion and culture: empirical studies of mutual influence*, pp. 89–130. Washington, DC: American Psychological Association Press.

(1994b). A collective fear of the collective: implications for selves and theories of selves. In D. Miller and D. Prentice (eds.), *Personality and social psychology bulletin.*( Special Issue on the Self and the Collective), 20, pp. 568–79.

Markus, H., and Zajonc, R. (1985). The cognitive perspective in social psychology. In G. Lindzey and E. Aronson (eds.), *The handbook of social psychology*. New York: Random House.

Marlowe, D., and Gergen, K. (1968). Personality and social interaction. In G. Lindzey, and E. Aronson (eds.), *The handbook of social psychology*. Reading, MA: Addison-Wesley.

Marsella, A., De Vos, G. A., and Hsu, F. (eds.). (1985). *Culture and self*. London: Tavistock.

Martin, J. M., and E. P. Martin (1985). *The helping tradition in the Black community*. Silver Springs/MD: National Association of Social Workers.

Martinez, R., and Dukes, R. L. (1991). Ethnic and gender differences in self-esteem. *Youth & Society, 22*, pp. 318–38.

McClosky, H. (1964). Consensus and ideology in American politics. *American Political Science Review, 58*, pp. 361–82.

McDonald, J. (1990). Some situational determinants of hypothesis-testing strategies. *Journal of Experimental Social Psychology, 26*, pp. 255–74.

McGrath, J. M. (1984). *Interaction and performance*. Englewood Cliffs, NJ: Prentice-Hall.

(1990). Time matters in group. In J. Galegher, E. R. Kraut and C. Egido (eds.), *Intellectual teamwork. social and technological foundations of cooperative work*. Hillsdale, NJ: Lawrence Erlbaum Association.

McIver, R. M. (1942). *Social causation*. New York: Harper Torchbooks.

McKinlay, A., and Potter, J. (1987). Social representations: a conceptual critique. *Journal for the Theory of Social Behaviour, 17*, pp. 471–87.

McKinlay, A., Potter, J., and Wetherell, M. (1993). Discourse analysis and social representations. In G. Breakwell and D. Canter (eds.), *Empirical approaches to social representations*, pp. 134–56. Oxford: Oxford University Press.

McLellan, D. (1986). *Ideology*. Milton Keynes: Open University Press.

McLoyd, V. C. (1990). The impact of economic hardship on Black families and children: psychological distress, parenting, and socioemotional development. *Child Development, 6*(1), pp. 311–45.

Menon, U., and Shweder, R. A. (1994). Kali's tongue: cultural psychology and the power of shame in Orissa, India. In S. Kitayama amd H. R. Markus (eds.), *Emotion and culture: empirical studies of mutual influences*, pp. 237–80. Washington, DC: American Psychological Association Press.

Mepham, J. (1972). The theory of ideology in capital. *Radical Philosophy, 2*, pp. 12–19.

Merkl, P. H. (1975). *Political violence under the Swastika*. Princeton, NJ: Princeton University Press.

Mesquita, B. Gomes de (1993). *Cultural variations in emotions: a comparative study of Dutch, Surinamese and Turkish people in the Netherlands*. Unpublished doctoral dissertation, University of Amsterdam.

Meyrowitz, J. (1987). *Die Fernseh-Gesellschaft: Wirklichkeit und Identität im Medienzeitalter*. Weinheim: Beltz.

Middleton, D., and Edwards, D. (1990a). Introduction. In D. Middleton and D. Edwards (eds.), *Collective remembering*, pp. 1–22. London: Sage.

(1990b). Conversational remembering In D. Middleton and D. Edwards (eds.), *Collective remembering*, pp. 23–45. London: Sage.

Miller, J. G. (1978). *Living systems*. McGraw-Hill: New York.

(1984). Culture and the development of everyday social explanation. *Journal of Personality and Social Psychology, 46*, pp. 961–78.

Miller, S. A. (1988). Parents' beliefs about children's cognitive development. *Child Development, 59*, pp. 259–85.

Molinari, L., and Emiliani, F. (1990). What is in an image? The structure of mothers' images of the child and their influence on conversational styles. In G. Duveen and B. Lloyd (eds.), *Social representations and the development of knowledge*, pp. 91–106. Cambridge: Cambridge University Press.

Molinari, L., Emiliani, F., and Carugati, F. (1992). Development according to mothers: a case of social representations. In M. von Cranach, W. Doise and G. Mugny (eds.), *Social representations and the social bases of knowledge*, pp. 104–11. Berne: Hogrefe and Huber.

Moreau de Bellaing, G. L. (1985). Mémires de la mémoire: la commenoration. *L'Homme et la société, 75*, pp. 237–44.

Morgan, D., and Schwalbe, M. (1990). Mind and self in society: linking social structure and social cognition. *Social Psychology Quarterly, 53*(2), pp. 148–64.

Moscovici, S. ([1961]1976). *La Psychanalyse: son image et son public*. Paris: Presses Universitaires de France.

(1972). Society and theory in social psychology. In J. Israel and H. Tajfel (eds.), *The context of social psychology: a critical assessment*, pp. 17–68. London: Academic Press.

(1973). Foreword. In C. Herzlich, *Health and illness: a social psychological analysis*. London: Academic Press.

(1977). *Essai sur l'histoire humaine de la nature*. Paris: Flammarion.

(1981). On social representations. In J. P. Forgas (ed.), *Social cognition: perspectives on everyday understanding*, pp. 181–209. London: Academic Press.

(1982). The coming era of social representations. In J. P. Codol and J. P. Leyens (eds.) *Cognitive approaches to social behaviour*, pp. 115–50. The Hague: Nijhoff.

(1984a). The phenomena of social representations. In R. M. Farr and S. Moscovici (eds.), *Social representations*, pp. 3–69. Cambridge: Cambridge University Press.

(1984b). The myth of the lonely paradigm: a rejoinder. *Social Research, 51*, pp. 939–68.

(1985). *The age of the crowd: a historical treatise on mass psychology*. Cambridge University Press.

(1987). Answers and questions. *Journal for the Theory of Social Behaviour, 17*, pp. 513–19.

(1988a). Notes towards a description of social representation. *European Journal of Social Psychology, 18*, pp. 211–50.

([1988]/1993). *The invention of society*. Cambridge: Polity Press.

(1990). Social psychology and developmental psychology: extending the conversation. In G. Duveen and B. Lloyd (eds.), *Social representations and the development of knowledge*, pp. 164–85. Cambridge: Cambridge University Press.

(1991). Die prälogische Mentalität der Zivilisierten. In U. Flick (ed.), *Alltagswissen über Gesundheit und Krankheit – Subjektive Theorien und soziale Repräsentationen*, pp. 245–68. Heidelberg: Asanger. (French translation: La mentalité prélogique des civilisés. In U. Flick (ed.), *La perception quotidienne de la Santé et la Maladie. Théories subjectives et Représentations sociales*. pp. 293–320. Paris: L'Harmattan).

(1992). *Influence sociale et cognition*. International Congress of Psychology, Brussels.

(1993a). The return of the unconscious. *Social Research, 60*(1), pp. 39–93.

Moscovici, S., and Hewstone, M. (1983). Social representations and social explanations: from the 'naive' to the 'amateur' scientist. In M. Hewstone (ed.), *Attribution theory: social and functional extensions*, pp. 98–125. Oxford: Basil Blackwell.

Moscovici, S., and Mugny, G. (eds.) (1985). *Perspectives on minority influence*. Cambridge: Cambridge University Press.

Mugny, G. (1982). *The power of minorities*. London: Academic Press.

Mugny, G., and Carugati, F. ([1985]1989). *Social representations of intelligence*. Cambridge: Cambridge University Press.

Mugny, G., and Pérez, J. A. (1991). *The social psychology of minority influence.* Cambridge/Paris: Cambridge University Press/LEPS.

Mugny, G., De Paolis, P., and Carugati, F. (1984). Social regulations in cognitive development. In W. Doise and A. Palmonari (eds.), *Social interaction in individual development.* Cambridge: Cambridge University Press.

Mugny, G., Lévy, M., and Doise, W. (1978). Conflit sociocognitif et développement cognitif: l'effet de la présentation par un adulte de modèles 'progressifs' et de modèles 'régressifs' dans une épreuve de représentation spatiale. *Revue suisse de Psychologie, 37*, pp. 22–43.

Nagata, D. (1990). The Japanese-American internment: perceptions of moral community, fairness and redress. *Journal of Social Issues, 46* (1), pp. 133–46.

Namer, G. (1983). *Batailles pour la mémoire.* Paris: Papyrus.

Neisser, U. (1988). Five kinds of self-knowledge. *Philosophical Psychology, 1*, pp. 35–59.

Nelson, K. (1981). Social cognition in a script framework. In J. H. Flavell and L. R. Ross (eds.), *Social cognitive development.* Cambridge: Cambridge University Press.

Nemeth, C. (1986). Differential contributions of majority and minority influence. *Psychological Review, 93*, pp. 23–32.

Nilsen, A. P. (1977). Sexism in children's books and elementary teaching materials. In A. P. Nilsen, H. Bosmajian, H. L. Gershuny and J. P. Stanley (eds.), *Sexism and language.* Urbana, IL: National Council of Teachers of English.

Nisbett, R. E. (1993). Violence and US regional culture. *American Psychologist, 48*, pp. 441–9.

Ochsenbein, G., and Schäres, M. (1994). *Tabus in sozialen Systemen.* Forschungsbericht 4/94. Berne: University, unpublished MS.

Ogbu, J. U. (1991). Minority coping responses and school experience. *The Journal of Psychohistory, 18*, pp. 433–56.

Ortner, S. B. (1984). Theory in anthropology since the sixties. *Comparative Studies in Society and History, 26*, pp. 126–66.

Oschanin, D. A. (1976) Dynamisches operatives Abbild und konzeptuelles Modell. *Probl., Erg. Psychol. 59*, 37–48. (Cited in W. Hacker (1986), *Arbeitspsychologie: Psychische Regulation von Arbeitstätigkeiten.* Berne: Huber.)

Owens, T. J. (1992). The effect of post-high school social context on self-esteem. *The Sociological Quarterly, 33*, pp. 553–78.

Oyserman, D. (1993). The lens of personhood: viewing the self, others, and conflict in a multicultural society. *Journal of Personality and Social Psychology, 65*, pp. 993–1009.

(1994). *School persistence versus delinquency: the role of the self.* Proposal submitted to the National Institute of Mental Health.

Oyserman, D., and Markus, H. R. (1990a). Possible selves and delinquency. *Journal of Personality and Social Psychology, 59*, pp. 112–25.

(1990b). Possible selves in balance: implications for delinquency. *Journal of Social Issues, 46*, pp. 141–57.

(1993). The sociocultural self. In J. Suls (ed.), *Psychological perspectives on the self* (Vol. IV), pp. 187–220. Hillsdale, NJ: Erlbaum.

Paez, D., and Gonzales, J. L. (1993). A Southern response to an insular critic: where to find the social and how to understand the use of clusters in our studies on social representations. *Papers on Social Representations, 2,* pp. 11–25.

Palmonari, A. (1980). Le representazioni sociali. *Giornale italiano di psicologia, 2,* pp. 225–46.

Parish, S. (1991). The sacred mind: Newar cultural representations of mental life and the production of moral consciousness. *Ethos, 19,* pp. 313–51.

Parker, I. (1987). Social representations: social psychology's (mis)use of sociology. *Journal for the Theory of Social Behaviour, 17,* pp. 447–70.

Peak, L. (1991). *Learning to go to school in Japan: the transition from home to preschool life.* Berkeley: University of California Press.

Peevers, B. H., and Secord, P. F. (1973). Developmental changes in attributions of descriptive concepts to persons. *Journal of Personality and Social Psychology, 27,* pp. 120–8.

Pennebaker, J. (1993). Creación y mantenimiento de las memorias colectivas. *Revista de psicología política. 5,* pp. 35–52.

Pepitone, A. (1981). Lessons from the history of social psychology. *American Psychologist, 36,* pp. 972–85.

Pérez, J. A., Mugny, G., Huguet, P. and Butera, F. (1993). De la complaisance a l'uniformisation: études perceptives. In J. A. Pérez and G. Mugny (eds.), *Influences sociales: la théorie de l'élaboration du conflit.* Paris: Delachaux et Niestlé.

Pérez, J. A., Mugny, G., Butera, F., Kaiser, C. and Roux, P. (1991). Integrazione tra influenza maggioritaria e minoritaria: conversione, consenso e uniformità. *Ricerche di psicologia, 4,* pp. 75–102.

Perret-Clermont, A. N. (1980). *Social interaction and cognitive development in children.* London: Academic Press.

Perret-Clermont, A. N. and Nicolet, M. (eds.) (1988). *Interagir et connaitre: Enjeux et régulations sociales dans le développement cognitif.* Cousset: DelVal.

Piaget, J. ([1936]1953). *The origin of intelligence in the child.* London: Routledge & Kegan Paul.

([1937]1954). *The construction of reality in the child.* London: Routledge & Kegan Paul.

([1941]1952). *The child's conception of number.* London: Routledge & Kegan Paul.

([1965]1995). *Sociological studies.* London: Routledge.

Pill, R., and Stott, N. C. H. (1982). Concepts of illness causation and responsibility: Some preliminary data from a sample of working class mothers. *Social Science and Medicine, 16,* pp. 43–52.

(1985). Choice or chance: further evidence on ideas of illness and responsibility for health. *Social Science and Medicine, 20,* pp. 981–91.

Poliakov, L. (1980). *La causalité diabolique.* Paris: Calmann-Levy.

Potter, J., and Billig, M. (1992). Re-representing representations. *Ongoing Production on Social Representations, 1,* pp. 15–20.

Potter, J., and Litton I. (1985). Some problems underlying the theory of social representations. *British Journal of Social Psychology, 24,* pp. 81–90.

Potter, J., Reicher, S. (1987). Discourses of community and conflict: the organization of social categories in accounts of a 'riot'. *British Journal of Social Psychology*, *26*, pp. 25–40.

Potter, J., and Wetherell, M. (1987). *Discourse and social psychology: beyond attitudes and behaviour*. London: Sage.

(1989). Fragmented ideologies: accounts of educational failure and positive discrimination. *Text*, *9*, pp. 175–90.

Potter, J., Wetherell, M., Gill, R., and Edwards, D. (1990). Discourse: noun, verb or social practices. *Philosophical Psychology*, *3*, pp. 205–17.

Pulver, U. (1991). *Die Bausteine des Alltags: zur Psychologie des menschlichen Arbeitens und Handelns*. Heidelberg: Asanger.

Putnam, H. (1988). *Representation and reality*. Cambridge, MA: MIT-Press.

Quinn, N., and Holland, D. (1987). Culture and cognition. In D. Holland and N. Quinn (eds.), *Cultural models in language and thought*. Cambridge: Cambridge University Press.

Radley, A. (1990). Artifacts, memory and a sense of the past. In D. Middleton and D. Edwards (eds.), *Collective remembering*, pp. 46–59. London: Sage.

Raspe, H. H., and Ritter, N. (1982). Laientheorien, paramedizinische Behandlung und subjektive Medikamentencompliance bei Patienten mit einer chronischen Polyarthritis. *Verhandlungen Deutsche Gesellschaft Innere Medizin*, *88*, pp. 1200–4.

Rebaudiries, P. (1987). De la question de l'identité culturelle a celle du sujet: pour une revision des paradigmes. *Enfance*, *1*(2), pp. 11–26.

Reeves, W. (1983). *British racial discourse: a study of British political discourse about race and race-related matters*. Cambridge: Cambridge University Press.

Reicher, S. (1984). The St Paul's riot: an explanation of the limits of crowd behaviour in terms of a social identity model. *European Journal of Social Psychology*, *14*, pp. 1–21.

Resnick, L. B, Levine, J., and Teasley, S. (eds.) (1991). *Perspectives on socially shared cognition*. Washington, DC: American Psychological Association.

Ricoeur, P. (1981). *Hermeneutics and human sciences*. Cambridge: Cambridge University Press.

Rijsman, J., and Stroebe, W. (1989). The two social psychologies or whatever happened to the crisis. *European Journal of Social Psychology*, *19* (5), pp. 339–44.

Riviere, A. (1985). *La psicología de Vygotsky*. Madrid: Visor.

Rohlen, T. P. (1989). Order in Japanese society: attachment, authority, and routine. *Journal of Japanese Studies*, *15*, pp. 5–41.

(1991). *A developmental topography of self and society in Japan*. Paper presented at the Conference on Self and Society in India, China, and Japan, Honolulu, Hawaii.

Roloff, M. E. (1981). Interpersonal and mass communcation scripts: an interdisciplinary link. In G. C. Wilhoit and H. de Bock (eds.), *Mass communication review yearbook* (Vol. II). pp. 428–44.

Roqueplo, P. (1974). *Le partage du savoir*. Paris: Le Seuil.

Rosenberger, N. (ed.) (1992). *Japanese sense of self*. Cambridge: Cambridge University Press.

Ross, L. (1977). The intuitive psychologist and his shortcomings: distortions in the attribution process. In L. Berkowitz (ed.), *Advances in experimental social psychology* (Vol. X). New York: Academic Press.

Ross, M., and McFarland, C. (1988). Constructing the past: biases in personal memories. In D. Bar-Tal and W. Kruglanski (eds.), *The social psychology of knowledge.* Cambridge: Cambridge University Press.

Rubinstein, D. (1982). Individual minds and social order. *Qualitative Sociology, 5* (2), pp. 121–39.

Rubinstein, S. L. (1977). *Grundlagen der allgemeinen Psychologie.* Berlin: Verlag Volk und Wissen.

Ruble, D. N., Feldman, N. S., Higgins, E. T., and Karlovac, M. (1979). Locus of causality and use of information in the development of causal attributions. *Journal of Personality, 47*, pp. 595–614.

Sacks, H. (1992). *Lectures on conversation.* Oxford: Basil Blackwell.

Sampson, E. E. (1975). On justice as equality. *Journal of Social Issues, 31*, pp. 45–64.

Schäfers, B. (ed.) (1986). *Grundbegriffe der Soziologie.* Opladen: Leske.

Schank, R. C., and Abelson, R. P. (1977). *Scripts, plans, goals and understandings: an inquiry into human knowledge structures.* Hillsdale, NJ: Erlbaum.

Schmidt, C. F. (1972). Multidimensional scaling of the printed media's explanations of the riot of the summer of 1967. *Journal of Personality and Social Psychology, 24*, pp. 59–67.

Schulze, G. (1992). *Die Erlebnisgesellschaft – Kultursoziologie der Gegenwart.* Frankfurt: Campus.

Schuman, H., and Scott, J. (1989). Generations and collective memories. *American Sociological Review, 54* (3). pp. 359–81.

Schütz, A. (1966). *Colletcted papers* (Vols. I–III). Den Haag: Nijhoff.

Schwartz, S. H. (1990). Individualism–collectivism: critique and proposed refinements. *Journal of Cross-cultural Psychology, 21*, pp. 139–57.

Schwartz, S. H., and Bilsky, W. (1990). Toward a theory of the universal content and structure of values: extensions and cross-cultural replications. *Journal of Personality and Social Psychology, 58*, pp. 878–91.

Schwarz, S., Weniger, G., and Kruse, L. (1989). *Soziale Repräsentation und Sprache: Männertypen. Überindividuelle Wissensbestände und soziale Kognitionen. Arbeiten aus dem SFB 245 'Sprechen und Sprachverstehen im sozialen Kontext'*, Nr. 4. Heidelberg/Mannheim: Bericht.

Semin, G. (1989). Prototypes et représentations sociales. In D. Jodelet (ed.), *Représentations sociales.* Paris: Press Universitaire de France.

Shweder, R. A. (1982). Beyond self-constructed knowledge: the study of culture and morality. *Merrill-Palmer Quarterly, 28*, pp. 41–69.

Shweder, R. A., and Bourne, E. J. (1982). Does the concept of the person vary cross-culturally? In A. J. Norsello and G. M. White (eds.), *Cultural conceptions of mental health and therapy*, pp. 97–137. Boston: Reidel Publishing Company.

Shweder, R. A., and LeVine, R. A. (eds.) (1984). *Culture theory: essays on mind, self, and emotion.* New York: Cambridge University Press.

Shweder, R. A., and Sullivan, M. A. (1993). Cultural psychology: who needs it? *Annual Review of Psychology, 44*, pp. 497–523.

Sigel, I. (1986). Mechanism: a metaphor for cognitive development? A review of

Sternberg's 'Mechanisms of cognitive development'. *Merril-Palmer Quarterly, 32* (1), pp. 93–101.

Singh, S., and Vasudeva, P. (1977). A factorial study of the perceived reasons for poverty. *Asian Journal of Psychology and Education, 2*, pp. 51–6.

Sinha, J., and Verma, J. (1987). Structure of collectivism. In C. Kagitcibasi (ed.). *Growth and progress in cross-cultural psychology*, pp. 201–3. New York: Swets North America.

Six, B. (1989). Stereotype in den Medien. In J. Groebel and P. Winterhoff-Spurk (eds.), *Empirische Medienpsychologie*, pp. 168–78. Munich/Weinheim: PsychologieVerlagsUnion.

Sommer, C. M. (1989). *Soziopsychologie der Kleidermode*. Regensburg: Roderer.

Sommer, C. M., and Wind, T. (1986). *Menschen, Stile, Kreationen*. Berlin: Ullstein.

(1991). *Die Mode*. Weinheim: Beltz.

Spears, R., and Shahinper, K. (1994). *The influence of linguistic context on the cognitive and strategic aspects of ethnic affirmation for an immigrant and a refugee group*. University of Amsterdam, unpublished Ms.

Spencer, S. J., and Steele, C. M. (1992). *The effect of stereotype vulnerability on women's math performance*. Paper presented at the Annual Convention of the American Psychological Association, Washington, DC.

Sperber, D. (1985). Anthropology and psychology: towards an epidemiology of representations. *Man, 20*, pp. 73–89.

(1990). The epidemiology of beliefs. In C. Fraser and G. Gaskell (eds.), *The social psychological study of widespread beliefs*. pp. 25–44. Oxford/New York: Oxford University Press.

Stacey, B. G. (1982). Economic socialization in the pre-adult years. *British Journal of Social Psychology, 21*, pp. 159–73.

Stacey, B., and Singer, M. (1985). The perception of poverty and wealth among teenagers. *Journal of Adolescence, 8*, pp. 231–42.

Stacey, B. G., Singer, M. S., and Ritchie, G. (1989). The perception of poverty and wealth among teenage university students. *Adolescence, 24*, pp. 193–207.

Steele, C. (1988). The psychology of self-affirmation. *Advances in Experimental Social Psychology, 21*, pp. 261–302.

Stein, M. (1984). The holocaust, the uncanny and the Jewish sense of history. *Political Psychology, 5* (1), pp. 5–35.

Steiner, J. D. (1986). Paradigms and groups. In L. Berkowitz (ed.), *Advances in Experimental Social Psychology, 19*, pp. 251–92.

Stephan, C. W., Stephan, W. G., and Pettigrew, T. F. (eds.) (1991). *The future of social psychology: defining the relations between sociology and psychology*. New York: Springer.

Sternberg, R. J., and Detterman, D. K. (eds.) (1986). *What is intelligence?* Norwood, NJ: Ablex.

Stevenson, H., Azuma, H., and Hakuta, K. (1986). *Child development and education in Japan*. New York: Freeman.

Stich, S. (1990). *The fragmentation of reason: preface to a pragmatic theory of cognitive evaluation*. Cambridge: MIT Press.

Strack, F. (1988). Social cognition: Sozialpsychologie innerhalb des Paradigmas der Informationsverarbeitung. *Psychologische Rundschau 39*, pp. 72–82.

Strauss, C., and Quinn, N. (1994). A cognitive/cultural anthropology. In R. Borofsky (ed.), *Assessing cultural anthropology*, pp. 284–300. New York: McGraw-Hill.

Sullivan, H. S. (1940). *Conceptions of modern psychiatry*. New York: Norton.

Taylor, C. (1989). *Sources of the self: the making of modern identities*. Cambridge, MA: Harvard University Press.

(1991). Lichtung oder Lebensform – Parallelen zwischen Wittgenstein und Heidegger. In *Der Löwe spricht . . . und wir können ihn nicht verstehen*, pp. 94–120. Frankfurt: Suhrkamp.

Thommen, B., Ammann, R., and Cranach, M. von (1988). *Handlungsorganization durch soziale Repräsentationen: Welchen Einfluss haben therapeutische Schulen auf ihre Mitglieder*. Berne: Huber.

Thommen, B., Cranach, M. von, and Ammann, R. (1992). The organization of individual action through social representations: a comparative study of two therapeutic schools. In M. von Cranach, W. Doise and G. Mugny (eds.), *Social representations and the social bases of knowledge* (Swiss Monographs in Psychologie, Vol. I), pp. 194–202. Berne: Huber.

Thompson, J. B. (1984). *Studies in the theory of ideology*. Cambridge: Polity Press.

Townsend, P. (1979). *Poverty in the United Kingdom: a survey of household resources and standards of living*. Harmondsworth: Penguin.

Triandis, H. C. (1987). Individualism and social psychological theory. In C. Kagitcibasi (ed.). *Growth and progress in cross-cultural psychology*, pp. 78–83. New York: Swets North America.

(1990a). Cross-cultural studies of individualism and collectivism. In *Nebraska Symposium on Motivation, 1989*. Lincoln, NE: University of Nebraska Press.

(1990b). *Theoretical and methodological approaches*. Paper presented for a workshop on Individualism–Collectivism held in Seoul, South Korea, July.

Triandis, H. C., Bontempo, R., Villareal, M. J., Asai, and M., Lucca, N. (1988). Individualism and collectivism: cross-cultural perspectives on self-ingroup relationships. *Journal of Personality and Social Psychology*, *54*, pp. 323–38.

Tukey, D. D. (1986). A philosophical and empirical analysis of subjects' modes of inquiry on the 2–4–6 task. *Quarterly Journal of Experimental Psychology*, *38a*, pp. 5–33.

Ugwu-Oju, D. (1993). Hers: pursuit of happiness. *The New York Times Magazine*, Sunday, 14 November.

Van Dijk, T. (1977). Context and cognition: knowledge frames and speech act comprehension. *Journal of Prgamatics*, *1*, pp. 211–32.

(1992). Discourse and the denial of prejudice. *Discourse and Society* (3), pp. 87–118.

Varela, F. J. (1990). *Kognitionswissenschaft – Kognitionstechnik. Eine Skizze aktueller Perspektiven*. Frankfurt: Suhrkamp.

Vygotsky, L. S. ([1934]1986). *Thought and language*. Cambridge, MA: MIT Press.

(1978). *Mind in society: the development of higher psychological processes*. M. Cole, V. John-Steiner, S. Scribner, and E. Souberman (eds.) Cambridge, MA: Harvard University Press.

Wagner, W. (1994). *Alltagsdiskurs – Zur Theorie sozialer Repräsentationen.* Göttingen: Hogrefe.

Wason, P. C. (1960). On the failure to eliminate hypotheses in a conceptual task. *The Quarterly Journal of Experimental Psychology, 12,* pp. 255–74.

Waterman, A. (1984). *The psychology of individualism.* New York: Praeger.

Watzlawick, P., Beavin, J. H., and Jackson, D. D. (1967). *Pragmatics of human communication: a study of internacional patterns, pathologies, and paradoxes.* New York: Norton.

Weber, M. ([1968]1972). *Economy and society.* New York: Bedminster Press.

Wegner, D. M. (1986). Transactive memory: a contemporary analysis of the group mind. In B. Mullen and G. R. Goethals (eds.), *Theories of group behaviour,* pp. 185–208. New York: Springer Verlag.

Weiner, B. (1985). 'Spontaneous' causal thinking. *Psychological Bulletin, 97,* pp. 74–84.

Weiner, B., Frieze, I. H., Kukla, A., Reed, L., Rest, S., and Rosenbaum, R. M. (1971). *Perceiving the causes of success and failure.* Morristown, NJ: General Learning Press.

Wertsch, J. V. (1985), *Vygotsky and the social formation of mind.* Cambridge, MA: Harvard University Press.

Wetherell, M., and Potter, J. (1988). Discourse analysis and the identification of interpretative repertoires. In C. Antaki (ed.), *Analysing everyday explanation: a casebook of methods,* pp. 168–83. London: Sage.

  (1992). *Mapping the language of racism: discourse and the legitimation of exploitation.* Hemel Hempstead: Harvester Wheatsheaf.

White, G. M. (1992). Ethnopsychology. In T. Schwartz, G. M. White and C. A. Lutz (eds.), *New directions in psychological anthropology,* pp. 21–46. Cambridge: Cambridge University Press.

Williams, G. A. (1960). Gramsci's concept of hegemony. *Journal for the History of Ideas, 21,* pp. 586–99.

Willke, H. (1991). *Systemtheorie: Eine Einführung in die Grundprobleme der Theorie.* (3. überarb. Aufl.) UTB 1161. Stuttgart: Fischer.

Winterhoff-Spurk, P. (1989). *Fernsehen und Weltwissen. Der Einfluß von Medien auf Zeit-, Raum-, und Personenschemata.* Opladen: Westdeutscher Verlag.

Witte, E. H. (1989). *Sozialpsychologie: ein Lehrbuch.* Munich/Weinheim: PsychologieVerlagsUnion.

Wittgenstein, L. (1953). *Philosophical investigations.* Oxford: Blackwell.

Woike, B. A. (1994). The use of differentiation and integration processes: empirical studies of 'separate' and 'connected' ways of thinking. *Journal of Personality and Social Psychology, 57,* pp. 142–50.

Wood, G. S. (1982). Conspiracy and the paranoid style: causality and deceit in the eighteenth century. *William and Mary Quarterly, 39,* pp. 401–14.

Wundt, W. (1900–20). *Völkerpsychologie: Eine Untersuchung der Entwicklungsgesetze von Sprache, Mythes und Sitte* (10 vols). Leipzig: Engelmann.

Wyer, R. S., and Srull, T. K. (1984). *Handbook of social cognition* (Vol. I). London: Erlbaum.

Young, K. T. (1990). American Conceptions of infant development from 1955 to 1984: What the experts are telling parents. *Child Development, 61,* pp. 17–28.

Zajonc, R. B. (1989). Styles of explanation in social psychology. *European Journal of Social Psychology, 19* (5), pp. 345–68.

Zhou, R. M. (1987). *Marquage social: conduites de partage et construction de la notion de conservation chez des enfants de 5–6 ans.* University of Aix-en-Provence, Doctoral Thesis.

Zukier, H. (1987). The conspiratorial imperative: Medieval Jewry in western Europe. In C. F. Graumann and S. Moscovici (eds.), *Changing conceptions of conspiracy.* New York: Springer.

# Author Index

# Subject Index